Mark
Octob

The Quaker Condition:
The Sociology of a Liberal Religion

Edited by

Pink Dandelion and Peter Collins

Cambridge Scholars Publishing

The Quaker Condition: The Sociology of a Liberal Religion,
Edited by Pink Dandelion and Peter Collins

This book first published 2008 by

Cambridge Scholars Publishing

15 Angerton Gardens, Newcastle, NE5 2JA, UK

British Library Cataloguing in Publication Data
A catalogue record for this book is available from the British Library

ISBN (10): 1-84718-565-7, ISBN (13): 9781847185655

TABLE OF CONTENTS

Part III: Meeting Culture

Part IV: Diverse Forms

LIST OF TABLES

LIST OF FIGURES

FOREWORD

This book explores many themes, but the most important is also one of the most basic: what is it to be a Quaker? In addressing this question, contributors also shed light on a more fundamental issue: what is religion, and what is it to be religious?

There is a long tradition of thought in the West which assumes that religion is primarily a matter of belief. The idea that being religious means 'believing twelve impossible things before breakfast' dies hard. We see its continuing force in the 'new atheism' of writers like Richard Dawkins, for whom religion is primarily a set of false propositions which must be replaced by the true belief of science. Its influence also continues to be felt in the academy, including in the Sociology of Religion. Two of the latter's most popular tools, the survey and the questionnaire-based interview, have a tendency to focus on matters of belief, and 'rationalist' approaches to religious secularisation focus on changing beliefs as the chief cause of religious decline.

This book shows that for Quakers, belief is relatively inconsequential. Different Quakers believe a whole host of very different things before breakfast, and the attempt to find some essence of Quakerism in a set of shared beliefs is doomed from the start. In searching for what it is which holds the group together and distinguishes it, a number of contributors point not to beliefs but to shared practices, including the central act of 'silent' worship, and a lifestyle based around 'plaining'. The idea that there is a distinctive Quaker *habitus* is aired, as is the finding that bonds of intimate community have a particular centrality for young Quakers. Such embodied social practices, it is suggested, help constitute the 'heterotopic' Quaker space.

The idea that religions offer a 'heterotopia' or, more simply, a social space in which it is possible to maintain a different form of social and individual existence than is possible outside it, is a vital insight. Taken together, the contributions to this book start to fill in the picture of what that existence involves. The overall impression is that it has a good deal to do with the maintenance of egalitarian relations of equal respect in which distinctions which might be important outside the group are downplayed or eliminated. Relatedly, it has to do with the creation of a peaceable community in which forms of domination are shunned in favour of collectivism. For Quakers, their heterotopia is a space which *goes beyond* everyday existence in terms of its truth and goodness, and which serves to resource and orient members when they re-enter non-utopian spheres of existence.

This gives us a useful clue about the nature of religion more generally. To define it solely in terms of beliefs – or even practices – concerning supernatural beings clearly will not do. Religion has more to do with creating alternative social worlds which transcend existing social worlds. As such, religions make it possible to live a different life than would otherwise be possible – and they may serve as force-frames for social change. Even the most Durkheimian sort of religion which throws a sacred canopy over existing social structures must have *some* element of transcendence, some sense that more is possible or desirable than has yet been achieved.

By developing this understanding of religion, *A Quaker Condition* shows that part of the task of the sociologist of religion is to identify what is distinctive about a particular heterotopia. It instructs us that this usually has less to do with belief than with what can be called an ethos, ordering, orientation or condition. Important though beliefs and practices are, they do not exhaust a religious order. Every dimension of religion points to, and helps establish, its distinctive heterotopia – whether rituals, doctrines, ethical injunctions, stories, emotions, use of space, distinctive social relations, symbols and symbolic objects, or dress and comportment – and the combinations will be different in different religions. (It is because each element of a religion participates in and contributes to its distinctive ontology that it is possible to remark of even, say, a hat or a car that it is 'very Quaker' or 'not very Quaker'.)

The Sociology of Religion is currently in an exciting phase, because it is broadening the way it thinks about religion. This book contributes to this task by drawing attention to many previously neglected dimensions of religion, and showing how they work together to create a distinctive alternate ordering.

Linda Woodhead
Department of Religious Studies
Lancaster University

INTRODUCTION

PINK DANDELION AND PETER COLLINS

This book focuses primarily on what we have termed the 'Quaker Condition'. It looks sociologically at the condition of present-day British Quakerism. 'Condition' is also a Quaker term for a personal or collective spiritual state and the title plays on this insider use of the term - the early Friends, as Quakers are also called, used the term 'condition' to refer to their inward spiritual state: for George Fox, 'Christ Jesus' spoke to his 'condition' (Nickalls 1952, 11) Finally, 'condition' can be understood as the conditional, the condition regarding what makes a social dynamic a Quaker one.

This original and innovative collection contributes to several different, though obviously connected, fields within the study of religion. It operates on five levels. In the first place, the volume is the first to represent, substantially, the contribution of social science to the study of Quakerism and should therefore provide useful comparative material for those whose focus is on other faith groups. Second , the book focuses largely on British Quakerism and so enriches the pool of resources relating to the sociology of British religion and British culture more generally. Third , there are very few sociological volumes dedicated to the analysis of a single faith group (Barker 1984, Beckford 1978, Wallis 1976, Walliss 2002). Fourth, the book represents an in-depth study of a liberal faith group, when liberal religion is the focus of much scholarly debate at present particularly with reference to the secularisation thesis. The study of British Quakerism is especially fascinating in this regard, given how the group can be described almost as hyper- or ultra-liberal, prefiguring many of the developments which may overtake currently more conservative groups. Fifth, the volume has a unique trajectory which is of great interest to all those concerned with the methodology of the social sciences. In this case, the authors met twice early on in the project in order to identify and discuss, in considerable depth, issues which are salient to the sociology of Quakerism. Abstracts were then written and circulated around the group. Our aim was to write with each of the other papers in mind in order to produce a meaningful dialogue, rarely captured in edited volumes. That dialogue (which involved lengthy consideration of obvious connections and compelling juxtapositions) was furthered by a third meeting of contributors where draft papers were presented and discussed at some length. Following that meeting, final drafts were collated and an introduction to the project written by Peter Collins and Pink Dandelion. This culminates in a book far more interwoven and layered than a typical 'edited collection.'

Quakerism in Britain

Quakerism began as a movement in Britain in the early 1650s and the Quakers were the most successful sect of republican rule. The first Quakers saw themselves as co-agents with God and confidently predicted the unfolding endtimes (Dandelion 2005). They were radical in a number of ways. They believed in the universal possibility of an inward, immediate, transformative, and ongoing encounter with God and gave this form of revelation higher authority than Scripture. Quaker worship reflected the need they felt to move away from outward forms towards the inward and was based in silence. Everyone, importantly for the time including women, was spiritually equal and anyone might 'minister' as part of worship, if led to by God. Whilst worship has got shorter by about half an hour a century, this has remained the basis for Quaker worship in Britain for over 350 years.

Out of their experience of *encounter* with God and divine revelation emerged a series of 'peculiarities' performed in everyday life. Most visible was plain dress, the adoption of plain clothing without embellishment, conveyed to most of us today through a porridge packet. Quakers also adopted 'plain speech', using only 'thee' and 'thou' to everyone instead of the deferential form 'you' to social superiors. They levelled all of society down before God. They refused to take their hats off to anyone except when in prayer, that is before God, and eschewed small talk for fear of its carnality and worldliness (Bauman 1973).

Over the centuries, British Quakerism adapted to new social and theological contexts. In the 1660s, Quakers talked less of the endtimes and in the eighteenth century focused more on 'peculiarity'. With the second and third generations, many waiting for their personal transformation experience, what had been consequences for an earlier generation became rules. Dress, speech, lifestyle all became codified and enforced. The rule of endogamy (only marrying other Members) was a particular cause of disownment and the loss of thousands of Members (Marietta 1984). During the mid-nineteenth century, British Quakerism became predominantly evangelical, saw itself for the first time as *part* of the true (Christian) church rather than the true church itself and relaxed its rules about marriage, dress, and speech. Numbers again rose. Lowering the 'hedge' however, also allowed modern ideas about religion into the Society[1] and by 1900, Quakerism had been re-visioned by its younger adherents as part of liberal Christianity. It was also redesigned as again distinctively Quaker: Experience was primary. Liberal Friends did not want to return to the earlier days and they envisioned a Quakerism relevant to the age, open to new ideas, and one which held to the idea of progressive revelation, that God necessarily revealed more over time. This is the basis of the Quakerism explored in this book. It is a Quakerism built upon the rational basis of liberal religion, permissive and fluid about doctrine, but still clearly identified as Quaker, through its use of traditional worship forms and insider language.

The Sociology of British Quakerism

Quaker studies as an organised field of academic study is a phenomenon of the last ten to fifteen years. Much of the work is within Quaker studies is historical (eg Kennedy 2001, Moore 2000), and in literary studies (Gill 2005, Hinds 1996, Hobby 1989, Peters 2005) contributing in a significant way to the study of the seventeenth century and in particular to gendered readings of the seventeenth century context and the onset or modernity (Trevett 2000, Mack 1992, Tarter 2001). Quaker studies too is sometimes theological or theo-historical (Bailey 1992, Davie 1997, Gwyn 1995, Spencer 2007). What this volume represents however is the important growth of the sociological within this area of academic study. In particular it reflects a significant focus on the sociology of British Quakerism, born partly out of the location of academic centres specialising in Quaker studies in two British universities (Birmingham and Sunderland). Nevertheless, the findings presented here offer both an indication of the condition of Liberal Quakerism elsewhere in the world, and set a research agenda for those studying Quakerism outside of Britain.

Three doctoral theses presented in the 1990s underpin this new interest in the sociological and anthropological aspects of Quakerism, those of Dandelion (1993), Collins (1994), and Plüss (1995). Working largely unbeknownst to each other, all three worked on areas of Quaker identity. Pink Dandelion explored patterns of believing in Britain Yearly Meeting.[2] He found that belief was both diverse (he argues British Quakers are best described as post-Christian) and marginal. Belief was not central to the creation of Quaker identity. Rather, the way in which

*of. his
scroll narrative.*

Quakers were Quakers, such as the way they worship, creates coherence within the group and maintains unity and identity. Dandelion calls this twin operation of a 'liberal belief culture' and a conservative and conformist 'behavioural creed' a 'Quaker double-culture'. Conservatism around form counterbalances the permissiveness around belief.

Peter Collins carried out an ethnographic study of a single Quaker Meeting. Although he subjected various aspects of the Meeting to anthropological analysis (the uses of gossip and scandal, ritual, the relationship between 'insider' and 'outsiders' he became increasingly interested in the means by which the continued existence of the Meeting was sustained. After a number of less than successful attempts to model the Meeting in various ways he eventually came to see the significance of stories and story-telling. He concluded that it was through the spinning of narrative threads that the Meeting maintained both its existence and its identity. These narratives, he argued, were of three orders: the individual, the vernacular and the canonical, reflecting the existence of various horizons of legitimacy. In later papers (1996b, 2001), Collins developed the concept of plaining – the active process which, he believes, is central to the generation of Quaker identity. Plaining, in Collins' terms, is both critical aesthetic and ethic.

Caroline Plüss looked in particular at theological debate within the group, advanced by two interest groups[3] within the wider body, between a view of Quakerism as necessarily Christian and a view that Quakerism was essentially 'universalist', ie that it could accommodate many different faith perspectives. She explored how unity was maintained within a group that claims to seek God's will without any paid clergy or fixed hierarchy and coined the term 'collective epistemology' to reflect how corporate insight was given greater authority over individual viewpoints. Indeed, her work shows how the idea that God's will is found in unity amongst the group both creates an ideal of agreement and casts disagreement into a lower or even secular epistemological basis. In other words, if the Meeting is not in agreement, nobody can claim the ultimate authority of having found God's will. Unity is thus generated by a deference to unity itself.

Since these theses, and the publication of Dandelion's in book form in 1996, these authors and others have worked further to explore the consequences of some of their findings. Dandelion has worked with Roger Homan on two methodological papers on the difficulty of asking Quakers survey questions about theological topics as their hesitation about theological language translates into a pedantry about theological terms used for such surveys (Dandelion and Homan 1995; Homan and Dandelion 1997). He has also conducted work on patterns of resignation within British Quakerism (2002). Dandelion has also produced socio-theological/historical work looking at the sociological trajectories over time of the modification of theological ideas about the endtimes (2005). One book chapter concluded that Quaker theology has become ahistorical and atemporal and driven by ethics, rather than theology (2001). This is not a theme he has taken up elsewhere although it is one which emerges in this volume (see chapters by Chambers, Scully and Best).

With specific reference to ethics, Scully first developed the model of the collage approach to making moral evaluations based on empirical work among British Quakers. She further developed this line of inquiry in a chapter on the 'secular ethics' of Liberal Quakers, which related Quaker practices of discernment to discourse ethics, concluding that Liberal Quakerism uses collective procedures of decision making that are recognisable within the formats of contemporary secular ethics (Scully 2007).

Peter Collins has continued to explore several of the themes first developed in his thesis. Apart from publishing a number of papers developing his understanding of the narrative character of the Quaker Meeting and on Quaker plainstyle, he has continued to write on ritual and symbolic aspects of Quaker worship, and on the potential value of Bourdieu's work in understanding the Quaker habitus. With Simon Coleman (a fellow anthropologist) he has been engaged in an ongoing comparative study involving Quakers and Charismatic Christians (Coleman and Collins 2000, 2006).

Collins and Dandelion also worked together on a book chapter (2006) picking up on Joy Hendry's insights on the Japanese practice of 'wrapping' (1995). Hendry, in her anthropological work in Japan noted how the everyday is wrapped, often serially, depending on its status and value. However, gifts for the Gods are unwrapped. Collins and Dandelion demonstrated how the most 'open' church rites, such as the 'free ministry' of Quaker Meeting, were, in contra-distinction to the Japanese practice, heavily wrapped. Quaker silence and the vocal 'ministry' which arises out of it, seemingly an open liturgy, is constrained and bound by a whole series of rules particularly about how often and in what way silence can be disturbed.

Plüss has recently looked at patterns of socialisation within non-doctrinal groups, using British Quakerism as a case study (2007). She shows how cognition is not a significant factor in socialisation but that affective and experiential components serve to strengthen novices' identification with institutional practice. However, most of her work now lies outside Quaker studies.

Gay Pilgrim has had two chapters published on her use of heterotopia as a sociological determinate and means of creating identity within Quakerism. Pilgrim uses this impulse to create an out-of-place juxtaposition as a key way of understanding early Friends' counter-cultural behaviour and the way they turned the everyday into a religious opportunity, eg a courtroom into a pulpit (similar to Collins' idea of 'playing the vis-à-vis' – 1994). Pilgrim argues that as Quaker insights have become more and more co-opted by mainstream ideology, the Quaker heterotopic impulse has become turned inward. The kinds of groups that Caroline Plüss investigated can be seen to represents the outcome of this internalised desire to create difference and juxtaposition. Circumventing 'collective epistemology' and the idealisation of unity, Pilgrim argues that Quakerism consists of sub-cultures that now operate by different personal and theological motivations. Thus, the generation of unity through the idealisation of unity is, Pilgrim argues, no longer a value shared by all British Quakers.

Statistical work by Bill Chadkirk, Charles Stroud and Pink Dandelion, has looked at both rates of decline of membership and how British Quakerism may disappear by 2032 at present rates. Work by Mark Cary and Anita Weber (2007), and Mark Cary and Pink Dandelion (2007), has taken survey results and, through latent class analysis, has attempted to see to what extent different composite Quaker identities emerge. Within their British sample, based on the rigorous but alas, unpublished work of Rosie Rutherford (2003), Cary and Dandelion found three kinds of Quakers: they termed these   1) 'Christian Quakers' (27%), who hold a traditional Christian theology 2) 'secularised Quakers' (37%), who do not consider themselves atheists, but whose conception of God is not personal, and 3) 'Inner Light Quakers' (36%), who emphasise the inner light and 'that of God in everyone.' Little else has been published to date within the sociology of Quakerism.

Contents

The book is divided into four main sections of three chapters each: Identity; Belief and Values; Meeting Culture; Diverse Forms. However, as we have already indicated,   the chapters can also be understood as a part of a complex and ongoing dialogue. We return to the dynamics between the chapters and the issues they raise at the end of this introduction.

A. Identity

This section is comprised of the theories, already outlined above, of Dandelion, Collins, and Pilgrim, whilst including their more recent insights.

In his 'The Creation of Coherence', Dandelion revisits the work mentioned above on the pattern of Quaker believing in Britain Yearly Meeting and the two phenomena he identified, that of post-Christianity but also that of the marginalisation of belief and the centrality of form. Under the 'mask' of the 'culture of silence' (the devaluation of language, the value of silence, and the consequent rules governing the breaking of silence with speech, or the 'wrapping' of rite), British Quakerism shifted its popular theology from a Quaker-Christian one to a post-Christian one. At the same time, the caution given words and the philosophical caution towards theology as a sufficient description of experience, had led to a marginalisation of theology and a permissive attitude to believing, a 'liberal belief culture.' Rather the group is held together by a conformist and conservative 'behavioural creed'. Adherence to form provides unity, undermined only by the possibility of the heterodoxy becoming so diverse as to undermine the basic tenets of part of the behavioural creed. Dandelion here identifies a further boundary function in the recent prescription of seeking, an attitude of 'absolute perhaps' towards theology whereby rationally, from outside the religious enterprise, Quakers know they can only be uncertain about their interpretation of experience within the religious quest. Quakers are thus less permissive than they first appear in terms of believing although the content remains individuated.

Peter Collins argues in his chapter, 'The Problem of Quaker identity' that the issue of Quaker identity is problematic in two senses. On the one hand it would appear to be a problem, a practical problem one might say, for Quakers themselves. Indeed, Quakers seem often to see the problem as a solution or in any case as a cause for celebration. It is a celebration with distinctly post-modern overtones in that a creedless Quakerism allows considerable scope for variation in belief and practice. With its explicit avowal of the importance of individuality, Quakerism would seem to be a religion for today. Quaker identity is, furthermore, sociologically problematic. Given that the Religious Society of Friends has sustained its identity for 350 years, how has this been possible? How can a voluntary organisation, like the Religious Society of Friends (Quakers) sustain a coherent identity without charter or creed - without an overt, unifying ideology? One possible answer, suggested by Dandelion, is the existence of a behavioural creed. In other words, Quakers are Quakers by virtue of *doing* rather than *believing* the same thing. Although an interesting hypothesis, it does not entirely convince. Empirical research (including that carried out by Dandelion himself) indicates that although Quakers (during Meeting for Worship) appear to be doing the same thing, they are not and are often aware that this is the case. The central problem remains, then: how is Quaker identity sustained? Collins' response to this question draws on three concepts: *narrative, plaining* and *habitus*.

In 'British Quakerism as Heterotopic', Gay Pilgrim suggests that Foucault's concept of heterotopia, as developed by Kevin Hetherington (1996), names a continuing thread which links the first Quakers (who emerged in the mid-17th century) with those in Britain today.   The diversity of belief amongst Friends today no longer supports the original religious basis for their utopian vision which resulted in their heterotopic stance, and which provided early Friends with their identity and unity. The chapter goes on to argue that, instead of an overarching belief, it is the sense of being 'other' and living out an 'alternate ordering' that is one of the key ways in which 21st century Friends obtain a sense of identity and unity.

B. Belief and Values

This section looks at the theological suppositions of sociologists of Quakerism, and offers two approaches to the examination of Quaker values and moral-decision-making.

In the 1990s, work by Dandelion suggested British Quakerism could only be accurately described as post-Christian. This was based in part on a large-scale survey of 32 Quaker Meetings. In 2003, Rosie Rutherford carried out longitudinal research using some of the same questions as Dandelion but adding new ones. Kate Mellor, in her chapter, 'The Question of Christianity', outlines the key findings on patterns of believing within a group in which explicit corporate theology is marginalised whilst personally extremely important. Mellor challenges the findings of Dandelion and Rutherford and raises methodological questions as well as ones about regionalism within British Quakerism. The chapter concludes with a discussion on how Quakers define Christianity and how Christian they can claim to be.

There has been little research into the workings of the testimonies in the model of Quaker double-culture advanced by Dandelion. Within this paradigm, Quakers hold a liberal outlook in matters of belief and doctrine, but are conservative in matters of form. The testimonies have elements of both. Helena Chambers' chapter, 'Quakers, Drugs, and Gambling: testimony as values that bind' is based on research which examined

Friends' attitudes and behaviours in relation to the testimonies on gambling and substance use. Previous research into other religions and denominations has suggested that the stronger the prohibition against a particular behaviour, the less it is likely to occur in adherents – particularly if they are strongly engaged. However, there are different views about whether this is the result of increased conformity alone, or whether those who undertake these behaviours within a strongly proscriptive sect are more likely to leave the group because of high levels of cognitive dissonance. The results of Chambers' study validate the importance of the level of prohibition: the strength of the testimony on gambling is reflected in high abstinence rates amongst the Quakers in the study, while the use of substances shows a broader spectrum of behaviour, reflecting the less stringent standard of 'moderation.' However, the study also discovered that behavioural non-adherence to testimony was not explicable solely by disengagement or deviance models - and that behavioural adherence was similarly nuanced. The findings led to the development of a new paradigm that is located within the over-arching model of Quaker double-culture. Chambers suggests that three major elements combine to enable Quakerism to offer a hybrid pattern in which abstinence from gambling and low use of substances are fostered, but behaviours outside these denominational norms can be accommodated without a weakening of the religious standard embodied in these testimonies. The three elements are, first, the Quaker liberal belief culture (with its emphasis on the importance of the individual spiritual path rather than doctrine or outward behavioural adherence). Secondly, key Quaker values (particularly 'that of God in everyone' and 'as long as thou canst'), which enable a valuing of, and a non-judgemental approach to all regardless of behaviour. Finally, an approach to moral reasoning that Jackie Leach Scully has defined as 'collage' (flexible, context-led moral reasoning, with a tendency towards virtue ethics that emphasise the intention of the individual). It is suggested that this combination results in a sense of inclusivity that enables Quakers of all behaviours regarding substance use and gambling to remain engaged without unacceptable levels of cognitive dissonance – and, often (including in the case of younger Friends), to modify their behaviour over time.   The form and content of the testimonies, however, positively reinforce the Quaker religious standard amongst the majority, and 'recruit' adherents with a similar outlook.

The current British Quaker condition is distinguished by, among other things, the authority given to personal experience of the Light, and a preference for defining oneself as a Quaker in terms of acts and behaviour rather than statements of belief. This is, however, in accordance with a model that sees behaviour as the outward expression of an inner orientation to God, so what Friends do becomes their testimony of faith. This connects ethical behaviour with religious identity in an extraordinarily direct way. Other Christian denominations of course see ethical behaviour as an important element of the Christian life, but the theological organisation is such that the moral life can be considered distinct from a person's belief. This is simply not the case for any Friend making the claim to be a 'good Quaker' in any sense of the term. In Jackie Leach Scully's chapter, 'Virtuous Friends: the Quaker approach to moral identity', Scully draws on the 'collage' model of Quaker approaches to ethical evaluation which she first outlined in *Quaker Approaches to Moral Issues in Genetics* (2002), and compares this with contemporary theories of development and identity in moral psychology, to consider how Quakers use their ethical procedures and practices to define themselves as Friends, to themselves and other Quakers as well as the world outside the Society.

C. Meeting Culture

This section looks at how Quakers face challenges arising out of the tension between the ideal and real not only in their Meetings but also in their everyday lives. In 'Congregational Culture and Variations in Gospel Order', Derrick Whitehouse suggests that the Quaker term 'gospel order' can also be used by sociologists of Quakerism to refer to the aspirational ideal of local Quaker Meetings. His study of nineteen local Meetings revealed huge variation in how far this ideal is manifest. Variations in congregational culture can be usefully analysed around three primary elements: the *worship life of the group*, the *degree of community realised within the group*, and its *social witness*. Whitehouse goes on to argue that the existence of these braided and inter-related elements is dependent on four further supporting elements: *functional participation, cultural architects, management style* and *resource availability* plus an overarching directional element, the *transforming trend*. Descriptive values are assigned, as 'functional styles', to each of the eight elements listed above, which when applied to a Quaker congregation articulate a unique 'cultural profile' that points towards the cultural character and quality of 'gospel order' in a specific Meeting.

Susan Robson's chapter looks at the dissonance of conflict within Quaker Meetings, whose testimony against war, and latterly for peace, has led to a self-image of a peaceable community. As she suggests in her chapter, 'Grasping the Nettle: Conflict and the Quaker Condition', conflicts that arise between Friends within Meeting are unexpected, even shocking: harmony is privileged above justice. In the community narrative, commitment to 'mend the world' is undoubted, but Robson argues from her interview data, that Friends respond to conflict within their own community with aversion. The result is that disputes between Friends remain largely unarticulated while the 'theory in use' is 'don't ask, don't tell, don't even think about it'. Quaker identity *as ideal* is cherished and challenges to it provide the rationale for intractable conflict sagas. The hesitation Robson sees as implicit in Dandelion's idea of the 'absolute perhaps' is visible in unwillingness to appear authoritative about tackling conflict. A different account is reported from Ireland Yearly Meeting where Quakers appear to be able to grasp the nettle of conflict and remain friends.

In, 'The Temporal Collage: how British Quakers make choices about time', Judy Frith introduces the concept of the 'temporal collage' as a descriptive tool for the compiled, interwoven elements of an individual's time that accommodates the complexities and paradoxes brought about by choice. It is pertinent to understand how British Quakers make choices about time when the Society is suffering (as indeed are many British churches) a decline in membership and a resulting reduction in the number of volunteers. This is critical since Friends have no paid clergy it relies heavily on time given voluntarily as service. The paper draws upon Scully's (2002, 212 and this volume) use of 'collage' to describe how Friends make ethical choices as there are similarities in the ways in which Friends make choices about time. For instance, individual collages are creatively compiled, but need not share a common language, and the outcome of choice is not always predictable. In her Quaker case study, the collage is built in three layers. The first is a foundation layer, taken here to be Friends' spirituality, because despite spending the greater part of their lives in the secular world, Friends who took part in the interviews and group work consistently declined to distinguish any part of their life as free from the spiritual. The second layer is built with the practical aspects of life including work, relationships, service and volunteering. Finally, there is an overlaying mesh of time spent in the networked Quaker community where the time Friends give builds the Society's social capital and where individuals develop their spiritual life, friendships and learning. Time is taken to be polychronic rather than linear in order to accommodate the varied qualities given in Friends' descriptions. Linear time is the time of clocks, calendars, and diaries, with specific beginnings and ends, but polychronic time is heterogeneous. By describing time as polychronic, its paradoxes, cycles, juxtapositions and interconnections and linear aspects can all be included in the collage and thus include the contradictions about time that individual's face.

D. Diverse Forms

This section looks at three examples of groups that exist within the larger national body of British Quakers but who operate alternative expressions of form and belief. All three operate as communities within the broader community with a clear sense of strong self-identity. They rest part of this identity on a 'culture of contribution' rather than the 'culture of silence' posited by Dandelion in his study of the larger group and, as such, their study points to a new and rich research agenda.

Giselle Vincett in 'Quagans in Contemporary British Quakerism' draws upon semi- structured interviews with four Quaker women, all of whom also identify as pagan. All the women were long-term Quakers (though none were raised in the tradition) and all emphasised that their paganism was in no way a rejection of Quakerism. Vincett introduces the term *Quagan* to refer to individuals who fuse Quakerism with neo-paganism. For these individuals Quakerism is not necessarily Christian, but is based upon '*how* you are, rather than what you believe'. Quakerism for these women, argues Vincett, becomes a way of life, a spirituality rooted in praxis, where praxis includes: ritual (both Quaker and pagan); spiritual experience; and forms of relating to others and the world (social and eco- justice actions, pastoral work, writing). Quakerism is supplemented with images, ritual and new forms of the divine. As one participant told Vincett, '…now I know ways to work with symbols, ritual, even micro-ritual… I have a bigger range than I did when I worked solely with the Friends'. This chapter examines how and where a pagan worldview may merge with Quaker praxis, and where the two spiritualities merge with difficulty.

Simon Best's research into the spiritual beliefs and religious practices of adolescent Quakers reveals that there is great variety of belief and the group does not have a unified theology but rather has a permissive attitude towards believing. However the popular theology can most accurately be described as non-Christian. For Best, adolescent Quakerism represents a 'Community of Intimacy', a collective grouping which places emphasis on inter-personal networks secured by friendships and the difference and separateness of the group both from other Quakers and from other young people. He uses the term 'Community of Intimacy' refers to both the visible community, as expressed in the separate space occupied by adolescent Quakers during 'Quaker-time' (the time Quakers are publicly

Quaker, for example at Quaker events) and to the variable, networked community of friendships between adolescents that exists beyond and between 'Quaker-time' gatherings. The 'Community of Intimacy' is central in terms of forming Quaker identity, provides the group with unity and is strictly bounded in terms of behaviour. Best explains that individuals' involvement in, and belonging to, the 'Community of Intimacy' is secured through networks of friendships and relationships based upon participation in a range of Quaker activities. Increased involvement and participation in events means that individuals are likely to be more closely integrated into the 'Community of Intimacy', to affiliate themselves with an exclusively adolescent Quaker group, and to identify their closest friendships as being with other adolescent Quakers. Best argues that these networks simultaneously separate adolescent Quakers and mark them as different. Communal worship with other adolescents, whether programmed or unprogrammed, imbues individuals with a heightened and passionate sense of their participation in the collective and is a significant factor in the formation and maintenance of the 'Community of Intimacy'.

Helen Meads argues that the 'Experiment with Light' initiative represents a radical spiritual wing of British Quakerism. Experiment with Light is based on the steps which led Seventeenth Century Quakers to their 'convincement' or encounter with God and the resulting dramatic changes in their lives. Experimenters do not, however, specifically seek 'convincement', because they do not want to assume that God will come when called. The Experiment is usually undertaken in 'Light groups' based in Quaker Meetings, although some Experimenters do practise individually. It consists of a forty minute meditation, consisting of six steps interspersed with periods of silence. Usually, but not always, the meditation is followed by silence for individual personal reflection. Finally, participants share what has come up for them. Experiment with Light represents the radical spiritual wing of British Quakerism and as such is not thriving. It is radical in that its aim is to lead participants (Experimenters) to 'Truth' and 'right relationship with God'. Meads found that Experimenters' experience in following the programme was often uncomfortable. Experimenters share intimate details of their lives and experience and this binds them together closely into local Communities of Intimacy (following Best), but not necessarily into their Meeting's formal structure. The dissemination of Experiment with Light has not been approved by any formally constituted business Meeting within Britain Yearly Meeting and often Light groups are established without using local Meetings' business process. Meads believes that the programme is not thriving partly because it is not supported by central administration and partly because of the antipathy of many participants towards formalizing its organisation. Furthermore, there is no structured accountability inherent in the programme, so that it does not properly comply with British Quakers' behavioural creed whose implicit behavioural conservatism opposes its radicality. The result, according to Meads, is a programme that is neither legitimated nor supported by the wider community of British Quakers.

Ongoing Debates

These chapters do not present a unified view of some unified and homogeneous whole. As stated above, the authors have met on three occasions and all presented their papers at the 2007 Quaker Studies Research Association conference. This enabled us to see both unity and diversity in what we have written. We have made the important dimensions of agreement and disagreement explicit in each chapter. The process of reading and writing, talking and listening has proved to be a thoroughly rewarding experience for all concerned.

For example, the first three chapters on the creation of Quaker identity fall into two camps initially, those (Collins and Pilgrim) who find sociological continuity running across time and into the present forms of British Quakerism, (whether it be the impulse to plain, to generate narratives or to create heterotopia), and Dandelion who represents modern British Quakerism as significantly discrete in terms of the tradition and operating its own sociological dynamics. At the end of her chapter, Pilgrim begins to conclude that perhaps her own theory is best used as an historical tool and that the presentday situation may indeed be deviant in relation to what has passed before.

The second main debate arising out of the scholarship presented here is the use of Dandelion's idea of 'double-culture', the liberal approach to believing and the conservative and conformist attitude towards form. This was originally used to define ways in which faith transmission differed in different aspects of Quakerism but has proved useful in analysing patterns of leadership and authority within 'Quaker-time', attitudes to the testimony, patterns of resignation (2002), and in the way the group adapts over time easily in terms of belief and slowly in terms of form (2005). Authors here, notably Chambers and Scully, use this model to take their work on locating values within Quaker faith transmission, further, whilst Best claims the double-culture does not fit the data from his study of adolescent Quakers. For his Quakers, a triple-culture, formed by ritual (the culture of contribution), the networked community and narrative and behaviour, better describes the elements of transmission.

Several of the papers in this collection suggest that narrative plays a significant role in the construction of Quaker identities. Collins has argued consistently since 1994 that it is the stories that Friends tell, particularly in and around Meeting, that bind them together. Best's innovative research among Quaker adolescents tends to support this claim, as does the work of Helen Meads and Giselle Vincett. All of the 'diverse forms' strongly emphasise a shared narrative within their communities. Susan Robson's work is based on the narratives of conflict avoidance and Judy Frith's work on Quakers and time articulates the close relationship between choices over time and narrative about time.

Kate Mellor raises significant questions about the validity of statistics used to demonstrate the theological direction of Quakerism which itself underpins the robustness of theoretical tools such as 'the double-culture' or heterotopia. Her survey work points to wider questions about sampling, survey design, and survey reliability. The gulf between her figures for Quakers who call themselves Christian and particularly those of the contemporaneous survey of Rutherford requires further investigation, preferably before the next longitudinal survey in the Dandelion/ Rutherford series in 2012. It also calls into focus what the meaning of 'Christian' is for those who have answered the surveys.

Helen Meads' work offers insights into why groups may appear to challenge the status quo and in what ways dissonance is minimised (See also Kline 2002 and Plüss 1995) and heightened. This could be usefully applied to other groupings within British Quakerism. In particular, if they are not physically and psychologically separated from the rest of Quakerism, as Best suggests of his adolescent sample, how much more likely is conflict? And following Robson, what is then done about that? Is conflict avoidance an alternative version of Dandelion's 'culture of silence' (Dandelion 1996, Chapter Six)?

Liberal Religion

Quakers, as stated above, are fascinating sociologically. They are doctrinally diffuse and denominational in such aspects, whilst sectarian in the way they place demands on participants (see Dandelion and Frith's chapters) and in the way, if Dandelion is correct, they demand (whatever) beliefs to be held by participants in a certain way. They are in some ways unusually liberal, in others clearly part of traditional, modern organised religion. This dichotomy connects with existing scholarship in two ways.

As an especially Liberal group (Dandelion has called them liberal-Liberal – see 2004a), Quakers fall within the sociological predictions surrounding liberal religious groups. Steve Bruce, for example, has predicted the end of Methodism by 2031 and Anglicanism in Britain by 2058 at present rates of decline (Bruce 2003, 61). As above, Chadkirk (2005), and Stroud and Dandelion (2005) have given British Quakerism a terminal date of 2032. Paul Burton has challenged these figures claiming decline is regional and urban (2006). In the wider sociology of religion, Garnett *et al* have challenged the generational accounts that have claimed that something dramatic has taken place within the history of secularisation within the last forty years (Brown, 2001; Bruce and Glendinning 2003; Voas and Crockett 2005). For Garnett *et al*, they are more interested in chains of transmission, the cultivation of fresh religious language, and less linear patterns of inter-generational change (2007, 12). Simon Best's work is especially pertinent here concentrating as it does on the creation by adolescent Quakers of a form of spirituality constructed along very different lines from the 'parent' organisation. Quagans (Vincett) and Experimenters (Meads) also offer diverse expressions that may point to future forms of Quakerism that stem decline. As a seedbed for new forms of expression, the group without any fixed hierarchy and without permissiveness around belief, may also find new recruits from those attracted to the 'holistic milieu' identified by Heelas and Woodhead in their 'Kendal study' (Heelas *et al* 2005). They positioned their Quaker sample as a congregation of 'experiential humanity', on the edge of religion, with its transcendent reference point (as they defined religion) and the holistic milieu, with its subjective reference point. In Pilgrim's terms, syncretists are emphasising the subjective value of attendance. Faced with similar membership figures (about 15,000) in 1859, British Quakers abolished endogamy. There is no equivalent structural solution this time but new forms may be one solution to prolong longevity.

Another possibility is that Quakers appear more 'serious' to those who enquire. Studies of affiliation and switching (Kelley 1972; Bibby and Brinkerhoff 1973, 1983, Perrin and Mauss 1991) show that seriousness is a compelling factor to those joining or switching. Their new spiritual home appears more serious about what it does than its old one. For the agnostics attracted to Quakerism, an organised framework for the possibility of religious doubt appears more serious than wholly domestic uncertainty. Heron has showed that 47% of newcomers to Quakerism come from no immediately prior religious affiliation (1992, 13). However, following Dandelion, if orthocredence was adopted as an explicit element of Quaker identity, the Liberal group would present as less permissive and more serious and may attract those switching from other churches. Within Bruce's analysis it is diffuse belief transmission which aids numerical decline (Bruce 2003). Dandelion has challenged Bruce elsewhere about how groups which appear liberal, such as the Quakers, may indeed be implicitly sectarian (given in this case the behavioural creed and the 'absolute perhaps' (2004b). If each denomination made its implicit seriousness explicit, Liberal religious groups might at least slow their rate of decline.

It is an equally fascinating question to ask how many other radical sects internalised a heterotopic impulse as they denominationalised. Can 'plaining' be identified as central to identity-generation in other radical sects such as the Strict and Particular Baptists? Does Robson's theory of conflict aversion apply equally to Mennonites and Brethren, the other historic peace churches?

What remains to be done? Perhaps there needs now to be a more explicit engagement of sociologists of Quakerism with some of the larger themes which have emerged in the broader sociology of religion during the last two decades. For example, although Collins has published papers on the historical context of Quaker plainstyle and plaining, and Walvin's The *Quakers: money and morals* (1997) touches on the subject, there has been very little work done on the relationship between Quakerism and modernity. Apart from the logging of decline in numbers mentioned above, there has been little systematic work carried out on Quakerism and its place within the 'secularization thesis' represented recently by Grace Davie (1994), Steve Bruce (1999, 2003) and others. While several attempts have been made to interpret the significance of the silence that best characterises Quaker worship (Bauman 1983, Bell and Collins 1998, Dandelion 2005), less has been written about the stillness of participants. Again, Collins' engagement with the work of Bourdieu (1977 in particular) is perhaps the only attempt to interpret Quaker practice (and especially worship) with reference to theories of embodiment. Finally, and although this is implicit in several of the papers in this volume, there has yet to emerge a systematic treatment of contemporary Quakerism as a near relative of some New Religious Movements. After all, Quakerism seems to emphasize individuality, a very loosely knit theology and a collection of testimonies that cover several NRM bases including environmentalism, healing and pacifism. Our feeling is, then, that future work in the social scientific study of Quakerism might engage more energetically with theories, themes and methodologies prevalent in the broader area of the sociology of religion.

Wider Sociological Perspectives

Having suggested, above, that sociologists of Quakerism should perhaps pay greater attention to the developments taking place in the discipline as a whole, we would claim that there are concepts and perspectives presented here which might also be taken up by others in the sub-discipline. Whitehouse's model, drawn partly on the work of Ammerman (1997) and Becker (1999), contributes to the growing field of congregational studies (Guest *et al* 2004) and perhaps also to organization theory. Chambers' work is necessarily useful for anyone looking at religious affiliation and drugs and gambling in demonstrating some of the ways in which psychological processes are linked with group functioning but presents findings of interest to wider sociology. Scully's and Frith's collage models can be applied beyond the sociology of religion. Scully's model of a moral collage may well work in other segments of the populations whilst her virtue ethics model needs to be tested in other religious groups. The study of values and notions of virtue needs to be expanded within Quaker studies, the sociology of religion, and more widely still. Returning to Garnett *et al*, they list 'Virtue' as the third organising element of religious life in contemporary times (Garnett *et al* 2007, 13).

In summary, this volume marks a significant point in the history of the sociology of Quakerism. This is the first book of its kind and is intended to be the beginning, rather than the final word. It adds considerably to the study of Quakerism but also to the study of Liberal religion per se. This volume devoted, as it is, to a single faith group raises many more research questions than it answers in relation not only to Quaker studies but also for those studying other faith groups as well as those engaged with the sociology of religion more generally. Furthermore, the book itself, as an interwoven collection, offers colleagues a more collaborative model of working and one we would recommend. Finally, we feel certain that many of the ideas in this volume have a significant currency in sociology generally, particularly the moral collage and temporal collage. In these, we have analytical tools useful for studying the population at large.

Notes

---

[1] After 1793, Quakers in Britain became formally known as The Religious Society of Friends.

[2] 'Britain Yearly Meeting' is the term for the national organisation of Quakers in Britain and also for its annual meeting. See the Glossary for a list of Quaker terms.

[3] These were the 'New Foundation Fellowship' and the 'Quaker Universalist Group', both membership organisations existing within the Yearly Meeting.

PART I:

IDENTITY

CHAPTER ONE

THE CREATION OF COHERENCE:
THE 'QUAKER DOUBLE-CULTURE'
AND THE 'ABSOLUTE PERHAPS'

PINK DANDELION

Work on the pattern of Quaker believing in Britain Yearly Meeting has revealed two phenomena, that of post-Christianity but also that of the marginalisation of belief and the centrality of form. Under the 'mask' of the 'culture of silence' (the value of silence, the devaluation of language, and the consequent rules governing the breaking of silence with speech), the Yearly Meeting has shifted its popular theology from a Quaker-Christian one to a post-Christian one. At the same time, the caution given words and the philosophical caution towards theology as a sufficient description of experience, had led to a marginalisation of theology and a permissive attitude to believing, a 'liberal belief culture.' Rather the group is held together by a conformist and conservative 'behavioural creed'. This double-culture can be traced within patterns of leadership and authority within 'Quaker-time', patterns of resignation, attitudes to testimony, and in the way the group adapts over time easily in terms of belief and slowly in terms of form. This emphasis protects the means to experience, the highest authority within this form of Quakerism. Adherence to form provides unity, undermined only by the possibility of the heterodoxy becoming so diverse as to undermine the basic tenets of part of the behavioural creed. A further boundary function has been identified in the recent prescription of seeking, an attitude of 'absolute perhaps' towards theology whereby rationally, from outside the religious enterprise, Quakers know they can only be uncertain about their interpretation of experience within the religious quest. This functions as 'orthocredence', a conformist approach to how beliefs are held. Quakers are thus less permissive than they first appear in terms of believing although the content remains individuated. These phenomena are considered in turn. The chapter concludes that Quakerism adapts its means to coherence over time rather than locating coherence in more stable tropes such as 'plaining', 'habitus', as suggested by Collins, or the heterotopic impulse described by Pilgrim (both this volume)..

The Liberal Project and the Primacy of Experience

As Isichei (1970), Davie (1997), and Kennedy (2001) have shown, the seeds of liberal Quakerism can be found in the Duncanite controversy of 1870 but became established with the public presentation of Liberal perspectives at the Manchester conference in 1895. The meeting between J. W. Rowntree and Rufus Jones in Switzerland in 1897 proved a critical moment in the spread of the vision from Britain across the Atlantic and in the combined energies to realise that vision.

Davie (1997, 67-72) sets out a list of features which characterised the Liberal Quakerism which emerged in Britain and parts of America at the end of the nineteenth century. Theologically, there were four main motifs to the modernist vision:

a) that experience was primary
b) that faith needed to be relevant to the age
c) that Friends were to be open to 'new Light'
d) that new revelation had an automatic authority over old revelation and that God's Truth was revealed to us gradually over time: the idea of 'progressivism'.

In some ways, this reaction to the evangelical Quakerism of the Liberal Friends' parents looked like a reclamation of early Quakerism but the emphasis on this set of characteristics was to create the biggest deviation from early Quakerism to date.

The primacy of experience accorded with the foundational experience of George Fox of 1647. Then, at a period of deep depression and having 'nothing outwardly to help me nor could tell me what to do, then, oh then, I heard a voice which said, "There is one, even Christ Jesus, that can speak to your condition". And when I heard it, my heart did leap for joy.' (Nickalls 1952, 11). Fox's experience signalled the possibility and reality of a direct inward connection between humanity and God. It required no human or textual mediation. However, unlike Liberal Friends, Fox also claimed that everything revealed to him was later confirmed by the scripture (Nickalls 1952, 33). What was new about Liberal Quakerism was the authority given experience alone.

The other three aspects of the Liberal project (that faith be relevant to the age; that Friends be open to new light; and progressivism) enshrined an

attitude of seeking never-ending revelation which was also new to
Quakerism. For example, in 1662 when John Perrot raised the possibility
of changing the form of worship, Fox and his allies were clear that Friends
had already been given their dispensation and that such innovation was
inappropriate (Gwyn 2000, 344). Whilst Quaker theology has changed
numerous times in the seventeenth, eighteenth, and nineteenth centuries,
such shifts had been protracted and sometimes bitter processes rather than
the result of an innate flexibility about doctrine. Whilst taken by Liberal
Friends as normative, the phrase 'be open to new Light' was invented by
the 1931 Yearly Meeting (Punshon 1989, 15). The importance of these
four characteristics is that they both represent a deviation from erstwhile
Quaker theology and are also difficult to regulate, lacking as they do any
external accountability beyond the collective interpretation of pure
experience. Theologically, they are tied to nothing in terms of doctrine, to
no particular text, no particular rendering of the tradition. Whilst based on
interpretations of the past, they allow and accommodate a Quakerism
potentially forever on the move.

Diversity and Post-Christianity, the Marginalisation of Belief and the Liberal Belief Culture

Martin Davie has charted the shift as being one from 'conservative' to
'radical', most visibly seen in the move from a Liberal Quakerism which
assumed Christianity to one in which it did not matter (1997). As early as
the 1930s, Rufus Jones was apparently asked whether you had to be a
Christian to be a Quaker. His answer is not known for certain but the
question itself is more interesting. In 1966 at London Yearly Meeting,
British Friends rejected draft membership regulations as too doctrinally
Christian. One Friend 'appealed for a place in the Society for those who,
like himself, were reluctant to define their attitude in terms only of
Christian belief' (*The Friend* 124 (1966), 672). Davie (1997) cites Janet
Scott's 1980 Swarthmore Lecture *What Canst Thou Say? Towards a
Quaker Theology* as symbolic of this shift. When faced with the question
as to whether Quakers need be Christian or not, Scott answers that it does
not matter: 'what matters to Quakers is not the label by which we are
called or call ourselves, but the life' (Scott 1980, 70).

After the Second World War, particularly as the endogamous and
dynastic Quakerism was replaced by an increasing number of Friends
joining as adults, belief diversified. Eighty-five per cent of participants
now join as adults (Dandelion 1996, 331), 47% directly from other
churches, the rest with no immediately prior religious affiliation (Heron

1992, 13). In a group with a diverse and consequently diffuse belief system, these converts interpret Quakerism in the context of their own faith experience. As the diversity of belief increased, so too did the points of contact for a wider diversity of new participant. By the 1990s, Muslim, Hindu, Buddhist (Huber 2001), and non-theist Quakers (Rush 2003) were all explicitly present in the group. The group is most accurately described as 'post-Christian' given the large numbers of alternative theologies present within the membership. In a 2000 survey, Rosie Rutherford asked over 1000 Friends whether they describe themselves as Christian: 45% responded that they do (2003). (However, at the same time, recent work by Kate Mellor has located Meetings where almost 90% of Friends have claimed to be Christian, with the term defined as they wish: see chapter 4, this volume) My 1989 survey found that 39% of British Friends claimed that Jesus was an important figure in their spiritual life with a further 32% for whom it varies, Thus, at any one point, as many as 71% could answer in the affirmative. Rutherford's statistics are very similar (2003).

Belief, in the permissive Quaker 'liberal belief culture' (Dandelion 1996, 123), is thus diverse. Unlike other religious groups, belief does not play a central defining role. Indeed, accommodated by an historical critique of creedal systems of belief, belief is marginalized as concept and content.

Conformity and the Behavioural Creed

Eleven reasons for not adopting a credal system of belief come easily and readily to Liberal Quaker groups. These can be grouped into five categories as follows:

1. The Limitations of Language.

 a) Religious experience is beyond linguistic codification and definition.

 b) Credal statements demean, in their limited linguistic form, the depth of religious experience.

2. The Limitation of God's Word.

 c) Credal statements operate to close off new religious expression and revelation.

 d) Credal statements encourage a complacency of attitude to religious life by giving an impression of finality and surety.

 e) Credal statements take on an authority of their own, belying the authority of God.

3. The Limitation of Quakerism.

f) It would be impossible, inappropriate and dishonest, because of the diversity of individual belief, to adopt a credal statement.

g) Credal statements, even if possible, would misrepresent the nature of Quaker religion.

4. The Exclusive Nature of Credal Statements.

h) Credal statements operate i) to exclude those outside the group, and ii) alienate those within the group, who cannot subscribe to them.

j) A credal statement would separate the group from those of other faiths by identifying the group with one particular faith.

5. The Practical Points.

k) There is no structural need to adopt a credal statement, eg a basis for Membership.

l) There is no mechanism for adopting a credal statement.

What is interesting in the way Liberal Quakers collectively agree and affirm these eleven values. Ambler has described six advantages of creeds. Creeds:

a) express faith in memorable words;
b) educate new members and the young;
c) symbolise unity;
d) define and defend the faith in relation to other beliefs;
e) maintain authority and discipline;
f) provide a church with a public identity (Ambler 1989, 11).

Faced with these advantages, Liberal Friends still affirm their opposition to creeds. If pushed, they resist more firmly. In other words, Liberal Friends collectively agree that they do not have creeds. This paradoxical collective affirmation of belief in not having creeds led me to the idea of a 'behavioural creed' (Dandelion 1996, Chapter 3) In other words, a credal attitude to form or practice exists, visible through its opposition to more traditional kinds of creed.

If we take the eleven reasons against credal systems of belief and apply them to attitudes to Quaker worship, the keystone of Liberal Quakerism, we find that the opposition falls away. Liberal Quakers do not feel concerned that maintaining a similar system of worship for 350 years demeans the experience of worship, undermines progressive revelation or leads to complacency and a false sense of surety. These Friends do not feel silent worship misrepresents Quakerism and its diversity or inappropriately links Quakerism with particular faith. If it excludes those outside the group or alienates those within, this does not seem to concern these Friends. Orthopraxy is used as a basis for Liberal Quaker commitment and membership. Prescriptive passages on practice form part of the Yearly Meeting book of discipline. In other words, the concerns over the consequences of belief creed are not present when Liberal Friends think about their adherence to a particular form.

The Quaker Double-Culture

This contrasting pattern, of a permissive approach to belief content and a conformist and conservative 'behavioural creed' comprising a 'double-culture,' is sociologically fascinating.[1] First, it is the behavioural creed, the way in which Quakers are religious, which acts as the social glue. Second, more detailed research may show that the two aspects of the double-culture operate in inverse relationship, so that when one is weak or permissive, the other is strong. Thus, we might identify a proto-behavioural creed in the Quietist period. The 'peculiarities' of plain dress and plain speech were the outward mark of the inward Quaker spirituality and they operated as a boundary marker of who was in and who was out of the group. The Evangelicals with strong belief content felt able to abolish the peculiarities and relax the behavioural creed surrounding worship, even in some cases replacing traditions such as unprogrammed worship. The Liberals with a permissive attitude to belief regrouped, according to Kennedy, on the peace testimony (2001) and latterly on process rather than belief content. The ways in which the two dimensions of the double-culture relate is illustrated in table 1-1.

Liberal Belief Culture ie Belief	Behavioural Creed Form
Non-credal	Credal
Religious basis	Pragmatic basis
Individually decided	Collectively agreed
Individually held	Collectively operated
Open to individual reinterpretation	Collectively changed
Accommodates diversity	Requires conformity
Diversity between participants	Commonality of practice
Inclusivist	Exclusivist
Syncretic	Conservative
Permissive	Conformist
Change of paradigm in last thirty years	Basically unchanged for 350 years
No official control	Official control (e.g. Clerks and Elders)
Unofficial leadership('weighty Friends')	Rule-defined (book of discipline)
Not discussed in Quaker-time	Discussed frequently
Not required for membership	Required for membership
Not central to perceived meaning of Quakerism	Central identification with Quaker identity
Subordinate	Dominant
Does not function as a framework	Meta-narrative

Table 1-1: The Quaker Double-Culture

In terms of sect/denomination typology, it can be argued that Liberal Quakers operate as both. The permissiveness afforded to belief content places low demands on participants: there is nothing to learn or get right, and no requirement for a confession of faith or conversion narrative. At the same time, participants are required to learn the rules of worship and 'Meetings for business'. These collective acts are by default more public and more central to Liberal Quaker identity. When these Quakers answer that 'dread question', 'what do Quakers believe?' with a list of negatives: 'we do not sing hymns', 'we do not have outward sacraments', 'we do not have a separated priesthood' (Dandelion 1996, 302), it looks as if they are avoiding the question. They are actually answering the question they think is being asked, 'What is at the core of your religion?' In other words, what defines you as a particular set of believers? Silent worship, in its open and inward form is what defines this form of Quakerism. It is the means to the experience, central to the Liberal Quaker project.

These twin cultures play out in terms of leadership and authority. Explicit roles in the Meeting are limited to those concerned with the maintenance of form and to step beyond those limits is itself breaking the form and can lead to censure. Resignations also follow the dichotomous pattern of permissive attitudes to belief and conformist and conservative attitudes to form.

Attempted resignations which emphasise a crisis of faith or doubt are unlikely to be successful. They do not contradict the liberal belief culture in which doubt is valid (*Advices and Queries* 1995, No. 5). When one Friend criticised 'Nominations Committees' (who 'discern' the names for those appointed to roles) as 'undemocratic', a tension was exposed between the individual and the behavioural creed. No longer seeing itself as the true church, the Meeting encouraged this Friend to go elsewhere as there seemed to be so large a gap in understanding of the fundamentals of the faith. In a group which places so much emphasis on continuing revelation, individuals resign not only because they feel disenchanted generally but because they feel left behind by a group on the move. Equally they can feel 'left ahead', that the group is moving too slowly in spite of being 'open to new Light.' Each of these three types of resignation operates in each aspect of the double-culture, belief and practice (Dandelion 2002).

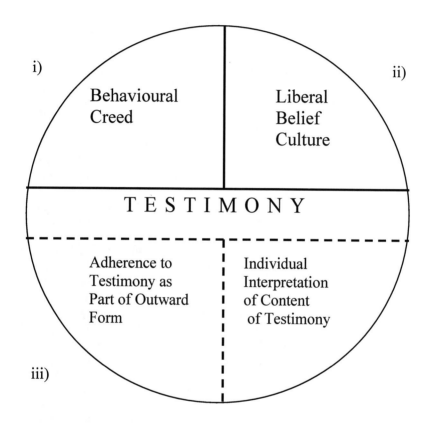

Figure 1-1 The Quaker Double-Culture and Testimony
the form of religion
the description of religious experience
the consequences of religious experience

Testimony cuts across both aspects of the double-culture. Today, in the liberal-Liberal setting, Friends interpret the beliefs associated with the peace testimony individually. What is interesting is that the testimony itself, seen as part of the Quaker tradition dating back to 1660, is rarely questioned. Some Friends join in spite of not agreeing with the Peace Testimony but it is not challenged as foundational for most Quakers. In this way, attitudes towards testimony reflect both sides of the liberal-Liberal Quaker double-culture, as illustrated in figure 1-1.

The Culture of Silence and the Potential for Heteropraxis

The double-culture also underpins the way in which silence has masked and accommodated the pluralisation of belief within Britain Yearly Meeting and other Liberal Yearly Meetings in the last fifty years. The 'Culture of Silence' (Dandelion 1996, Chapter 6) is created through the high value given silence, the low value given language, and the consequent rules about breaking the silence. Superficially, silence marks the boundaries of the collective worship. It is also, in Quaker orthodoxy, the medium through which God's will is heard, voiced, and discerned.

It is through the silence that:

1) God is experienced by the individual and thus, authority for belief in God is given

2) the silent approach to discerning God's will is validated through the fact that participants claim they experience God in the silence

3) God's will is discerned by the individual through 'leadings'

4) ideas of what might constitute God's will are shared and tested through ministry

5) action consequent to God's will is devised and accepted through business Meeting decisions

6) the names of those playing roles are thought of (in nominations committee), decided upon, and are given their authority (the appointment of Officers or committee members by the appropriate Meeting for Worship for Church Affairs).

Within the Liberal liturgy of silence, speech is devalued by consequence of the theological role given to collective silence. Its status is also diminished by the popular Quaker view on the impossibility, and the inappropriateness, of speech, to communicate belief. Words are not of practical use in expressing spirituality.

Second, it is not appropriate to try and verbalize religious belief. This view is based on the premise that the nature of language and the nature of God are qualitatively distinct. Language limits the understanding of God.

For many of us, I feel sure, putting 'God' into words at all is to trivialise the very thing we are seeking to convey . . . the silence of meeting means so much to me. Where else can I go to share with others what is beyond words? (Letter to *The Friend* 150 (1992), 471).

In this sense, this Quaker group sets itself apart from both a text-bound tradition and an oral one.

The value placed on silence devalues speech and also increases attention on the role of vocal ministry (Kelly 1944, 12). Present-day Friends are confronted by two challenges. The first is to identify what is and what is not true ministry. The second is to deliver God's word in the right way. Zielinski neatly summarises the problem of discerning the legitimacy of vocal ministry: 'if there is any doubt in the mind of the speaker as to the value of his message, then he should remain silent' (1975, 31).

In addition to discerning whether or not the message is from God, Friends need to submit to the cultural and theological rules around when and how the silence can be broken by speech if they are not to risk public interruption or a private word from an Elder. Seven aspects of normative ministry are readily identifiable. They are: i) length; ii) style; iii) frequency; iv) timing; v) content; vi) thematic association; vii) linguistic construction. Davies found in a survey of 14 Meetings that the total length of ministry ranged between 7.5 and 20.25 minutes for a whole Meeting. Individual ministries ranged between 0.25 and 10.25 minutes. Seventy per cent of the spoken contributions were less than three minutes in duration (1988, 123). Ministries which are of a length greater than ten to fifteen minutes are subject to public interruption by an Elder.

There are four consequences to the rules around speech and silence in worship. The first is that the correct use of silence and speech is a skill to be learned. Second then, conversely, silence can be misused. Participants try to minimise differences between their 'performances'. Third, fear of not having learnt the normative style of, or misusing, speech acts as self-censor within worship. Fourth, fear of conflict and ostracism within a pluralistic group where theology is often kept private impedes 'talking-God' outside of the worship event. If theology is not mentioned within ministry, it is even less likely to be mentioned in contributions which lack the divine potential of ministry. It is not only fear of getting the form of ministry wrong which constrains, but fear of expressing ideas which will not be approved of. Quakers learn in silence too. Over half of those who have been involved with Friends for less than three years have not ministered (Dandelion 1996, 254). Changes in belief content remain hidden.

Quaker religious experience occurs within the silence, and types of individual belief are constructed to help make sense of that experience. Belief may be vocalised in ministry but frequently is not, either through a lack of opportunity or lack of courage (with the silence used as a form of self-censor or defence against ostracism). The lack of regular and explicit vocalisation of belief means that there is no reaction in these terms. The silence operates at this stage of the process as a consequence of a) silence used as a form of worship, and b) silence used as a defence. In this way, changes to popular belief, as newcomers enter the group or as participants change the language of the theology, occur covertly. This process is repeatable and changes in individual and group belief remain hidden (silence masks reality) whilst the common form of worship presents a picture of unity.

Thus heterodoxy has been accommodated by orthopraxy. Orthopraxy creates coherence in a group without an orthodoxy. Orthopraxy conceals diversity but may get unpicked by it. Whilst the form of worship operates as a means of cohesion for the group, its varying interpretations may at some stage begin to unpick the form. The Meeting for Worship for business, for example, also based in silence, has been traditionally seen as a means to the discernment of the will of God. For those modern Liberal Friends without a God or without a God with a will, this formula becomes anachronistic. Instead, for some of these Friends, the business method becomes secular, simply a temperamental or political preference. What was once a heretical query, 'why can't we vote?' becomes a legitimate question.

The Prescription of Seeking: the absolute perhaps

To try and understand its shifting dynamics, there have been various attempts to model Liberal Quakerism. In 1992 Fran Taber suggested a dynamic Quakerism in tension between Liberal and Conservative impulses (1992). She argued that this was a healthy Quakerism with spin-offs or aberrations the result of losing the counterbalance. In the British context however, the model fell short as much of what was normative in Britain had been described by her as an aberration.

Emlyn Warren focussed on the nature of believing within Liberal Quakerism. His models depict a shift from a Quakerism with a central core of belief in the 1660s, to one with a more diffuse pattern of believing in the 1990s. His projection was of different clusters of belief affinities operating in the periphery of Quakerism, independent of each other.

This is similar to Gay Pilgrim's model of the future of Quakerism (see this volume, Chapter 3). She uses the term 'heterotopic' to describe the way in which some social groups such as the Quakers have defined themselves by creating dissonant contexts, such as by turning the courtroom into a pulpit. She argues that Quakers have maintained unity and identity through their heterotopic stance. Pilgrim argues that for world-affirming Liberal Friends in a Quaker-affirming culture, the heterotopic impulse has become turned inward. In other words, the desire to create difference and dissonance becomes internalised when the world no longer readily affords Quakers the possibility of defining themselves in opposition to it. This results in the celebration and even prescription of mutual difference between participants. The ability to be different has become a normative expectation. She argues that three kinds of Friends have emerged as distinct groupings, akin to Warren's clusters. The first group are exclusivists, who maintain a doctrinal unity, some of whom have left the 'larger body' such as the Yearly Meeting of Friends in Christ. The second group is that of the inclusivists who manage the Liberal belief culture by continually adding new layers to their theology but who also uphold the conservative and conformist behavioural creed. The third group is that of the syncretists who follow a self-serving path through Quakerism.

The main problem with all these models is that they over-emphasise *belief content*. It is the behavioural creed which remains definitional for Liberal Friends, with belief, 'belief stories' of semi-realist interpretation, marginal and individual. Only the idea of 'that of God in everyone' is shared, acting as i) an underpinning of form (e.g. the free ministry), ii) an underpinning of testimony, iii) a common element of the belief stories, and iv) a boundary function in that anything which transgressed this idea would be challenged. Its meaning, what the 'that', the 'God' and the 'everyone' means, nevertheless remains individual.

More recently, I identified an additional boundary function to Quaker identity in the idea of the 'absolute perhaps', the prescription of seeking as the normative mode of belief, a rigorous and conformist aspect of the otherwise liberal belief culture which ultimately makes Liberal Quakerism less permissive than it first appears (Dandelion 2004). In other words, Liberal Quakerism is held together not by what it believes but by *how* it believes. Caroline Pluss identified this epistemological collectivity in the 1990s but I argue that it has since become prescriptive. The set of characteristics that allowed this kind of Quakerism to be forever on the move have become normative. The possibility of difference has become a prescription. The idea of progressivism and of being open to new Light have become translated into the idea that the group cannot know Truth, except personally, partially, or provisionally. Thus Liberal Quakerism is not just about the possibility of seeking, it is about the certainty of never finding. I have suggested that these kinds of Friends can seek anywhere where they are sure they will not find. All theology is 'towards', a 'perhaps' kind of exercise. In a rational philosophical understanding of the nature of religion, these Friends have decided that religious truth claims are problematic, perhaps even neither true nor false but meaningless. From outside the religious enterprise they are sure of this. In other words, they are absolutely certain (rationally) that they can never be certain (theologically). They operate a doctrine of the 'absolute perhaps' and they operate it in a prescriptive way. In other words, these Friends are zealous, even fundamentalist, about their theological stance (Dandelion 2004). Those who find theological truth or who wish to share it with the rest of the group feel increasingly uncomfortable. One of the ironies for such a permissive group is that this position holds that any group or any individual who claims to have found the final truth, for all people or for all time, is wrong. All religious groups have to be partly wrong theologically: Liberal Quakers operate an orthocredence, a conformist approach to how beliefs are held. The 'absolute perhaps' is the defining characteristic of the Liberal Quaker and is the key difference between these Friends and the whole of the rest of Quakerism, worldwide today and historically.

Alex Wildwood depicts Quakerism as straddling the worlds of Christian theism, and multi-faith and new age spiritualities and the area of overlap between the two. Historically, Liberal Quakerism has shifted away from Christian theism in the last fifty years but Wildwood contends that at present the group straddles both worlds. This contradicts the work of Linda Woodhead and Paul Heelas who in their work on the town of Kendal identified Quakerism as part of 'religion', i.e. emphasising the sacred as transcendent or 'other', rather than 'spritual' where the sacred is part of the subjective (Heelas *et al* 2005, 6). In Wildwood's analysis, Woodhead and Heelas are right to include Quakerism at the experiential end of religion (Heelas *et al* 2005, 21-22) but wrong not to have it overlapping into their 'holistic milieu'. Theologically or devotionally, Quakers need to address how to live in this multi-faith world whilst those who are more exclusivist, in Pilgrim's terms, leave from either side. Pilgrim's inclusivists and syncretists can lie at any place on the spectrum but those believing in a corporate structure based on divine guidance are likely to be grouped more towards the traditional end with more diffuse spiritualities towards the innovative end. The model is helpful too in letting us see that whilst particular theologies within Liberal Quakerism may not be distinct from those of other Christians or Buddhists, this form of Quakerism as a whole transcends any single faith definition or identity. Wildwood's model also leaves open the question of what constitutes the nature and boundary of Quakerism. It can thus accommodate Pilgrim's idea of heterotopia, mine of the 'absolute perhaps' or Collins' idea of 'plaining', a deeply enculturated construction of 'the plain' as a counter-cultural aesthetic impulse in everyday Quaker life (1996b).

Shifting markers of Quakerism

Membership is falling in Britain Yearly Meeting in line with Bruce's predictions that Liberal religion is contributing to its own demise through diffuse belief systems, poor belief transmission, and the lack of seriousness identified by Kelley (1972) that encourages conversion. Liberal Quakerism *does* offer a stepping stone on the ladder of religious seriousness to the 47% who come from no immediately prior religious affiliation, but in time some leave because of the very permissiveness which first attracted them (Dandelion 2002). The 'absolute perhaps' with its zealous uncertainity requires conformity amongst participants in the Quaker group and the demands placed on members may be less denominational than the idea of a liberal belief culture might at first suggest (Dandelion 2004). Having said that, even this implicit sectarianism, seems to be failing to stem the fall in membership. Chadkirk (2004) and Stroud and Dandelion (2004) have both suggested that there will be no Quakers left in Britain within the next 30 years if present trends continue. Unlike the reforms of the 1860s which abolished endogamy and the 'peculiarities' as compulsory, which halted falling numbers, there is little major structural reform open to British Quakerism to reverse the trend. Quaker numbers are not falling because of disownment but because of a failure to attract new participants.

However, as the last two decades have shown, Liberal Quakerism, is highly adaptable. Freed from the constraints of a singular or fixed pattern of believing, it can mould its interpretations of the divine in wide variety of ways. Even form can ultimately be changed, as the growth of all-age semi-programmned worship in some local Meetings reveals. Indeed, the boundary function of the 'absolute perhaps' allows Friends to now experiment more fully with form, given that the creation of coherence has, in my view, shifted from orthopraxis to orthocredence, a normative approach to the credibility of belief, if not belief content. Counter-cultures (see the chapters by Helen Meads, Simon Best, and Giselle Vincett) could be co-opted or rejected. Quakerism is not immutable.

This shifting pattern around creating coherence suggests that Collins' ideas of plaining and of a Quaker habitus, and Pilgrim's ideas of heterotopia may need to be revisited as tropes which cut across centuries of Quakerism, or at least as ones which can be predicted to continue to operate as normative and foundational. In this reading, Liberal Quakerism and its enshrinement of seeking means it is far too flexible to be tied to any one particular form of coherence-creation, especially if they have been historically normative. Maybe Pilgrim's idea of heterotopia has actually begun to play with itself to the point that even it can no longer adequately describe the group. Certainly twenty-first century liberal Quakerism is reaching out into new self-creations and interpretative identities that fly in the face of Quaker tradition. It is the most truly radically deviant form of Quakerism to date.

Notes

---

[1] Culture has been described in a multitude of ways, and the literature on organisational culture is extensive (Pettigrew 1979, 1986, Child 1984, Schein 1985, Ouchi and Wilkins 1985, Clegg 1990, for example). Allaire and Firsirotu have identified eight schools of cultural definition (1984), divided by whether or not culture is seen as an 'ideational' or 'socio-cultural' system. That is, whether or not culture and social structure are distinct from each other (ideational) or not (socio-cultural). In organisational terms, this distinction translates as whether or not a culture is something an organisation has (ideational), or whether or not the culture is something that the organisation is (socio-cultural) (Meek 1988, 464). Functionalist writers have traditionally viewed culture as a socio- cultural phenomenon in which culture and the social system in which it exists cannot be separated (Parsons 1960, 20). However, culture, here, is used to describe a transmission system of shared meanings, values, and informal rules. Reference in this chapter is made to a 'culture of silence', for example. In this instance, the term refers to the transmission system of meaning, values, and cultural rules surrounding the understanding and use of silence in the Quaker context. In this sense, culture is ideational, and operates as a transmission system component of the organisation. It is thus a) not identical with the organisation, and b) can be divided into separate components concerned with separate areas of organisational life. Thus, the division of attitudes towards belief and behaviour/form, is described in terms of the operation of a Quaker double-culture, comprised of a liberal non-credal belief system (liberal belief culture) and the behavioural creed (the meaning attributed to the organisational and behavioural rules). In this way, the double-culture functions as twin components of the culture of the organisation, thus operating within the organisational life of the group.

CHAPTER TWO

THE PROBLEM OF QUAKER IDENTITY

PETER COLLINS

Introduction

'What is a Quaker?' This is the apparently simple question that I have been trying to answer for over a decade. It is a question which I believe requires a multiperspectival approach. Quakerism is a subtle, and complex process, one that cannot be determined either by individual or social agency. Furthermore, I assume from the outset, that in order to understand Quakerism it is necessary to understand Quaker faith *and* practice and this is only possible in terms of the individuality of particular Quakers. As Tony Cohen avers in a different context, how can we possibly understand the social (Quakerism) if we make no effort to understand the individual (Quaker) (Cohen 1994)? How, indeed?

The issue of Quaker identity is problematic in two senses. On the one hand it would appear to be a problem, a *practical* problem one might say, for Quakers themselves. This is so because of the heterogeneity of Quaker belief (witness the chapters comprising this volume). Indeed, Quakers seem often to see the problem as a solution or in any case as a cause for celebration (Dandelion 1996). It is a celebration with distinctly post-modern overtones in that a creedless Quakerism allows considerable scope for variation in belief and practice. With its explicit avowal of the importance of individuality, Quakerism would seem to be a religion for today. Quaker identity is, furthermore, sociologically problematic. Given that the Religious Society of Friends has sustained its identity for 350 years, how has this been possible? How can a voluntary organisation, like the Religious Society of Friends (Quakers) sustain a coherent identity without charter or creed - without an overt, unifying ideology? In this chapter I revisit three perspectives that I have myself developed during the past ten years or so: 'narrative', 'plaining' and 'habitus'. Together, these quite different means of interpretation when brought together result in a synergy that helps us further understand Quaker identity and may illuminate religious identity more generally.

Meeting Narratives

During ethnographic fieldwork undertaken in a Quaker Meeting in the north of England (given the pseudonym 'Dibdenshaw') I was struck, at first, by the irony of the sheer quantity of talk at Meeting. I later I described this talk in typically anthropological terms, as a tripartite event comprising a 'before', a 'during' and an 'after', each relating to the 'fixed point' of worship itself (Collins 1994). The quantity of talk was both intriguing and from a fieldworker's point of view, alarming. How to make sense of it? After many months of fieldwork, it was clear that talk was neither heterogeneous, (i.e. not entirely random) nor homogeneous (i.e. determined by some narrow purpose, e.g. spiritual development). The idea eventually dawned on me that that the talk was purposeful and orderly: the Meeting was, I found, alive (and enlivened) with stories. I argued for the first time (Collins 1994) that however else one might characterise the Quaker Meeting, narrative is at least partially constitutive of it. In other words, without stories the Quaker Meeting (and necessarily therefore, Quakerism) is nothing. I sketched out nine 'threads' (it is interesting how often the metaphor of weaving is used in presenting narrative analyses). However, I further noticed that while talk tended to be about straightforwardly substantive topics (music, Meeting, 'business', football, gardening, family, travel, and so forth) but that they could be more interestingly characterised in terms of certain tensions: inward/outward, inclusive/exclusive, sacred/profane, faith/practice, unity/diversity, individuality/corporate, tradition/change, equality/hierarchy, unity/diversity (Collins 1994, 416). All talk, I argued could be characterised as an exploration or attempt to resolve these tensions. I argue, further, that these particular tensions have characterised Quaker faith and practice since the beginning of the movement in the 1650s. Although talk may have varied as to precise subject matter, Quakers have *always* been talking these tensions and it is that, above all else, which determines their identity as Quakers. Quakers are less interested in resolving these tensions than they are in exploring them - they constitute what is centrally important to Quakers as Quakers. At the time I imagined that I was mapping the foundations of Quakerism but realise now that this, despite its analytical 'looseness' is still too deterministic. My theory was that all religions might be characterised by the 'tensions' their talk exposed. This may be true but would take considerable comparative work to prove.

In my first published paper (1996a) I attempted to develop further the idea that Meeting is constituted primarily in and through narrative. Although I discovered that the Quaker Meeting could be modelled in a variety of more or less fruitful ways, narrative seemed increasingly to be that which bore the greatest verisimilitude to Meeting as I experienced it as a participant observer. Developed as a strategy for understanding texts in literary criticism, narrative analysis had become, during the 1980s and 1990s, an increasingly widely used means of social analysis; for instance, in sociology (Franzosi 1998), history (White 1987), psychology (Sarbin 1986), psychiatry and psychotherapy (Spence 1982; Schaefer 1992), law (Jackson 1990), political theory (Roberts 2004), economics (McCloskey 1990) and organisation theory (Roe 1994). One characteristic shared by these disciplines however, is their focus on written texts. In each case, it was a matter of merely applying a mode of analysis common in interpreting novels to other forms of printed texts. Extending this mode of analysis to talk was a relatively straightforward second step to take.

Indeed, in my initial analysis I took what can now be seen as a rather conservative view of narrative form, placing it entirely in talk, conversation, spoken dialogue. As I continued to rake through my fieldwork notes I saw that narrative threads were sustained through the material culture of the Meeting House. I realise that this is not at first at all easy to understand and that empirical examples are more likely to convince. The narrative 'pacifism' was communicated not only through discussions of what became a more or less annual peace vigil and related issues during formal and informal Meetings in and around the Meeting House, but also through the peace vigil itself, during which it could be argued, 'pacifism' as discourse was embodied by those Quakers who processed from the Meeting House the steps of the town hall where they lined up alongside one another and behind banners. I might add here (after Cohen 1986) that this was indeed a vernacular narrative as it presented itself to onlookers and also to those in the procession – in the case of the latter, in particular, there were just as many prototypical narratives as their were individuals – in other words there is demonstrated an external homogeneity (the message of pacifism), simultaneously, an internal heterogeneity – though some individual narratives would be bound to overlap. The story of pacifism was further narrated through posters around the Meeting House (one including a quote from Martin Luther King), from leaflets and flyers deriving from organisations like QPS (Quaker Peace and Service), CND (Campaign for Nuclear Disarmament) and CAAT (Campaign Against the Arms Trade). I have already written in rather more detail about the pacifism narrative as developed during the weeks preceding Remembrance Sunday – indicating how the three narratives levels come together, both substantively and analytically (Collins 2003, 257-8). Each of these elements contributes, constructs, reconstructs the narrative 'pacifism' – a single instantiation can be plotted on the model, indicating the extent to which it is individual, vernacular or canonic.

These narratives, spun with varying degrees of vigour and creativity by all participants in Meeting, were not, however, 'free-floating'. They were threads which no sooner spun were woven into the social fabric of the Meeting and of Quakerism more generally. They are woven (either by the narrator or audience, and most often by both) into the fabric of Quakerism, into the testimonies - those fundamental narratives which are grounded in the faith and practice of the first Quakers and rehearsed in innumerable ways since then throughout the Quaker movement. I became increasingly interested in what appeared to be different 'levels' of narrative. Clearly the stories I heard were presented by individuals, either alone, or in consort - family members, for instance, might present an almost choral performance telling of a holiday in Spain. Then there were those stories which seemed already to exist, or rather which formed an existing context into which the narratives of individuals were embedded. These contexts were, I argue, of two kinds – the local and the national – although I feel it is rather misleading to base them on crude spatial co-ordinates. This is the primary reason for calling them 'vernacular' and 'canonic' in that these terms speak more of 'reach', 'status', 'authority' and 'power'. Local or vernacular narratives include 'Oak House' (a Quaker nursing home situated not far from the Meeting House), 'the old Meeting House' (out of which the Meeting moved in the 1960s), 'Meeting history' and so forth. National or canonic narratives coincide approximately with the 'testimonies' – a moral code including 'pacifism' and 'social justice' for example. These narratives are codified in texts legitimated by the group as a whole. I have outlined the ways in which these stories (and 'story levels') are articulated - and would argue that they have been, and indeed are, brought together under one religio-moral roof - an important issue which I return to below.

Although I suggested earlier that Quaker narratives might be understood in terms of their 'distribution' it took me some time to work out how to plot these 'levels'. I came eventually to plot Quaker discourse within a space bounded by three points, each representing a 'level' of discourse: the canonic, the vernacular and the prototypical (or individual). This model was helpful in that it pointed to a means of transcending the individual/social dichotomy which has always plagued sociology and anthropology. In this model each narrative spun by an individual Quaker is always and already a part of a vernacular and canonic narrative (Collins (2002a, 2003, 2004). The point in this triangular space in which narrative plotted is inevitably approximate, and indeed different agents might plot the narrative differently. In any case, each narrative is necessarily prototypical, vernacular and canonic - and what is more, has in every case the potential to become more or less any of these. At the same time, it is true that the model is misleadingly static. It is the work carried out constantly by Quakers that provides for and ensures the vernacular and canonic character of the narratives generated by individuals.

Let me provide an ethnographic example. An established Quaker testimony related to the 'right use' of the world's resources: this is a canonic narrative. One way in which this is so, is its presentation and development in the text *Quaker Faith and Practice* (*QFP*). Crucially, then, this means that the discourse of 'sustainability' is a component part of *QFP*. It has been legitimated (given authority) at Yearly Meeting, that is at the highest tier of Quaker decision making. And is therefore incorporated into *QFP* which commits to writing what might be seen as 'essential Quakerism'. The text, substantially revised every 25 years or so, comprises texts extracted from a variety of Quaker sources, including minuted decisions and comments recorded during business Meetings, passages from the writing of individual Friends and so forth. *QFP* is distributed both to Quaker Meetings and to individuals - most often when they are accepted into membership. In the current edition, Chapter 25 is entitled 'Unity of Creation' and deals especially with environment or 'green' concerns. For instance, the first extract is from the works of John Woolman (a noted 18th century Quaker), who wrote in 1772: 'The produce of the earth is a gift from our gracious creator to the inhabitants, and to impoverish the earth now to support outward greatness appears to be an inquiry to the succeeding age.' (*QFP* 1995, 25.01)

During the course of my fieldwork, discourse relating to the right use of resources (green issues) was generating through a number of initiatives. For instance, several Friends persuaded the Meeting to establish a 'wild garden' at the rear of the Meeting House. This involved a good deal of discussion both within and outwith formal business Meetings. Reference was made both to Quaker testimonies (primarily as presented in *QFP*) and also to local agencies involved in sustainability issues. Before very long, an idea mooted by an individual participant had become a local or vernacular narrative. Further threads woven into this narrative was the decision to replace all bulbs in the Meeting house with 'long-life' bulbs which, it was agreed, were less objectionable than the existing high wattage bulbs. During the same period, reports were given to preparative

Meeting relating to green issues discussed at various Quaker Meetings, conferences and workshops. In this way the individual's stories and those of the Quaker movement as a whole are mediated (and sometimes metamorphosed) by the Meeting, that is, at the level of the vernacular.

Plaining: from product to process

Although I believe that the creation and exchange of stories is a key element of Quaker faith and practice I suspect that there is something more, something which patterns these narrative threads so that each derives from and contributes to the more or less coherent discourse called Quakerism. The pattern is 'plain'. Quakers have always exhorted one other to be 'plain' and others have often characterised Quakerism in terms of the plain. Indeed, the proscriptions multiplied to such an extent in the late seventeenth century as to stir Margaret Fell/Fox to rail against the whole shebang. And, certainly, the plain (or simple) is well-represented in the key canonic text. For instance, the 41st of the current Advices and Queries:

> Try to live simply. A simple lifestyle freely chosen is a source of strength. Do not be persuaded into buying what you do not need or cannot afford. Do you keep yourself informed about the effects your style of living is having on the global economy and environment. (*Quaker Faith and Practice* 1995)

Let us focus on the first sentence, which urges the reader to 'Try and live simply'. Clearly, this calls for an extraordinary interpretive effort on the part of individual Quakers, given the steady growth of consumer capitalism at least since 1900. The question is whether it is possible in any absolute sense to live simply in the Britain of the 21st century. Is it possible, nowadays, engulfed as we are by consumer culture to make consistent choices between the plain and not plain any more: do we have the cognitive powers to make the millions of choices necessary to properly fulfil our obligation to 'live simply'? There seems little doubt that early Friends believed they were up to the task - with a little help from their Friends. It must have been a help to individuals to be told which commodities could be acquired without blighting one's attempt to live the simple life. Even so, predominantly middle class Quakers were left to make innumerable choices. Up until now, it seems that we are clearly dealing with particular products - with individual items (from coats with cross-pockets to umbrellas, from the use of certain pronouns to playing the flute) that are deemed 'prohibited'!

This is a claim built on empirical grounds and is hardly controversial. The common-sense view would have it that the world comprises two types of thing: the plain and the not-plain. This resolutely objectivist view holds that it is the world (comprising complete and clearly delineated 'things') that imposes itself on the individual. There is a disturbing inevitability about characterising Quakers in this way. One becomes a Quaker and is then taught or told which bits of the world are plain and therefore acceptable. In this view Quakers are almost entirely passive individuals, except that they need to identify and set aside those things which are intrinsically 'not-plain'. The corporate character of Quakerism must once have been of practical help here, at least up until the mid 19th century. There then came a point at which business Meetings could no longer name the not-plain on a case-by-case basis: is gaslight plain or not? And what about bicycles, automobiles, patios, aubergines and cameras? Given the rapid increase in the number and variety of consumer goods, naming the not-plain on a one-by-one basis became an impossible task.

After the mid-nineteenth century, what had been implicit was necessarily made explicit: the centrality of 'the plain' to Quaker faith and practice gave rise to the associated *process*, that is, *plaining*. Plaining is a learned and cognitive tendency to classify the world in terms of the distinction plain/not-plain. Quakers, as they mature, become more or less conscious of practising such discrimination. I remember a long conversation between Friends after one Meeting for Worship in 2003 which was explicitly about the pros and cons of various cars. I have time here only to note that the comments could only be understood in the context of the Quaker tendency to plain. The fact that each Friend involved in the conversation preferred a different car in no way weakens my argument: plaining is a process which enables Quakers to justify the choices they make. For instance, a commodity which might seem far from plain to one Friend can be justified as plain in terms of its good safety record, because of the savings it will generate in the long run or because of the employment its manufacture provides. The criteria used to define the plain or not-plain are neither fixed nor essential. There is nothing necessary about, or inherent in, those things which are perceived to be plain. Things are constructed as plain by Friends.

I have tried to show the relevance of this idea to our understanding of Quaker identity in two ways – by giving empirical examples, that is by presenting examples of plaining in action as it were; and by showing how Quaker plaining meshes with processes that have been identified as more all-embracing. I will present three examples of theories which seem to lend plausibility to my idea of plaining, two of which (the work of Peter

Auksi, and Wolfgang Welsch) I have presented before, while the third
(drawing on the work of Bruno Latour and Webb Keane) is presented here
for the first time.

It was something of a revelation to come across Peter Auksi's brilliant
Christian Plain Style: the evolution of a Spiritual Ideal (Auksi 1995). In
this book, Auksi places 'the plain' in its historical context arguing that the
plain and not-plain (elaborate, ornamented) have been implicated in
struggles between people ever since the Ancient Greeks, and especially in
religious disputes. Auksi supports my claim that 'the plain' is more
usefully reconstituted as a process, that the term is better conceived as a
verb rather than a noun.

A second connection with modern social theory occurs at the point at
which we realise that plaining is not merely a pragmatic response to the
complexity of the modern life but can also be regarded as spiritual, moral
and ethical. Furthermore, plaining provides a singular opportunity for
Quakers to stand in the vanguard of those who are able to critique one of
the more damaging consequences of modernity: aestheticisation (Collins
2001). Astheticisation is the glossing of our environment with the thinnest
veneer of 'the beautiful' - a gloss so pervasive that the German
philosopher Welsch has argued that it blinds us to the difference between
the beautiful and the ugly (and probably between 'the good' and 'the bad')
(1997). I argue that the propensity to plain might provide Quakers with the
means to see through this process and avoid the an-aestheticization that is
its harmful result.

I shall go on, now, to introduce a third contextualisation. The French
sociologist, Bruno Latour argues that the term 'modern' (used to describe
life in the West since around 1750) designates two very different sorts of
practice: *translation* creates mixtures between entirely new types of
beings, hybrids of nature and culture; the set of practices he calls
purification, on the other hand, creates two entirely distinct ontological
zones: human beings on the one hand and nonhumans on the other (1993).
Purification and translation, so long as they are kept separate, define what
it is to be modern. In this section I draw out the parallels between what
Latour calls purification and what I call plaining.

Webb Keane, an American anthropologist, argues that a key question
that we moderns have had to consider is 'What beings have agency?'
(2007). A question which can only be answered by sorting out the proper
relations among words, things and subjects. This sorting out is fraught
with moral implications and involves the work of purification. The
paradigmatic case is the antiritualism of Reformation Protestantism,
though such reform movements have taken place in all major world

religions. Such reformers aim to purify religion by replacing ritual with beliefs and the resulting reforms are identified with modernity itself. Several groups helped to complete the Protestant Reformation through their explicit rejection of ritual (or liturgy). Quakers purified the practice of worship through denying the possibility of the eucharist and of the sacraments in general. It was primarily the fetishistic elements of the eucharist, the principle of 'real presence' or transubstantiation, which Friends objected to: material things (Kantian 'things-in-themselves') are just that, *they cannot also be God*, no matter how this is couched, theologically. Things cannot be agents and it is the possibility of this (awful) misconception that drove some protestants, Zwinglians and Salvationists as well as Quakers, to deny the capacity of things to bear the weight of the sacred. In Quakerism, ritual is replaced, from the outset, primarily by practice ('let your lives speak').

Keane goes on to make two important points: first, that the assertion of purification can never be entirely successful. He refers to Latour who observes that even while moderns are trying to separate things, hybrids are proliferating, things that mix nature and culture, things and humans: psychotropic drugs, hybrid corn and frozen embryos for example. But Latour tells us little about why this is happening. Keane suggests that both the ubiquity of so-called hybrids and the sense of scandal they can generate have sources beyond the history of science and technology and can be traced, ultimately, to the religious sphere. Signs terminate in things after all. The materiality of semiotic form cannot be entirely eradicated and to the extent to which it mediates even inner subjectivity, it renders full purification impossible. Things endure and plaining requires such things in order to make them symbols of less material qualities.

Keane's second point is that there is a significant moral element to Latour's characteriston of modernity, specifically, that purification is driven by 'the sense that there is something scandalous or threatening about the mixing of humans and things, culture and nature' (Keane 2007: 23). Modernity, he argues, is often represented as the outcome of a story of moral redemption (as in Quaker plaining). Latour, in focusing on the role of science in the creation of modernity, largely ignores (according to Keane) the significance of religion by assuming that it is just one more thing affected by purification. God, he observes, is eliminated from the public scene and exiled to the individual's heart ('the light within' in Quaker terms). Keane argues that if we place the work of purification within the context of the Reformation attack on certain aspects of semiotic form (of Catholic faith and practice for example), we may recognise a major source of its moral impetus. It is not only the sociologist and anthropologist who position themselves where roles, actions and abilities are distributed, those that make it possible to define one entity as animal or material and another as a free and conscious agent - this is also the task of the religious reformer, of George Fox and his proseletyzing supporters for example, who, perceiving themselves as standing on the religious frontier, set about making these distinctions. In doing so, they make some of the core assumptions of their Euro-American world visible and reveal some of the moral imperatives and anxieties these entail. And in struggling with the proper place of objects in the lives of individuals, with the possibilities and limits of human agency and with what is ethically acceptable, or even simply believable, they take on problems which lie at the heart of modernity.

At the time of the Reformation, if words were bodily forms for meanings, they were nonetheless superior to nonlinguistic forms - ritual, for instance. It became a major issue to understand the nature of words and their distinction from concepts and from things. However, in considering the Quaker case we must further consider the belief that there is that which is beyond words. The proper treatment of language called for purification, which in the Quaker case meant its eradication - at least up to a point. Language cannot be suppressed entirely and in Quaker liturgy (for there are vestiges of liturgy remaining) language forces its way back in through spoken ministry. Here we glimpse, at very close range, the parallels between what I call plaining and what Keane (after Latour) calls purification.

However, the Reformation churches had the creed, a paradigm for subjective agency. By taking the textual form, the creed makes religion highly portable across contexts (it relies far less on material context). Although Quakers eschewed creeds, they generated other forms of textualisation, including minutes of business Meeting, advices and queries and testimonies. The point is, however, that Quakers, like other contemporary believers, opted for codification (Collins 2002). Whereas Keane talks of the 'creed paradigm', we may talk of 'the codification paradigm' - which is, in the same way, a part of the purification process identified by Latour. But the work of purification goes well beyond the content of doctrines. Creeds or if we wish to include Quakerism here, codification, make beliefs available in the foreground. To put it bluntly, codification (along with socialisation) serves to operationalize belief.

The view accorded to transcendance in traditions like Calvinism encouraged efforts at abstraction, to play the materiality of semiotic form in order to arrive at a disembodied spirit, a pure idea, or an unsullied faith. This goal, however, cannot reproduce itself without generating new semiotic forms. Latour says that the work of purification inadvertently produces new hybrids. But why should that be? Well, once semiotic forms are introduced into a social world, they become available as materials for experience on which further work is carried out. They can become objects of reflection, sources of disciplinary practice, points of contention, or sources of anxiety. In 'doing away with' the material aspects of religion the reformers could not help but produce new forms - creeds, sermons, hymns, houses of worship - even clerical garb. Such forms could never be fully confined to their original contexts or definitively subordinated to their 'true' immaterial meanings. They risked being fetishized, producing new hybrids. So, while purification contributed to the creation of the modern world, it can never, as Latour argues, entirely succeed. The impossibility of attaining complete purification lies precisely in the materiality of semiotic form - note the continual attempts to achieve religious purification by the religions 'of the book'. The efforts of reformers, such as Fox, to 'strip away superstitions, instrumental reason, idolatry, and fetishism' are justified in the name of greater spirituality on the part of individuals. Even the most mystical of religions are bound to involve some semiotic medium; in the case of Quakerism, the very denial of words begins as a response to words and includes various ways of displaying that denial. Semiotic form requires material instantiation and even though purification can never fully succeed, it continues to appear. This helps us understand why plaining is necessarily a process - it is a project than can never reach completion.

Meeting/Habitus

Quaker identity is learned and the learning process continues for as long as the individual wishes it to. Some are, of course, more eager and diligent learners than others. Having convinced at least myself that it was the economy of narrative grounded in an obligation to plain that best characterised Quakers and Quakerism I began to wonder increasingly about the details, and especially the details relating to the social processes through which these things are learned. In recent years the term 'socialization' has fallen out of favour among sociologists. The reason for this, most probably, is the rise and rise of Bourdieu's influence on the discipline. In elaborating his theory of practice, Bourdieu wrote prolifically on a wide variety of subjects (education, elites, photography, TV, suffering, art, social stratification - to name just a few) but in doing so always drew on the same small group of analytical constructs or 'tools' as he preferred to call them: habitus, practice, capital and doxa. Habitus is not easy to define, and Bourdieu's often dense, sometimes obtuse, prose does not help. He explores the idea in considerable detail in *Outline of a Theory of Practice* (1977). Here he writes:

> The habitus, the durably installed generative principle of regulated improvisations, produces practices which tend to reproduce the regularities immanent in the objective conditions of the production of their generative principle, while adjusting to the demands inscribed as objective potentialities in the situation, as defined by the cognitive and motivating structures making up the habitus (Bourdieu 1977, 78).

Given that Bourdieu specifically endows the habitus (and not the individual) with agency, those who criticize the concept for its determinism would seem to have a point. His attempt to transcend unhelpful dichotomies which have stymied progress in social theory, such as those generally abbreviated as objective/subjective and agency/structure, ultimately fails. However, there is much in his development of the notion of habitus which is thought-provoking and helpful. Probably the most significant strength of the habitus as a means of representing the process of socialization is the fact that is it embodied, and that Bourdieu, himself, paid a great deal of attention to this particular characteristic. Secondly, the habitus is clearly established partly through interactions with the (built) environment. In relation to the Quaker Meeting and its participants these are extremely useful insights. In relation to Meeting for Worship, the epitome of what Dandelion (1996) economically calls 'Quaker time', both body and environment play a significant part, in both the generation of stories and in acts of plaining. This mode of analysis (focusing on the habitus) confirms my earlier argument underlining the role of non-discursive interaction in and around the Meeting House. One's habitus is itself embodied (one carries it around in one's head as it were), but is embodied in a more complete and convincing sense: Bourdieu introduces a second term *hexis* to fix this aspect of embodiment. In the following passage he relates the embodiment of the habitus directly to socialization:

> The child imitates not 'models' but other people's actions. Body *hexis* speaks directly to the motor function, in the form of a pattern of postures that is both individual and systematic, because linked to a whole subsystem of techniques involving the body and tools, and charged with a host of social meanings and values: in all societies, children are particularly attentive to the gestures and postures which, in their eye, express everything that goes to make an accomplished adult - a way of walking, a tilt of the head, facial expressions, ways of sitting and of using implements,

always associated with a tone of voice, a style of speech, and (how could it
be otherwise?) a certain subjective experience (Bourdieu 1977, 87).

Let me comment on this extremely provocative account. First, much of
this rings true in relation to my fieldwork among Quakers. I would
substitute 'newcomers' (or some such term) for children in that everyone
new to Meeting embarks on what is colloquially know as a 'steep learning
curve'. Although, it is possible that hexis may on occasion be a motor
function purely and simply that need not always be the case. It is apparent
in Meeting for Worship that participants observe one another, sometimes
cautiously but on other occasions boldly - children may jump down from
their chair, walk across to another (adult) participant and stare at them,
quite unselfconsciously. Which raises another point - the degree to which
hexis is assimilated consciously. During Meeting for Worship Quakers sit
in a circle - the chairs or benches prearranged thus. Hexis (orientation of
body in this case) is 'given' and is adopted largely unconsciously by all
but newcomers. My field-notes suggest that the process cannot be entirely
unconscious at least. It is possible for a participant to be 'disciplined'
(spoken to by another, usually senior, Member) if they transgress the
norms of behaviour during Meeting for Worship. Having said that, it is
equally possible that one's posture in Meeting, after attending for several
years say, may well be adopted unconsciously on each occasion. The point
is that I think we must at least allow for the possibility of the conscious
assimilation of hexis by Quakers in Meeting. Clearly, hexis is a means of
not only representing but of constructing one's identity whether as a
Quaker, a Sikh, Muslim, or Shaker. In each case, the bodily disposition of
the adept (at least during worship) speaks of ones belongingness to this or
that community.

An interesting coda to this argument relates to Dandelion's interesting
argument that the unity of Quakerism depends not so much on an overt,
unifying theology but on a behavioural creed. It is an argument that
chimes strongly with Bourdieu's idea of an embodied habitus. Dandelion
is quite correct in pointing out that Quakers appear to be doing the same
thing (in Meeting for Worship) so long as he acknowledges that
participants in Meeting are *not* doing the same thing, and perhaps not even
the same kind of thing. Participants in Meeting for Worship at
Dibdenshaw claimed to be praying, worrying, drawing up shopping lists,
reading, breathing evenly, meditating, puzzling things out, and so on.
Whatever can be said about them, they are not doing the same thing,
despite appearances to the contrary. Dandelion's own fieldwork bears this
out (see, for example Dandelion 1996, 111; see also the booklet produced
by Newcastle Meeting 1998).

Bourdieu establishes a close link between the embodiment of habitus and the built environment:

> But it is in the dialectical relationship between the body and a space structured according to the mythico-religious oppositions that one finds the form par excellence of the structural apprenticeship which leads to the embodying of the world (1977, 89).

The extent and depth of socialisation processes would be far greater in the case of the Kabyle among whom Bourdieu conducted fieldwork, however, the processes described by Bourdieu are present in the Quaker case though less explicit. Practically speaking, the Quaker habitus is at its most overt on Sunday mornings. And although Quakers remain Quakers when they leave the Meeting House, the habitus is reduced: they may be the only Quaker in their family, they may work in a place where membership of any religious group is derided. Historically, however, the Quaker habitus would probably have been as all-embracing and homogeneous at the Kabyle during the first 150 years of the movement.

I have written a good deal on the topic of the Meeting House and I don't intend to repeat those arguments and observations here (Coleman and Collins 1996, 2006; Collins 1996a, 2006a). I have tried to show how the narratives of Meeting are manifested in the very fabric and furnishings of the Meeting House itself - as I have already argued briefly above. The Meeting House concretises the identity of Quakers. Habitus, as presented by Bourdieu, manifests both strengths and weaknesses when applied to actually existing communities but it is far too monolithic to account entirely for individual identity in the 21st century (Collins 2008).

Concluding Remarks: understanding Quaker identity

In Dandelion's terms (this volume, Chapter 1), plaining, habitus, narrative (or heterotopia for that matter, see Pilgrim's chapter, this volume) may indeed be relatively stable tropes manifested by Quakers across the centuries and I believe that there is plenty of evidence to suggest that they are. However, the point I wish to emphasize here is that there can be no single overarching interpretation by which we can come to understand Quaker identity. The research undertaken by Simon Best (this volume, Chapter 11) on adolescent Quakers and Giselle Vincett on 'Quagans' (this volume, Chapter 10) is of particular interest here. The practice of adolescent Friends in particular seems in various ways to confound generalisations made of Quakers in general. Understanding or even describing the identity of individuals in the first years of the 21st

century is a difficult, perhaps impossible task. Nevertheless, this is the project in which I have been primarily engaged during the last decade. It just so happens that, in my case, it was the Quaker Meeting and its participants that sparked this interest and which provides my starting point for each new excursion into identity. Quaker identity is sustained primarily through the generation and regeneration of stories, primarily in and around the Meeting House but also elsewhere: these stories, it should be remembered are presented not only through the spoken and written word, but through many other media: the body, the built environment, clothing and other consumables, leisure pursuits and so on. It is just *this* concatenation of stories which comprise the Quaker Meeting and which lends an individual their Quaker identity, their Quaker self. While Quakers live in the world and interact both with those who are Quakers and those who are not Quakers, this does not mean that Quaker narratives are suspended away from the Meeting. However, when presented they are more implicit than they once were and are therefore far less likely, nowadays, to be acknowledged and regenerated, restored, rejuvenated, revitalised. In the seventeenth century, Friends manifested Quakerism very explicitly, to wear the Quaker grey, to eschew the standard greetings, to refuse to doff one's hat, to thee and thou everyone one met regardless of their social status, was to allude to narratives which were widely recognised, and more often than not, condemned. The response of the non-Quaker, though sometimes violent, was often equally overt and necessarily served to regenerate those narratives. Nowadays, religious faith and practice is primarily private: the stories that are woven are primarily for the consumption of the group itself, and are legitimated by further stories, by those drawn from the canon, which are, of course, also generated from within the group. Whatever the advantages and disadvantages of this process are for Quakers, fewer and fewer people find it fulfilling, and membership has been in decline since the 1960s. Meeting narratives have always been, at least to some extent, interwoven with those threads spun in the context of wider society. Writing both as social scientist and Quaker, I believe that it will be this process which, if sustained, may yet revitalise what remains an extraordinary group.

CHAPTER THREE

BRITISH QUAKERISM AS HETEROTOPIC

GAY PILGRIM

Introduction

This chapter suggests that Foucault's concept of heterotopia, as defined by Kevin Hetherington (1996), names a continuing thread which links the first Quakers (who emerged in the mid-17th century) with those in Britain in the 21st century. The diversity of belief amongst Friends[1] today no longer supports the original religious basis for their utopian vision which resulted in their heterotopic stance, and which provided early Friends with their identity and unity. The chapter argues that, instead of an overarching belief, it is the sense of being 'Other' and living out an 'alternate ordering' single inverted commas please that is one of the key ways in which 21st century Friends obtain a sense of identity and unity.

Heterotopia

Heterotopia is a word first coined by the medical profession, who used it to refer to those parts of the body which are out of place, missing altogether, extra or alien; features which were unexpected, incongruous and unsettling. Michel Foucault appropriated this word, using it to describe spaces that disturb, shock or unsettle, writing most fully about his concept of heterotopia in *Of Other Spaces* (1986)[2] where he discusses spaces, (physical and mythical) and the way in which spaces (or sites) can be used to subvert or invert normal relationships. He argues that spaces or sites which contradict or invert relationships are of two main types: utopias and heterotopias. According to Foucault, utopias are 'fundamentally unreal spaces', whereas a heterotopia is a countersite (1968, 24), a real space which highlights issues of order and power through the confusion it creates by its unexpected and incongruous use; for example the holding of a fun fair in a prison.

Alternate Ordering

Kevin Hetherington takes up Foucault's suggestion that the concept of heterotopia might illuminate the 'spatiality of the social ordering of modernity' (1996, 40).[3] Hetherington uses the term heterotopia to denote 'sites of alternate order (which are) constituted through their incongruous character and (their) relationship to other less incongruous sites' (1998, 31). He defines heterotopia as:

> Spaces of alternate ordering (which) organise a bit of the social world in a way different to that which surrounds them. That alternate ordering marks them out as Other and allows them to be seen as an example of an alternative way of doing things (1996, 2).

This is the definition which provides a link between mid-17th century Friends and contemporary Quakers, and is the definition I am working from when I use the term heterotopia. My understanding of this concept has been furthered and broadened by its use in other disciplines, in particular cultural studies and geography (see Shields 1991; Rose 1993; Keith and Pile 1993; Cresswell 1996) where the discourse is about how space, conceptual or actual, marginal or central, illustrates power relations and therefore social ordering. The discourse on marginality and on the opportunities that being marginal provides to rehearse an alternative social ordering is relevant to Friends, both in the past and the present.

The margins, whether geographical or social, offer opportunities for empowerment through practices of resistance, protest and transgression (Shields 1991; Rose 1993). They are spaces where alternative ways of living and ordering can be played with and practised, demonstrated and witnessed to. Louis Marin (1984, 1992) in particular explores the concept of spaces which can be experimented in and where ideas can be played with. He points out that Thomas More's word *utopia* was coined by bringing two Greek words together, namely *eu*-topia and *ou*-topia. One meaning a 'good place', the other 'no place or nowhere'. In other words, Utopia is defined as an ideal world which does not, and cannot, exist. Marin is interested in what happens in the gap that exists between the 'nowhere place' (the ideal that cannot be achieved) and the 'good place' (the good that can be achieved), that he terms the 'neutral' (1984). He posits that in this gap it is possible to imagine and attempt to create utopias within the confines of the modern world. He created the word 'utopics' to describe what occurs in this gap. What Marin calls the neutral is where Hetherington believes heterotopias exist. Hetherington states 'Heterotopias are not quite spaces of transition ... but they are spaces of deferral, spaces where ideas and practices that represent the good life can come into being ...' (1996, 3).

However, Hetherington also points out that:

> Difference, while being different to the accepted norm within a culture, while it is indeed a source of marginality and resistance to marginalization, is always also implicated in social ordering, even if at the most fundamental level, it is opposed to everything that society, seen as a social order, stands for (1996, 7).

Providing a significant alternate ordering necessitates being *simultaneously* marginal, and embedded in the prevailing social order, since heterotopias, or sites of Otherness, express their alternate ordering directly through the society whom they seek to be different from. They must be juxtaposed to something to be heterotopic.

The Rise of Quakerism

It was in the gap created by the collapse of traditional society and the failure of the Commonwealth to implement the envisioned new society, that Quakerism came into being. Its leading figure, George Fox, struggled with the contending religious ideas of his time, eventually experiencing a profound emotional crisis, during which he had a 'visionary' experience. This vivid personal encounter with God inspired him to begin preaching. He had some success in the Midlands but it was in the North of England that he found large numbers of followers. These were people who, realising that the Civil War was not ushering in God's Kingdom as they believed it would, had retreated to the margins of society until the arrival of Fox galvanised them (Nickalls 1952; Dandelion *et al* 1998, 20).

This northerly part of England was largely ungoverned by religious or civil authorities and its marginality permitted the exploration and creation of an alternate ordering. A 'nowhere' place which provided the space to consolidate an alternate ordering; a space where the 'good place' could be discovered and lived with confidence. Such a space was a site of resistance to the prevailing social order; a space which enabled people to 'raise their voices to be heard', and led them to move out from the margins into more central sites where they could not only be heard, but be 'seen to live different, alternative lives, openly hoping that others will share their vision ....' (Hetherington 1996, 7). Fox and other gifted leaders began to travel around the countryside spreading the message of their utopian vision and modelling, through their behaviour and actions, an alternate social ordering

Few, if any, of the beliefs which became central to Friends were unique, but what Fox and the early Quakers did was to bring them together in a cohesive way. The driving force of early Friends' actions was religious and they sincerely believed that they were 'called' to re-recreate society as God intended. But the congruence of their ideas with others around at the time about what constitutes a 'good society' indicates that they were aware of the prevailing cultural influences (Barbour 1964; Bauman 1983; Baines 1998; Carter 1999; Moore 2000a) and illustrates that sites of Otherness do not emerge out of a vacuum, but are stimulated by the very society against which they are reacting.

In the breakdown of civil society during the Civil War, there was no control over what people could say and publish, and Quakers were by no means the only group who sought to bring about a radical change in society based on religious precepts. The establishment of the Commonwealth government re-instituted control and censorship (Bauman 1983; Hill 1961; 1998; Lamont 1969; Acheson 1993) and those who continued to write and speak of an alternative way of ordering society were apprehended and dealt with severely by the authorities. Quakers were steadfastly uncompromising, thereby forcing the authorities to take action against them, which provided many opportunities for Friends to demonstrate their Otherness and alternate social ordering (Nickalls 1952; Hill 1972; 1998; Bauman 1983; Reay 1985; Gwyn 1995; 2000).

The Heterotopic Impulse

Heterotopias, or sites of Otherness, express their alternate ordering of society directly through the society whom they seek to be different from. To do this effectively, they need to inhabit spaces which are sufficiently central to render their alternate ordering visible.

The re-establishment of civil authority found Fox, along with others, imprisoned. However imprisonment did not dampen their convictions but rather provided them with a platform for their preaching and dissemination of the Truth (Nickalls 1952; Bauman 1983). Far from being intimidated, marginalized and properly subordinated as the judicial system intended, Friends used their trials as a space in which to evangelise and inspire. They treated the courtroom as a 'church' which was not only unexpected, but incongruous and confusing. A space designed to impose a proper respect for the social order was instead used to challenge the prevailing power relations, encourage resistance to the prevailing culture and witness to an alternate ordering. It became a heterotopic site.

A long standing heterotopic site was provided for Quakers by Margaret Fell, the wife of a Judge who had considerable social and material standing in Lancashire. Having heard George Fox preach she invited him to stay, and ultimately Swarthmoor Hall, the home of the Fells, became the unofficial headquarters of the Quakers. As such, it was a space consisting of real civil authority (being the home of an active, government appointed circuit judge), *and* determined protest and resistance to that same authority by Friends. It was a space which encompassed both the socially central and the socially marginal. It was both a site where law, order and the establishment were upheld and reinforced, and a site from which resistance, challenge and protest were formulated and enacted.

Hetherington points out that:

> Heterotopia exist when the relationship between sites is described by a difference of representation defined by their modes of social ordering. For example, holding a festival next to a prison would constitute a heterotopic relationship, each space being used to order the social in very different ways. Either site could be taken as heterotopic in relation to the other, but the likelihood, given that prisons are sanctioned within society whereas festivals are not, is that the festival will be seen as the heterotopia (1996, 6-7).

In just the same way, Swarthmoor Hall was used to order the social in very different ways, the one being sanctioned by society, the other definitely not.

Churches were another space turned into a heterotopic site by Quakers. These orderly places, controlled and organised by religious authorities backed up by the civil government, were central to the upholding and maintenance of social order and normativeness. A place where nothing unexpected happened, where people understood what was required of them, how to behave, what to wear, what to say and when to say it. Into this space came Quakers, interrupting the sermon, jumping onto the furniture, denouncing the priest and the established church and challenging people to a debate; (Nickalls 1952; Bauman 1983). The familiar church was transformed into a place of Otherness, a place where something excessive and incongruous occurs.[4] The Quakers' treatment of this space was in direct contrast to its normal usage, setting up disturbing and unsettling juxtapositions to normal social relations.

Quakers' worshipping style also witnessed to their Otherness. They met in ordinary houses, barns, or outside, gathering together in silence, waiting for the spirit of Christ to move them to 'minister' (speak). As they waited it was not unusual for people to shake, murmur, moan, or otherwise display peculiar behaviour (Higginson 1653, 15). There was no order of service, no organised sermon, no singing, no gender differentiation, no apparent heirarchy or leader. This was a site of Otherness established through its relationship of difference from other worshipping groups, and from other church spaces, though related to them by the concept of worshipping God. Quaker Meetings unsettled social and spatial relations, whilst simultaneously providing an alternate representation of the same. That they were regarded with great suspicion and seen as transgressive is borne out by the extreme measures taken to break them up and outlaw them (*Quaker Faith and Practice* [*QFP*] 1995, 19.35).

Otherness and Power

Sites of Otherness and alternate ordering do not occur in a vacuum. It is their difference *in relation to* other sites and orderings that makes them heterotopic, and such difference is not separate from the society in which it exists, but is construed by and participates in the construction of that society. The existence of sites of Otherness as visible alternatives in social ordering have an impact on the prevailing norms, and, in their turn, are influenced by the reaction of society towards them. Social relations are not isolated constructs, but are constantly shifting in subtle response to the society which produces them. That some groups within society have more power than others and determine the predominant social relations has implications for what is defined as a site of Otherness, and what represents an alternate ordering. Even within the group who constitute the site of Otherness, power relations are central to their understanding of what it is they are claiming as Other, and the freedom with which adherents to the group can express and practice their `otherness'.

Early Friends' were no exception, but eventually a system of organisation and control was set up which cleverly managed to sustain the centrality of the belief that every individual could be directly guided by God, whilst putting alongside it a process of testing discernment which squarely placed the responsibility for action on the group as a whole. Thus no one person could be seen to claim more power or knowledge than another. But, as Hetherington points out, alternative modes of ordering `.... have their own codes, rules and ... generate their own relations of power' (1996, 24) and the outcome of this system of organisation was that Quaker Otherness became institutionalised.

Up to the mid to late 19th century Quakers were still distinctively `Other' through their dress, speech, lifestyle and form of worship. They continued to challenge and highlight power relations and the social ordering of their time through their engagement with issues such as capital punishment and crime, the mentally ill and the abolition of the slave trade (Isichei 1970; Punshon 1984).

However, from about 1830 to 1885 the evangelical and methodist movement swept up many Friends, and their insistence on the centrality of the Bible began to blur the theological distinctiveness of the Quakers (Isichei 1970). The internal conflicts generated eventually resulted in a conference in Manchester in 1895 where Friends came together to consider and discuss late 19th century Quakerism. Ultimately, Friends returned to their distinctive theology of the centrality of the Inward Light, but their continuing engagement with the new scientific, philosophical and religious thinking gave rise to a questioning of religious certainties, and brought about a reinterpretation of this concept to mean individual personal experience (Isichei 1970, 5). This reinterpretation paved the way for the increased diversity of belief which has become the hallmark of contemporary Quakerism (Dandelion 1996).

By the end of the 19th century, Quakers' clear outward identifiers of speech and dress had fallen away and there was little outwardly visible to signify their alternate ordering. It took the First World War in 1914 to vividly demonstrate Friends' alternate ordering through their conscientious objection to participation in that war. Once again Friends used the courts as a heterotopic space; a place of witness to their peace testimony, enduring public vilification and imprisonment for their transgressive behaviour, which was viewed as shocking, excessive and incongruous. It was a minority of Quakers who were active conscientious objectors, but their steadfastness and courage made a significant impact, not only in the public arena, but within the Religious Society of Friends itself. It has been claimed that without the advent of the Great War (and the consequent elevation of the peace testimony to a central organising motif) the Religious Society of Friends would have ceased to exist as a distinctive religious group (Kennedy 2001, 414).

The Diminution/Attenuation of Conviction

The first Quakers did not have a vision of the world as it *ought* to be because of an ideology about social justice, peace and equality. It was *God's* vision for the world and humanity's place and purpose within it that was the inspiration and foundation for their otherness and alternate ordering (Gwyn 1995). Their experience of being convicted by Christ was utterly transforming, visibly altering their lives. It was an obligatory point of passage, without which a person could not be admitted to full participation in the life of the Religious Society of Friends. Victor Turner (1969) terms such experiences of transition as liminal, observing that they promote strong bonds and strengthen relationships and obligations within the group.

By the mid 20th century, Quaker certainty about Christianity as the only true and proper faith was collapsing (Isichei 1970). The experience of being convicted by the Light was certainly no longer regarded as an obligatory rite of passage and the liminal was replaced by the liminoid (Turner, 1982) whereby the rite of passage becomes optional rather than essential. Liminoid rites of passage are much weaker as they do not carry the same weight of obligation and consequently do not strengthen the integration of the group as effectively as the liminal, nor produce such a strong sense of identity. I would argue that they also allow a much greater degree of diversity, since it is no longer necessary for everyone to have participated in a similar experience to be part of the group.

At the end of the 20th century the Quaker culture of openness made taboo any certainty about Christ, God, divine will or the sacred (Heron 1992; Dandelion 1996). This 'death of conviction' (Lynch 2002) also leads to an openess to a range of beliefs which are based not so much on the truth claims involved in them, as the kind of life they make possible (ibid). Today, whilst many Friends remain committed to working towards peace and social justice (*QFP* 1995), it cannot be claimed that this is a consequence of a commonly shared religious experience. It owes more to the concept of an elect moral status (Phillips 1989; Hetherington 1998) a concept describing those who believe they have access to a heightened sense of experience, resulting in the expression of moral values to do with better ways of living and interacting with one another[5].

Contemporary British Quakerism

Friends' determination to be open to everyone and anything,[6] whilst certainly marking them out as Other, also creates uncertainty about what they are about and who they are. It can no longer be assumed that those attending Meeting for Worship or applying for membership of the Religious Society of Friends are Christian, even in the very loose Quaker interpretation of that label (Heron 1992; Dandelion 1996). There is no longer a commonly shared religious belief and this breakdown of an overarching religious paradigm has led to Friends' sense of identity and unity resting on their heterotopic stance itself; their sense of themselves as being Other and offering an alternate ordering to the rest of society (Dale 1996; Wildwood 1999).

However Friends' concerns are no longer exclusively, or even mainly, Quaker issues. Mainstream society has largely caught up with them and at the start of the new millennium, the Religious Society of Friends mirrors the pluralism, individualism and crisis of meaning common in the West (Flanagan and Jupp 2001). The absence of a creed or statement of belief, their seemingly non-heirarchical organisational structure, their clear statement of the necessity to be 'open to new Light from whatever source it may come' (*QFP* 1995, 1.02.7) and the weight given to experience rather than belief, attracts those who are searching for a faith path or spirituality that 'encourages (them) to forge their own unique life ... and spiritual paths in their own unique ways' (Heelas *et al* 2005, 21).

Contemporary Friends are likely to describe themselves as 'seekers', and talk about being on a spiritual journey, a pilgrimage. They desire a more spiritual, meaningful, integrated and life-revivifying existence enabling them to express freely all that they are. They could also be described as attempting to escape the routines of everyday life which they find oppressive, soulless, ethically and morally unsatisfying (Cohen *et al* 1987; Cohen and Taylor 1992). Both pilgrimage and escape attempts are transitional processes, occurring in a space in which a new identity can be constructed. The spaces best suited to this transitional process are marginal, although they will always have a social centrality for those inhabiting them. They are likely also to be spaces of occasion where the re-forming identity can be rehearsed (Shields 1991, 1992; Hetherington 1998).

The Quaker Meeting for Worship provides such a space of occasion, allowing identity performance through the expression of the values and principles of the group -- what Friends term 'ministry'. The Meeting for Worship is the primary space where Friends come to recognise and know one another, where they develop a sense of belonging and communitas (Turner 1969). The acceptance into membership of Friends who bring with them the mores and ethos of a culture committed to the personal, rather than a corporately shared spiritual path (Heelas 1996), is having a profound effect; not only on the understanding of what it is to be Quaker, but on the way in which identity and belonging are experienced and learned. The diminution of corporate authority has meant that identity performance no longer has to be expressed in terms of Quaker theology, and this, combined with uncertainty about what Quakerism is or should be, has created an unboundaried space which may be colonised by anyone espousing an alternate ordering. As a consequence, this is an ideal utopic site, enabling the development of an expressive identity whilst simultaneously developing ideas about how to create a better world, the practical progressing of which 'fit' with Quaker ideology and the contemporary Quaker vision quest.

The 21st Century

Contemporary Friends in Britain can be described as falling, approximately, into three groups; the Exclusivists, the Inclusivists and the Syncretists. All consider themselves 'proper' Quakers, though not necessarily each other as such.

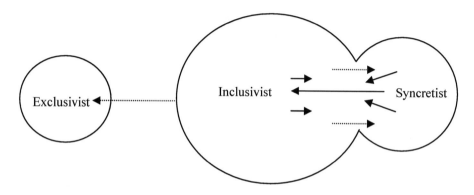

Figure 3-1: Relationship Between Exclusivists, Inclusivists, and Syncretists

The Exclusivists are a discrete, very small group, who find the lack of an explicit Christian religious enterprise in the mainstream of Britain Yearly Meeting (BYM) unacceptable. The most extreme (and largely unknown) example of this group is Friends in Christ (FiC). They seceded from BYM in 1993 because they consider it irremediably 'out of the Light' (*The Call* 1996, No1). They are emphatically Christocentric, seeking a return to 'primitive Christianity', 'gospel order' and Meetings for Worship which are not timed or constrained to one hour. Their utopian vision quest is religiously inspired and they seek to make visible their heterotopic stance by the use of 'plain' speech (the use of 'thee' and 'thou') and 'plain' dress (*The Call* 2000, No 1). The continual questioning of the concept of the 'one true church' by those within BYM, and their conviction that the only certainty is being absolutely *un*certain, (what Dandelion (2004b) has termed the 'absolute perhaps') has no warrant within FiC. They have reconstituted clear boundaries and offer a very specific identity. There is some crossover with members of the larger mainstream Yearly Meeting who are concerned about the loss of explicit Christianity within BYM (such as the New Foundation Fellowship) but FiC are too certain and their clearly defined faith position too 'exclusive' to attract a widespread following amongst most contemporary Quakers.

The Inclusivists, the core of Britain Yearly Meeting, consist of those who hold to the mainstream traditions and adhere to the 'behavioural creed' (Dandelion 1996) which permits enormous flexibility of belief, but constrains the performance of Quaker identity. They are still corporatist in their outlook and are loosely Christian, though Jesus may not be considered divine; his value lying more in his teachings and example than in his divinity. Members of this group may express understanding of and sympathy with the Syncretists' pluralism, but continue to value the discipline and authority of the corporate body over and above the individualised personalised spirituality of the Syncretists.

However, with increasing numbers of people coming to Quakerism because of its perceived lack of boundaries, 'you don't have to believe anything' (Pilgrim 2003) and its provision of a space in which to rehearse their personal spirituality, the behavioural creed is coming under considerable pressure. It is noticeable that over the last few years the annual gathering of Quakers (BYM) has become more clearly an explicitly religious enterprise and this is possibly a contributing factor to the decline in numbers attending (*Proceedings of Britain Yearly Meeting* 2001, 2006). Inclusivists are not unhappy to see Quaker values taken up by society since they see themselves as leading the way. Their heterotopic stance rests on continuing to live at the radical edge, but not so far out of mainstream society that they lose their influence and voice.

The Syncretists are much more amorphous, and appear to be concerned about their personal spiritual quest, rather than corporate theological certainties. Many of them have a sense of disconnection from traditional sources of meaning and are sceptical about fixed systems of belief which obscure more than they reveal. They seek and value comfort, healing and hope, wherever it might be found and often pursue non-Quaker religious and quasi-religious activities, as well as attending the Quaker Meeting for Worship (Pilgrim 2003; Heelas *et al* 2005). There is some overlap between Inclusivists and Syncretists (see Figure 3-1), but whilst Inclusivists may have a syncretic approach to belief, they are not *essentially* syncretist because of their adherence to the behavioural creed which acts as a fixed boundary. Syncretists place great emphasis on freedom, authenticity, the recovery of rejected knowledge and a synthesis of spiritualities. They include those who are drawn by a *lifestyle* but *not* a religion (who will in fact, often explicitly reject religion); those who are interested in *religion* but *not* in a belief system; and those who *have* a religion of some kind, but who seem to need to appropriate a belief system with which they have some familiarity.[7] They wish to locate themselves in a group providing a powerful sense of social solidarity within which it is acceptable to construct a highly personalised spiritual belief system. They are attracted by Friends' heterotopic stance and the utopic space it offers, rather than an explicit religious enterprise. Their identity as a Quaker is but one among many, and signifies an alternate ordering rather than a particular religious belief. The heterotopic stance sought by this group is not so much about an alternate ordering as alternate *orderings*, and it reflects the spiritual marketplace attitude of the wider society.

Conclusion

The organisational structure of the Religious Society of Friends arose out of a need to contain the anarchic, individualised expression of God's call to action. It also addressed the issue of social and power relations within the group, as major disputes between various segments of the Quaker movement brought it perilously close to disintegration (Gwyn 1995). The regularising of what constituted Quaker Otherness' and alternate ordering served to consolidate the movement and ensured its survival. But on exploring the historical sweep of Quakerism, it is apparent that the alternate ordering highlighting the 'otherness' of Friends has constantly shifted, depending on which group dominated social and power relations. The periods of greatest contention have arisen when their visible alternate ordering is becoming submerged, and their sense of being Other increasingly hard to maintain. This is a state of affairs which presently prevails.

The nature of modern, or post-modern, Western culture is pluralist and individualist, allowing for multiple identities, lifestyles and beliefs; what Ritzer (1983) refers to as a 'supermarket society'. There is no one overarching cultural myth or paradigm, but several to many competing 'stories'. The utopian vision quest of Quakerism with regard to peace, justice and social equality is no longer singular, or even unusual. Charities such as Oxfam, Action Aid, Fair Trade and others, are equally active in these areas. Even their testimony to living simply has become conflated with environmental and 'green' issues; the success of organic farming produce and government and local authority provisions for recycling being indicative of its acceptance in the wider society.

If a heterotopia is about offering a utopic space; a place where alternatives can be played with and practised, then Quakers still have one. But what of their overarching sense of being Other, and offering an alternate ordering to 'the world'? I have previously argued that over the 20th century, Quaker 'Otherness' has become internalised and individualised, and British Friends' energies are now directed towards negotiating the playing out of their heterotopic stance within their own organisation, rather than in the world at large (Pilgrim 2003).

To some extent this is still the case. Recent research by Best and Meads illustrate how at least two small groups within the Yearly Meeting see themselves as being `other', in Best's case, not only within the Quaker group, but also outside it. His research on adolescent Friends, leads him to describe the group as a `community of intimacy'. He writes that this group `places emphasis on belonging to the group, community, inter-personal networks secured by friendships and the separateness of the group *both from other Quakers and from other young people*' (my italics) (this volume, Chapter 11). Interestingly Best's research indicates the primacy of worship as experienced by Young Friends at their national events, `For adolescent Quakers, participating in worship with other adolescents is ... transformative' (ibid) and `adolescent Quaker ritual is an embodiment of the community and transforms individuals into members of the community, this transformation is crucial to creating a sense of belonging (and) is vital to the creation and sustaining of a networked community which continues between events'(ibid) Could Young Friends have rediscovered the liminal rite of passage that now escapes the majority of adult Quakers? Best argues that for the adolescent group unity is achieved not by orthopraxis but rather through the community of intimacy'(ibid). If that is so, is it powerful enough to be sustained once they have matured past being an exclusively adolescent group which `practice(s) in different ways and gather(s) in different places'?

Meads' research explores an experimental form of worship (this volume, chapter 12) which the Quaker theologian Rex Ambler believes was instigated by George Fox (Ambler 1997a, 14). Over the last decade his understanding and practice of a similar method has percolated amongst Friends. To date it has remained low-key, but Meads is clear that it is a transformative and liminal experience. She writes that participating in the Experiment with Light `binds (Friends) with each other at a subtle level and differentiates them in their own understanding from ... other Friends ... who have not had similar experience' (ibid). She further argues that `Friends who Experiment, by their Experimenting, potentially challenge those Friends who are comfortable, who do not want to examine their lives and have deeper spiritual experiences'; she suggests that they are, albeit in a small way, offering an `alternate ordering' and therefore creating a heterotopic site within their Meetings (ibid).

In 2002 I posited that if the Inclusivists acted to curb the utopic space Syncretists had become accustomed to, the latter would leave. It was perhaps too broad an assumption, failing to take into account sufficiently the variable nature of the Syncretist group. Vincett's research on Quaker Pagans

(Quagans) indicates this, although it also confirms my thesis that some syncretists are drawn to the Religious Society of Friends precisely because it provides a framework for their beliefs. She states 'their Goddess Feminism is shaped by and enclosed within their commitment to the Friends. But ... it is the *form* of Quakerism, the discipline or behavioural creed ... which encloses the beliefs and ritual of Goddess Feminism.' (this volume, Chapter 10) and argues that Quagans 'take the behavioural creed very seriously'(ibid) Given that this is the case, this particular group of Syncretists are not truly heterotopic to the Inclusivists.

Vincett points out that one of the key aspects of the Liberal Quaker project is that faith be relevant to the age and the present age privileges independence and autonomy. Given that this is the case, it is perhaps unsurprising that fewer and fewer people seek membership of the Religious Society of Friends, preferring to remain attenders. [8] Unpublished research reprising Dandelion's original thesis (1996) demonstrates that today many Friends feel connected to their local Meeting and the global network of Quakers, but have little to no sense of connection, or interest in their Area or the Yearly Meeting (Rutherford 2003). This may explain why it is no longer easy to perceive competing heterotopias within the Yearly Meeting.

It may also be that Friends are increasingly content to belong to an organisation within which people who share congruent spiritual and ethical values can draw support and encouragement. In 2002 I wrote '...Outwardly ... Britain Yearly Meeting might look much the same, but in fact it would be a very different kind of Quakerism, possibly signified through being renamed the Spiritual Society of Friends.' In 2006, the Assistant Clerk of a large Area Meeting publicly made just such a recommendation.

This desire to change the nomenclature of the Religious Society of Friends to the Spiritual Society of Friends, gives credence to Dandelion's argument that contemporary Quaker theology allows for 'a Quakerism ... forever on the move' (this volume, chapter 1) and that 'Quakerism adapts its means to coherence over time rather than locating (it) in more stable tropes such as ... the heterotopic impulse' (this volume, chapter 1) But he also says '(Quakers) believe in a very different way from most religious groups and hold belief as a category in a very different esteem ... The 'absolute perhaps' is the defining characteristic of the Liberal Quaker and is the key difference between these Friends and the whole of the rest of Quakerism, worldwide today and historically. (this volume, Chapter 1) But such a key difference is also something 'Other', an 'alternate ordering'; a heterotopic impulse.

Notes

[1] I use the terms 'Friends' and 'Quakers' interchangeably. It should be noted that this chapter is solely focused on the Quaker group in Britain.

[2] See also *The Order of Things* (1977) in which Foucault illustrates how incongruous juxtapositions challenge preconceived assumptions by using Borges' quote from a Chinese encyclopaedia. The ordering of the text in the *Encyclopaedia* is at odds with a Western understanding of logical sequencing and relationship (Foucault 1977, xv). This different ordering is confusing and unsettling.

[3] Although Hetherington points out that it has largely been applied to ideas about *post*modernity and been used in a variety of ways (Connor 1989; Soja 1990, 1996, Delaney 1992, Bennet 1995; Gennocchio 1995).

[4] Foucault refers to two principle modes of ordering: resemblance and similitude. Similitude is an ordering that takes place through a juxtaposition of signs that culturally are seen as not going together, either because their relationship is new, or because it is unexpected (as in Borges' use of a Chinese encyclopaedia); what is being signified cannot easily be attached to a referent. In contrast, ordering represented by what is being signified, refers to a known referent.

[5] See also Scully's account of Quakers and virtue ethics, (this volume, Chapter 6).

[6] Examples abound in the letters pages of *The Friend*, eg 26 May, 2000, 16 'All Inclusive'.

[7] Ongoing fieldwork currently substantiates this.

[8] The term given to people who attend Meeting for Worship regularly, but who have not applied for membership.

PART II:

BELIEF AND VALUES

CHAPTER FOUR

THE QUESTION OF CHRISTIANITY

KATE MELLOR

Both Pilgrim and Dandelion refer in this volume to the loss of or very low incidence of Christianity within British Quakerism. Pilgrim refers to 'the collapse of Quaker certainty about Christianity as the only true and proper faith...,' (this volume, Chapter 3) and Dandelion contends that 'Under the 'mask' of the 'culture of silence' (the value of silence, the devaluation of language, and the consequent rules governing the breaking of silence with speech), the Yearly Meeting has shifted its popular theology from a Quaker-Christian one to a post-Christian one,' (this volume, Chapter 1). I make an alternative claim: British Quakers remain Christian.

Research into Quaker belief structure conducted by Dandelion in 1989 and repeated by Rosie Rutherford in 2003 have helped to solidify the belief that British Quakers are no longer Christian. The first survey, Dandelion's (1996), claimed that 51% of British Quakers 'would describe themselves as Christian.' Rutherford's survey showed similar results; 46% of her sample 'think of themselves' as Christian (2003). However, in 2005 and 2006 I conducted a survey that included 1006 Members and Attenders of Britain Yearly Meeting, 80% of whom indicated that they consider themselves to be Christian. 87% of those who answered the question indicated that they would answer that they are Christian on a census-type survey. Fewer than 5% of those who took part in the survey are clearly, in my analysis, not Christian. Additionally, 90% of those who answered the question believe in God. This research contradicts the two earlier surveys that show a low incidence of Christian identity and also a low incidence of theism. It thus sheds new light on the ongoing debate about the nature of belief within Britain Yearly Meeting. This research strongly suggests that the Religious Society of Friends in Britain is still Christ-centred and theist.

In this chapter, I first examine the surveys carried out by Dandelion and Rutherford, with which I compare my results. Second, I describe and explain my research methods. Third, I introduce the idea of three types of Christian, as evidenced by my survey. And, fourth, I look at some of the questions I used and, more importantly the answers I received, giving examples from written comments.

Quakers and Christian Identity: other surveys of belief

The relatively small population of British Quakerism has answered three major surveys of their patterns of believing in fewer than twenty years. Dandelion conducted the first in 1989. Rutherford conducted the second survey in 2003, using Dandelion's research as a pilot study. Their results provided the starting point for my research.

Dandelion asserted from his survey, participant observation and interviews that 'the group has become post-Christian in the sense that so many Friends use non-Christian language to describe their religious experience that it would be intellectually dishonest to claim the group as Christian' (1996, xv). His work was the first important survey of belief of British Quakers and it fell neatly into a thirty-year discussion into the nature of Christian belief. This debate, which raised a concern about the loss of Christianity within the group, is summarised in Alastair Heron's book, *Quakers in History: a century of change 1895-1995*. Heron explains that in the late 1960s Quakers in Britain 'still held a distinctive Quaker Christian position' (1995, 75). By 1980, the position had changed. Heron draws attention to Janet Scott's 1980 Swarthmore Lecture, a lecture which he considered to be 'a significant event' because it raised a debate about whether Quakers had left Jesus behind in creating a new theology which was more monotheist (1995, 96).[1]

Dandelion's results provided evidence to support the claim that Quakers had moved away from their Christian identity. The debate, and claims about the non-Christian and Atheist nature of the Religious Society of Friends in Britain continues today in the pages of the weekly British Quaker newspaper, *The Friend*, under headlines such as 'Are Quakers Christian?', 'Where is Jesus?', and 'Do Quakers Need God?' (*The Friend* 164 (23): 10-11, 165 (31): 8, and 165 (44): 8).

In his survey, Dandelion found that:

> only around one in two claim Jesus as an important part of their spiritual lives. Whilst this could rise to two in three at any one time, by adding those in certain sub-samples who gave a positive response to the question with those for whom it varies…this figure could reduce to less than 1 in 6 for those with less than three year's participation within the group (1996, 146).

Dandelion's research also showed that approximately two thirds (66.2%) of the respondents claimed that Jesus' ethical teachings were an important part of their spiritual life (1996, 147). He concluded that,

> The concept of the liberal Quaker belief culture is supported by the diversity of opinions and views and it is apparent that Quaker Christianity is no longer the dominant framework for Quaker belief. Furthermore, the numbers of those who do hold Christian or Quaker-Christian beliefs are lower than their counterparts in other groups (1996, 176).

In 2003, Rutherford conducted a rigorously sampled survey of 48 Quaker Meetings across Britain, using Dandelion's questions as well as her own. In asking her question about identity, each respondent was allowed to choose as many from the following as possible: Quaker, Christian, Universalist, Pacifist, Atheist, Buddhist, Agnostic, Humanist, and/or a spiritual person. 46% of Rutherford's respondents indicated that they 'think of themselves as' Christian (2003).

In the following sections I consider the following: the way 'Christian' was defined by Dandelion and Rutherford; their question choice and question phrasing; the questionnaire design; the number of questions; question order and transparency.

The Surveys Conducted by Dandelion and Rutherford

Dandelion's 'Quaker Questionnaire' was in the form of a 15-page booklet. It included 72 questions with 436 variables, along with a cover sheet, a letter, a response slip, and two additional unnumbered pages for comments. Because they contained so many questions and variables, both Dandelion's and Rutherford's questionnaires represented a major undertaking on the part of the respondent.

Dandelion estimated that his questionnaire would take 'up to an hour to complete' (1996, 341).

In his introductory letter, Dandelion explains that,

> many of us within the Society of Friends are interested in trying to build up a picture of what Quakers in Britain really believe and how we pass on these beliefs to enquirers....you will find questions not only directly about yourself and your religious background and beliefs, but also more generalised questions on your ideas about the world, about other churches, about moral issues....the results will be useful in compiling a comparative picture of Quakers today (1996, 341).

Dandelion's aims were much broader than mine in so far as he was looking for a 'comparative picture' as opposed to discovering specifically whether or not Quakers consider themselves to be Christian. He strove:

a) to identify the normative belief system of Quakers;
b) to construct a model of Quakerism in terms of its patterns of belief and investigate the consequences of this model for the sociology of religion;
c) to investigate the process by which this belief system is imparted and the effectiveness of the process, coupled with an analysis of the system of authority within Friends (1996, 29).

Consequently, his question choices about Christian belief and theism cannot be taken as distinct units. They form part of a larger endeavour.

Rutherford used Dandelion's survey as a pilot survey. Since she intended to compare her answers directly to Dandelion's she did not substantially change the questions.

Dandelion's and Rutherford's Definition of Christian, Question Phrasing, and Use of 'Unique'

In considering Dandelion's and Rutherford's definition of Christian, I examine two distinct elements used in determining the conclusions. First, I consider Dandelion's use of a minimum definition of Christian. Second, I consider the way in which his direct question about Christianity was phrased. Third, I look at how Rutherford defined and asked the question.

Dandelion adopted a minimum definition of Christian. In discussing the question of Christianity within Quakerism, Dandelion (after Hampson), used belief in *Jesus as unique* as definitional of Christianity (1996, 178). He used the question on self-identification as a contributory part of the overall definition of Christianity. That 'Jesus as Unique' was his minimum definition was not disclosed to the participants.

Dandelion's Direct Question About Christianity

Although Dandelion did ask his participants to self-identify as Christian, his question phrasing is indirect. Question 37 asks, 'Would you describe yourself as any of the following?' one of the choices for which was 'Christian' (1989, 13). He writes,

The question was coined in the subjunctive to elicit frequencies of self-description, as opposed to the potential self-description of a 'could you...?'

question. In this example, both the question and the response items were ambiguous (1996, 60).

Dandelion noted this as a problem with his survey question, 'Would you describe yourself as a....Christian?',

> Various hesitations were expressed about this question either in interview or in note-form at the end of QQ. The main problem was the lack of a definition of the word 'Christian'. Some Friends claimed they were Christian, but would not tick the box because they were not Christian in the sense that the question might mean.
> *I do not know what 'Christian' here means – I do not believe in Christianity as most people seem to speak of it.*
> Others claimed they were Christian, but not Christian in the sense that the data analyst might understand the term. A third group claimed that they were Christian, but that, while I would understand the sense in which they described themselves as such, they were concerned that non-Quakers who might read the results would not understand the sense in which the respondents had called themselves 'Christian'.
> *When I'm filling in a questionnaire I am mentally addressing two sorts of audience: a)the researcher, and b)the reader for whose benefit the researcher may try to transmit some interpretation of what my responses meant.*
> A fourth group claimed they would not normally call themselves Christian, but that they followed the teachings of Jesus, which is how they perceived the meaning of the question. The reaction to the term 'Christian' highlights the difficulties of ambiguity within survey design (Dandelion 1996, 6).

Rutherford did not have a fully developed definition of Christian when she started her survey (personal communication). Following Dandelion's example of placing 'The most sensitive, and potentially threatening, questions on individual belief...in the middle of the questionnaire' (Dandelion 1996, 69), Rutherford placed her Christian question in amongst different kinds of questions concerning, for example 'To what extent do you agree with the idea that Quakers can be helped in their spiritual journey by hearing about the religious experience of...' and 'Has your Quaker life affected the way you use your vote in general elections?' (Rutherford 2003).

Interestingly, both Dandelion's and Rutherford's participants responded to the question whether they consider themselves to be Quaker at the same rate, 86%. Further, both groups of participants were equally unlikely to choose that they considered themselves to be Christian. In Dandelion's sample 50.7% answered that they 'would describe' themselves as Christian and in Rutherford's sample, 45.5% answered that they 'think of themselves as Christian'.

Dandelion's and Rutherford's Distribution Methods

Dandelion sent his questionnaire to thirty Preparative Meetings (now called Local Meetings), each of which had agreed to participate in the survey. The Clerk of each Meeting left them in a public place to be taken and filled in by those interested.   Dandelion also distributed his questionnaire to Meeting for Sufferings in 1989 and to members of the Young Friends Central Committee (1996, 72).   Dandelion distributed approximately 1,000 questionnaires and achieved a response rate of 60%.

Rutherford refined Dandelion's distribution method. Rutherford listed all the Meetings in Britain Yearly Meeting in order by size. She divided this list into groups of Meetings that have roughly the same number of Members, which gave her six groups. From each of the five groups of Meetings that had the most Members, she chose eight Meetings to approach. From the remaining group of Meetings, those with the smallest Meeting memberships, she chose ten Meetings. As a result Rutherford contacted forty-eight Meetings.

In each of the forty-eight Meetings, Rutherford asked the Clerk to help distribute the questionnaire to twenty-two people by counting off everyone present (excluding visitors and enquirers) and using a random number generation table to give random participants a survey form. If the Meeting did not have twenty-two people, then fewer people could fill it in. Only people who attended the Meeting for Worship on the distribution day could fill in a survey. The participants were given a questionnaire, asked to take it home to fill it in, and then asked to return it to Rutherford as soon as possible by post. From this method, she achieved a response rate of approximately 75% (Rutherford 2003).

Summary

I suggest that Dandelion ordered his questions and chose the wording to ensure that he got the fullest possible range of answers from all participants to help him create a very broad understanding of belief within Quakerism. Evidence of this is found in his introductory letter in which he asks for multiple variables to create a 'comparative picture'. Further evidence of this is found in the length and scope of his survey, which contained 15 pages and 72 questions. Whether Quakers are Christian or not was not a specifically stated aim for his research. Even so, he had a minimum definition of Christian to help determine that designation.

Dandelion was very successful in achieving his aim of building a comparative picture. Following Dandelion's lead, Rutherford had similar success with her survey and was confronted with a similarly wide range of beliefs. Unfortunately, Rutherford did not write up her work after completing the survey and as a consequence, we do not have her analysis of her research.

Mellor's Survey

My original intention was to conduct a relatively small-scale survey among the 80 or so Members and Attenders of Poole Meeting. I hoped to use the research to write one short paper as coursework for my MPhil. My familiarity with my target audience, which included all Members and Attenders in the local Meeting address book, informed many of the decisions I made about definition, question choice, question phrasing, design, order and transparency. Additionally, I made decisions about distribution methods based on sending to this initial small group, such as sending the questionnaire to everyone, rather than exclusively to those who are active and/or experienced Members and Attenders. As mentioned above, I relied heavily on Dandelion's and Rutherford's research questions to provide the groundwork for devising my own questionnaire and determining my methods.

My Questionnaire was two pages long, printed on the front and back of one sheet of A4 paper. It included twenty-two 'Yes' or 'No' questions; I estimated it would take five minutes to complete. I did not leave room on the page for comments. Each questionnaire included a brief explanation of my position as a researcher. The brief instructions also explained that the respondent should skip questions that he or she did not understand. I asked all respondents to remain anonymous. Because I wanted the questionnaire to be answered quickly, I asked respondents to return their completed questionnaire within four weeks.

My design reflected my original intention for the questionnaire. I thought I would only send it to Members and Attenders of Poole Meeting. However, having looked at the results, I decided to test the questionnaire further by sending it to other Quakers. I chose those local Meetings with which Poole has the closest affiliation, the other Preparative Meetings in the Bournemouth and Swanage Monthly Meeting. I sent the same questionnaire so I could compare the Monthly Meeting data directly with the Poole responses. Later, when I distributed the questionnaire nationally, I again used the same questions in order to facilitate comparison with data already collected. This would have been an opportune moment to improve my questionnaire. However, since I had no idea that I would get such a good response from those I approached outside of my own Monthly Meeting, I wanted to keep my original data. Unfortunately, this meant keeping my original questionnaire and data collection methods as well.

Question Order and Aims

I anticipated that the data from Members and Attenders might be different and the first question asked the respondent to specify which they are. Next, I asked 'Do you believe in God? (you can use your own definition) and then 'Do you consider yourself to be Christian? (you can use your own definition of Christian)'. These were my two most important questions, since I wanted to know specifically whether British Quakers consider themselves to be theist and/or Christian.

On the second page, I included the question 'If you had to answer a Census question that asked whether you are Christian or another faith, but did not allow you to choose unsure, would you choose Christian? (if you had to choose something)'. I hoped that three types of respondents would answer this question:

1. Those who had already said 'Yes' to question 4.
2. Those who did not answer 'Yes' to question 4 because they did not necessarily trust that I would understand the answer.
3. Those who did not answer 'Yes' to question 4 because within Quaker circles they would not call themselves Christian, while in non-Quaker circles they might.

I intentionally and transparently phrased the questions to try to get a 'Yes' answer to the participants' Christian identification. Given the results obtained by Dandelion and Rutherford, I expected that most of the respondents would answer 'No' to the question 'Do you consider yourself to be Christian?'. Therefore my aim was to use other questions to show that Quakers would either:

1. Self-identify as Christians if given a flexible definition of Christian, or,
2. Be shown to be Implicit Christians due to their answers to other questions.

Consequently, in phrasing the questions, I chose: a) to make the wording as inclusive as possible, b) to ask the participants directly if they consider themselves to be Christian, but provide backup questions, and c) not to give multiple-choice answers.

I also restricted the number of alternatives to 'Christianity' by giving few non-Christian references. I wanted to be as clear as possible that I was looking for an answer to one key question: Are Quakers Christian?

Definition of Christian and Use of Unique

Since I am a Quaker, this was 'insider research'.[2] I used definitions that I felt Quakers would understand. For example, I intentionally left out references that might seem paramount in other Christian faith groups, such as to the Virgin Birth, Resurrection, and the Trinity, since these ideas are not in common use in *Quaker Faith and Practice* (2nd Edition 1999, hereafter *QFP)*.

When referring in this chapter to whether or not someone is Christian, I use my definition, namely that if a Quaker calls him or herself Christian then I do too, no matter what their definition of Christian might be. It is important to note that I do not use any particular definition of Christian. In my opinion, the single factor that contributed most to my receiving such a high incidence of Christian responses was the definition, or lack thereof.

In analysing my data, I used the term 'Christian' to describe a person who answered affirmatively to the following question:
a) Do you consider yourself to be Christian?
Those who answered 'yes' to this question I call 'Explicit Christians'.

Likewise, in analysing my data, I used the term 'Implicit Christian' to describe any respondent who answered at least two of the following questions affirmatively:
b) Do you believe that Jesus' ethical teachings are meaningful to you?
c) Do you believe that Jesus' spiritual teachings are meaningful to you?
d) Do you use Jesus' teaching or example to help guide the way you live your life?
e) Would you identify yourself as Christian on a census?
f) Are you a 'Humble Learner in the School of Christ'?
and who also answered the following question negatively:
g) Do you follow another faith, such as Buddhism, Islam, Hinduism, Zen, etc.?

Through personal experience, I rejected Dandelion's minimum definition of Christian as someone who considers 'Jesus to be unique'. I included the question 'Do you believe Jesus was unique?' so I could test it. Contrary to Dandelion and Rutherford, I did not have a minimum definition other than self-definition. Indeed I explicitly added 'You can use your own definition of Christian'. The participants were free to distance themselves from any mainstream definition of Christianity.

I derived my questions from *The Oxford Dictionary of the Christian Church* (Cross 1957), from *QFP* (1999), and from personal knowledge drawn from my recent participation at Poole Meeting in the workshop *Hearts & Minds Prepared*, a study programme designed to examine the elements of Quaker faith. I incorporated parts of Dandelion's questions.[3] I also included suggestions from Members of Poole Meeting.[4]

I chose questions that were as direct as possible but at the same time gave the respondent maximum scope for definition. I did not want the participants to give me partial or qualified answers; consequently the questions could be answered only with 'Yes' or 'No'.

Distribution Methods

When I decided to test my initial, local results by taking my questionnaire to a national audience, I contacted Preparative Meeting Clerks and Monthly Meeting Clerks so that I could gain access to their databases of Members and Attenders. In each case I needed access to all Members and Attenders in the database so I could compare my results directly. The various Monthly Meeting Clerks all interpreted the Data Protection Act the same way, insofar that each person who agreed to be on the mailing list for that Monthly Meeting had *de facto* agreed to receive anything that the Monthly Meeting decided was Monthly Meeting business. In each case all Members and Attenders had agreed to have their names included on the Monthly Meeting database or directory as per *QFP* 11.44-11.46 (1999).

In each of the six participating Monthly Meetings, I posted a questionnaire and return self addressed stamped envelope directly to the home address of each and every Member and each Attender listed in the Monthly Meeting database or directory. In the case of five Monthly Meetings I had assistance from a local Member in addressing the envelopes to ensure that I did not contravene the data protection act by having direct access to the database. All envelopes were posted directly back to me.

The Data

Table 4-1 includes the collated answers of Members and Attenders. The percentages take into account only those people who answered the questions. Those who left it blank might have been trying to give me a message in their passive refusal to answer, but I did not include their answers. The percentage of those who answered the question is included in the table after the question.

Table 4-1: Frequencies of Responses to Mellor's Questionnaire

Yes	No	Question
72%		Are You a Member?
28%		Are You an Attender?
90%	10%	Do you believe in God? (You can use your own definition) *94% Answered*
80%	20%	Do you consider yourself to be Christian? (You can use your own definition of Christian) *93% Answered*
96%	4%	Do you believe that Jesus existed as a historical figure? *94% Answered*
27%	73%	Do you believe that Jesus 'existed', but maybe not as a historical figure? *53% Answered*
97%	3%	Do you believe that Jesus' ethical teachings, as you understand them, are meaningful to you? *98% Answered*
91%	9%	Do you believe that Jesus spiritual teachings, as you understand them, are meaningful to you? *92% Answered*
91%	9%	Do you use Jesus' teaching or example to help guide the way you live your life? *94% Answered*
49%	51%	Do you believe Jesus was unique? *89% Answered*
34%	66%	Would you generally use the title Christ? *91% Answered*
21%	79%	Do you believe Jesus died for Atonement (in other words to save your soul)? *83% Answered*
42%	58%	Do you believe Jesus was or is the Son of God? *78% Answered*
46%	54%	Are you a Universalist? *64% Answered*

53%	47%	Are you a Christian who might also be Universalistic? *64% Answered*
18%	82%	Are you Agnostic? *86% Answered*
11%	89%	Do you follow another faith, such as Buddhism, Islam, Hinduism, Zen, etc.? *94% Answered*
87%	13%	If you had to answer a Census question that asked whether you are Christian or another faith, but did not allow you to choose unsure, would you choose Christian? (if you had to choose something) *95% Answered*
58%	42%	Do you think the Evangelist churches have hijacked the word Christian? *78% Answered*
67%	33%	Are you a 'Humble Follower of the School of Christ'?[5] *75% Answered*
74%	26%	Does George Fox's (the 'founder' of Quakerism) famous quote 'There is one, even Jesus Christ, who can speak to thy condition' ring true for you? *84% Answered*
79%	21%	If you were describing Quakerism to someone who knew nothing about it, would you describe Quakerism as a Christian Faith (as you define Quakerism)? *92% Answered*

My questionnaire shows that 80% of the respondents declared themselves to be Christian and 90% indicated that they believe in God. This is in contrast with Dandelion's results that showed 50.7% declared themselves to be Christian and 74% declared that they believe in God. My results are also in contrast with Rutherford, who had 45.5% declare themselves to be Christian and 73.5% declare that they believe in God.

Explicit Christians, Implicit Christians, and Those Clearly Not Christian

I planned my research to be based primarily on the quantitative results of the questionnaire. My questions were of the Yes/No type and there was no space on my questionnaire for notes. Despite the lack of provision for it, many respondents chose to clarify their answers with notes to me. Some changed the questions so that it fit their own meanings better and I could not then use these responses. And, some respondents wrote a note about the whole survey so that they could expand on the questions I asked. Some participants told me in person about their experience of answering the survey. They also told me why they answered certain questions in the way that they did. Although I did not request it, I found that the qualitative data helps explain the quantitative results.

The qualitative data helped me distinguish the three different distinct types of 'Christian' answers that emerged from the questionnaires: 'Explicit Christian', 'Implicit Christian', and 'Clearly Not Christian'. Each of these designations is expanded below.

Explicit Christians

Those whom I term Explicit Christians are the group that answered my questionnaire by stating 'Yes' to the question 'Do you consider yourself to be Christian? (You can use your own definition of Christian)'. This group comprised the 80% whom I call 'Christian' for the purpose of my research so 'Christian' and 'Explicit Christian' are synonymous.

One such person wrote a letter regarding my research that included the following:

> I am a Christian Quaker and feel comfortable with many of the ideas of George Fox, who did use the Bible widely, but also came up with some very important new insights on the ways we explore faith and spirituality, as well as his contributions to the problems of Peacemaking (which for some Quakers is all we really stand for). I also find the life and teachings of Jesus to be central to my ability to face the problems of the World we live in....Yours in Christ, T.C. (letter, 12/6/06).

In the margins of the questionnaire, Lymington 1[6] wrote 'I try to follow Christ's Teaching'. Lymington 27 added 'Jesus was a great person, one of several. Our cultural background (UK) is Christian.' Bolton 2 wrote 'Yes, Just!', as did another, Muswell Hill 9. Crawshawbooth 13 wrote 'But my definition may be completely different to someone else.'

Sudbury 10, an attender, wrote 'I have never thought of myself as a Quaker, "Christian" would probably be the most appropriate word.'

Golders Green 24 wrote, 'having originally been brought up in a Roman Catholic home, schooled in a convent, the language of the RC Church came easily. I have learned (and been asked) to take care about describing my spiritual experiences in language that other Quakers would find alien...But believe me we would be a stronger organisation with a greater commitment to the Christian Ethic.' Hampstead 43 added, 'One who tries to follow the teaching of Jesus'. Muswell Hill 32 wrote, 'I am very concerned about what others would perceive about the word Christian and would never use it unless I knew there is an understanding.'

These comments indicate that the category of 'Explicit Christians' includes a wide range of views.

Implicit Christians

Many of the respondents who replied that they were not Christian fell into my original criteria for my definition of Christian, influenced by *The Oxford Dictionary of the Christian Church* (Cross 1957). It gives the following in its definition of Christian:

> The name was orig. applied to followers of Christ by outsiders...As the name for which the martyrs suffered (cf. LK 21.12) and as containing the name of Christ, the term easily came to fill the proper name by which the Church could designate itself as distinct from Jews and Pagans (and later from Moslems, etc.)... (Cross 1957).

What is striking about this definition is that it does not suggest any creedal statement. Rather, it suggests that simply by following Christ and not another one can be considered to be Christian (although this is to assume that we all mean the same thing when we say 'following Christ'). Additionally, this definition is one that is *applied to* the individual, *not applied by* the individual. Therefore, it is a definition that I argue can be used to apply to those Quakers who identify that they follow Christ and at the same time do not describe themselves as following another faith or religious practice (such as Islam or Buddhism).

The 15% who make up the group of Implicit Christians are nearly indistinguishable from the Explicit Christian group. I am *not* going to label these individuals 'Christian', even considering the definition of Christian I have given above, since that would be contradictory. But it is interesting to note that in most cases the questionnaire responses of the Implicit Christians were similar to the respondents I call Explicit Christians, with the one exception of the answer to the question 'Do you consider yourself to be Christian?' In other words, the Implicit Christian group answered the questions so similarly to those who were Explicit Christians that without asking the question 'Do you consider yourself to be Christian' the difference between them would be negligible.

Some of the Implicit Christians chose to add written comments in the margins of their questionnaires. Bournemouth 4, for example, added 'I follow Jesus, but do not like to say I am a Christian'. Hampstead 69 added, 'Depends who I'm speaking to'. Telford 6 wrote, 'Follower of The Christ, but not a Christian.'

Telford 29, who wrote a comment on each question wrote, 'I would say that my Quakerism is becoming more Christ-centred.'

The comments that Implicit Christians wrote show a great deal of commitment to Christianity, but little commitment to the label. This further validates my application of the designation 'Implicit Christian'.

Non-Christian Theism and Atheism

I was surprised at the size of the population who answered my survey who were clearly not 'Christian', 4.5%. Before I started this research I imagined it would be a larger group. Of them, eight Members and eight Attenders answered that they believe in God, however tentatively, and yet are clearly not Christian. Of these, seven of the Members and two of the Attenders indicated that they are Universalist. As an example, Lymington 27, a Member, circled the 'Yes' answer for 'Do you believe in God?' with dots and then added to the question about Jesus' ethical teachings '[Yes], but incomplete'. Lymington 27 answered 'Yes' to the question about Evangelist churches. In replying to the final three questions, this person added 'sounds soppy' to the 'Humble Learner in Christ' question, 'not a lot' to the George Fox quote question, and 'Quakerism has its roots in Christianity' to the last question. Lymington 27 also wished me a cheery 'Good Luck!'.

A further ten Members answered that they do not believe in God and do not consider themselves to be Christian. Thirteen attenders answered the same way. There are some written comments on these questionnaires, which help us better understand why they answered these questions the way they did. When asked if they would describe Quakerism as a Christian faith, Telford 12 added 'sprung from but not of it'. Telford 13 wrote in large capitals, 'I AM A SPIRITUAL ATHEIST!'

These and the many other comments prevent me from drawing a clear conclusion. This is not surprising, since my intention was to explore the possibility that many Quakers are actually Christian and theist, rather than the opposite. Most of those who answered that they were Atheist and Non-Christian did not add comments.

Responses to my Use of 'Unique' and Question Choice

The question 'Do you believe Jesus was unique?' was the question most likely to be qualified by my respondents. Of those who answered, 51% replied 'No' and 49% replied 'Yes'. These figures are similar to Dandelion's overall analysis of Christianity within Quakerism, based on his claim that the uniqueness of Jesus needs to be definitional of Christianity. Additionally, seventy-three Friends wrote some message in the margins of this question. Their notes tended to be 'We're all unique,' or 'Each of us is unique,' or 'As we all are,' or 'Every human being is unique,' or I am not sure.' These comments along with the survey results further suggest that asking whether or not Jesus is 'unique' is a question too open to interpretation to be used as a definition of Christian belief within the Quaker population.

Most Friends who quibbled with my question choice did so gently. They changed a word here and there or inserted a phrase into one of my questions to fashion it more to their liking. Twenty-three Friends wrote substantial comments on my use of Yes/No answers. Many of them echoed the sentiments of Bournemouth 33, 'Almost impossible to answer some of the questions with yes/no answers honestly without some qualification' or Bournemouth 37, 'These questions are far too profound for "yes" "no" answers.'

Bradford 9 arrived at a similar conclusion with, 'I'm not sure about this questionnaire. Surely it is the reasons behind the questions and answers which are important not the number of yes/no answers. I have found it very easy to complete at one level, but I am concerned about the superficiality of the answers I have given.' Bewdley 13 wrote,

> I think you are using a computer, which is defeating your own ends; as you see, I cannot answer all your questions with a simple 'yes' or 'no', and other Bewdley Friends say the same. I can't really think that something as important as religion can be computerised! Perhaps as M.C. Barnes remarked, "Is there a need for all these words about something which began in a manger and is as simple as love?"

My analysis of these comments is that the people who wrote messages were trying too hard to predict what I might do with the data. I believe that they did not trust me simply to stick with the answers people gave me; and they clearly did not trust the Yes/No process. Even though I, perhaps naively, felt that my aims for the questionnaire were clear, in hindsight I can see I was not clear enough for these individuals, which reflects the complexity of faith and practice. My desire to see whether Quakers would self-identify as Christian or not is subsumed in this case into a larger debate about whether we can truly understand what another is saying.

Conclusion: British Quakers are Christian

The aim of my research was to determine whether Quakers consider themselves to be Christian, by whatever definition. In doing that I succeeded. I argue that two factors influenced the results: my definition, or lack thereof, of Christian and my questionnaire design. I believe that my definition struck a chord with British Friends; it enabled them to identify themselves as Christian without compromising their belief system in other ways. My questionnaire design reinforced my 'definition'; by not trying to achieve a full picture of Quakerism or to hide the aims of my questionnaire, I enabled Friends to be 'Explicitly Christian' in a Quaker context. This leads me to wonder whether it might be possible that even more Friends would self-identify as 'Explicit Christians' if I had communicated my 'lack of definition' in a better way.

My findings suggest that Dandelion and Rutherford probably underestimated the extent to which the Religious Society of Friends is a Christian group. I did not anticipate or even intend to challenge Dandelion's and Rutherford's results so fully, but having done so, further research should be completed to determine more about the nature of Quaker Christianity. It would be interesting to know more about what affects Quakers in their decision to describe themselves as Christian or not and whether the definition is different for internal and external conversations, as Gay Pilgrim suggests (this volume, Chapter 3). Either way, any further research must take into account this new benchmark: most British Friends consider themselves to be Christian.

Notes

[1] See also Davie 1997, who makes a similar point about the significance of Scott's Lecture.
[2] I am using Dandelion's definition. 'The term 'insider research' is used in this book to refer to research undertaken on a group or constituency by a member of that constituency (Becker 1963, Polsky 1967, Ianni and Reus-Ianni 1972, Krieger 1985, for example) (Dandelion 1996, 36)'
[3] I referred specifically to Questions 22, 24a and 24c in Dandelion's 1989 Quaker Questionnaire and his definition of Christians as believing that Jesus is unique.

[4] One Member in particular indicated a strong belief in Christ, but as a non-historical figure. Another Friend suggested that I include the 'Humble follower of Christ' question since it had particular meaning to her.

[5] The question should be are you a 'Humble learner in the school of Christ' as per *QFP* 11:18 (1999).

[6] The questionnaires were anonymous. I labelled each questionnaire with the name of the Preparative Meeting (PM) and the order in which it was received. Lymington 1 means the questionnaire was the first I received from Lymington PM.

CHAPTER FIVE

MODERN TESTIMONIES: THE APPROACH OF QUAKERS TO SUBSTANCE USE AND GAMBLING

HELENA CHAMBERS

This chapter outlines a study into Quaker attitudes and behaviours in relation to the testimony of abstinence and moderation and that regarding gambling and speculation. The background to the Quaker testimonies is summarised, and relevant research in the substances/gambling fields about denominational influences on personal behaviours is briefly outlined. The questions raised by recent Quaker scholarship represented in this volume are considered, and the study results are outlined in relation to the theory of Quaker double-culture (Dandelion 1996, and this volume) and the suggestions of Scully regarding virtue ethics among Quakers (2002, and present volume). It is suggested that whereas the liberal belief culture (Dandelion 1996) and the spiritual/belief diversity within Quakerism (Pilgrim this volume, Chapter 3) have some fragmenting effects theologically, in relation to these testimonies, these diversifying elements are counter-balanced by core (deontological) values. These values are spiritually-based and widely-held among Friends, and are perceived as being specifically Quaker. It is argued that diversifying and unifying factors are thus held in tension in a way that has some distinctive effects, both in terms of individuals and in relation to the denominational profile. It is further argued that the results of this balance are largely benign in terms of substance using and gambling behaviours, and that this may have useful applications beyond a Quaker context.

Introduction

Position as Researcher

The starting point for this investigation was my appointment as Project Leader by Quaker Action on Alcohol and Drugs (QAAD), which is a Quaker charity with a long-standing concern about these subjects. This gave me 'insider status', as part of the broad group on which I was conducting the research (Becker 1963; Krieger 1985). Dandelion (1996) has classified insider research that is overt (known to all participants) into two categories: 'insider to the group' (eg Hobbs 1989) and 'insider to the context' (eg Heilman 1976). Prior to my appointment I had no previous connection with Quakers, though I have subsequently developed a personal interest in Quakerism. Although I had many of the characteristics of the insider, then, I was an insider to the context rather than to the full range of experiences of the group that I was researching. During the research investigation and analysis, I was positioned on the research discourse, the professional discourse, and that of the enquirer about Quakerism. The result is, of course, a composite but I have tried to make these strands as clear as possible.

Historical Background to These Testimonies

The Quaker testimony on the use of alcohol dates back to George Fox and the beginnings of Quakerism. Fox's journal shows him drinking 'small beer' only in so far as it was necessary to quench his thirst, and disassociating himself from a situation where others who 'professed' to be religious began to drink to excess:

> And when we had drunk a glass apiece, they began to drink healths and called for more drink, agreeing together that he that would not drink should pay all. I was grieved that any that made profession of religion should offer to do so.... wherefore I rose up to be gone, and putting my hand into my pocket, I took out a groat and laid it down upon the table before them and said, 'If it be so, I'll leave you'. So I went away.... (Nickalls 1952, 2-3).

There is also early evidence of care being taken to avoid smoking tobacco in public places, in order to avoid 'the appearance of evil':

> It being discoursed that the common excess of smoking tobacco is inconsistent with our holy profession, this meeting adviseth that such as have occasion to make use of it do take it privately, neither in their labour

nor employment, nor by the highways, nor in alehouses, nor elsewhere too publicly. (Minutes of Hardshaw Monthly Meeting 1691, 17 ix)

Gambling, too, was avoided, for some similar reasons: 'Are friends careful to avoid all vain sports, places of diversion, gaming, and all unnecessary frequenting of alehouses or taverns, excess in drinking, and intemperance of every kind?' (London Yearly Meeting 1783, 196).

In the nineteenth century, Quakers were strongly associated with the Temperance movement, and many eschewed alcohol completely. By the twentieth century, the emphasis tended back towards moderation rather than total abstinence, and *Quaker Faith and Practice* gives advice on the use of substances under the heading of 'abstinence and moderation': 'In view of the harm done by the use of alcohol, tobacco and other habit-forming drugs, consider whether you should limit your use of them or refrain from using them altogether' (*Quaker Faith and Practice,* 1995, 1.02.40).

As regards content, the Quaker testimony on gambling and speculation has modulated somewhat less than that on substances over the last two centuries, and a consistent stance against any gambling has been maintained: 'Resist the desire to acquire possessions or income through unethical investment, speculation, or games of chance' (*Quaker Faith and Practice* 1995, 1.02).

The advent of the National Lottery brought gambling into particular focus for Friends: a public statement of opposition to it was issued in 1995 and reaffirmed in 2004. This gave the testimony on gambling a higher profile, both among Friends and more widely.

Studies of Other Denominations

Evidence in the field of substance use and gambling shows that both behaviours are related to religious affiliation (Jessor and Jessor 1977). Research in Christian denominations indicates that those with strong standards that proscribe these behaviours tend to show higher rates of abstinence and lower rates of engagement in these activities. Protestant groups (which have proscriptive traditions) tend to show lower rates of substance use and gambling than people in society generally, while Catholicism (which does not strongly proscribe either alcohol use or gambling) tends to show patterns that are more congruent with wider society (Rooney 1977; Jolly and Orford 1983).

The evidence relating to the problem use of substances or problematic gambling is a little more variable. Some studies suggest that among those who depart from the standard of abstinence in proscriptive sects, problem levels can be higher – and it has been suggested that 'normlessness' may be one reason for this (Mizruchi and Perrucci 1962). Other studies have found lower rates of problems and dependencies among such sects, as well as lower rates of use (Krohn *et al* 1982).

Much debate has taken place about the causes and processes that might be involved in the religious engagement-use relationships. It is thought that individual adherents internalise the moral normative standard through the teaching of religious leaders, texts and sermons, and that this will be reinforced through social interactions that reward conformity and provide sanctions against non-conformity. Sanctions could also include internal psychological processes such as self-criticism and guilt when the adherent departs from the norm (Nelsen and Rooney 1982). This framework would suggest that a strong standard of prohibition results in both less use and less misuse for the majority of adherents. An alternative theory (posed by Mullen *et al* 1996) suggests that religious groups with strongly proscriptive standards tend to 'lose' those people who do not conform to the religious norm because those individuals cannot contain the emotional discomfort – or cognitive dissonance – that is caused by the awareness of the gap between their own behaviour and the denominational stance. In this reading, groups such as Catholics do not necessarily have standards or interactions that result in generally higher levels of use and misuse - but simply tend to retain the adherents who would tend to leave other sects.

Finally, it has also been suggested that asceticism – a distrust of worldly and sensual activities or the pursuit of pleasure – may a key element in the relationship between religiosity and lower substance use and gambling, particularly as regards Protestant sects (Burkett and White 1974). It has also been suggested that spirituality (Miller 1998), rather than religious engagement as such, may be a significant element both in prevention and recovery from substance problems: spiritual programmes (of Alcoholics Anonymous, for example) are often associated with recovery from addictive behaviours.

Questions Posed by Research in Other Denominations and Quaker Scholarship

When these findings from other denominations are coupled with Quaker history and the currents in modern Quakerism that are discussed in this volume, several questions arise about the operation of these testimonies by contemporary Quakers. Quakerism has its origins in the puritan/Protestant tradition, and normative ascetic standards that advise abstinence in the case of gambling and abstinence or moderation in the case of substance use. However, the silent form of worship and the lack of sermon and institutionalised authority would tend against the mechanisms that are held to reinforce the normative standard in some other denominations. Another fundamental factor is the traditional Quaker stress on individual experience of the Light as paramount, rather on than external authority (Dandelion 1996). The Liberal belief culture Dandelion defines de-stresses belief and allows a wide latitude for individual interpretation. When this is taken in conjunction with Pilgrim's analysis of the many 'different understandings of spirituality' in modern Quakerism, and 'the extremes of openness which mainstream Quakerism permits' the potential for post-modernist 'shopping' as regards these testimonies becomes a real one (Pilgrim this volume, Chapter 3). This is particularly the case since these testimonies do not have the profile or centrality of the peace testimony – and now that Quakers are no longer identifiable as such, they are enacted in non-Quaker, private time.

A linked point is that both testimonies were heterotopic for early Quakers in the terms Pilgrim outlines. The carefulness about drinking or gambling *in public* reflects the intention to mark 'themselves as Other' (Pilgrim this volume, Chapter 3) and manifests an 'alternate ordering.' If, as Dandelion suggests, testimony is no longer used to 'mark the separate identity of the group *against* the non-Quaker world.' (Dandelion 1996, 121; Scully this volume, Chapter 6) questions arise as to how those on gambling and substance use are considered by Friends, and used to structure 'the Quaker role in the world.'

In Dandelion's framework, 'Quaker double-culture' suggests that contemporary Quakerism is liberal in terms of belief but conservative in matters of form: and in these terms, the testimonies have a locus in both, but are defined by neither:

> In terms of Quaker double-culture, dimensions of the testimonies... are split between the two areas of belief and form. As part of the tradition, they are maintained within the behavioural creed. In terms of their content and usage, adherence to them is left up to the individual. (Dandelion 1996, 122)

All of these considerations raise questions about the role and operation of these testimonies in modern Quakerism. They can be summarised as follows:

Does the liberal belief culture and the spiritual 'openness' of Quakerism mean that these testimonies do not act as 'normative standards' for Quakers? Is this reflected in a wide range of individualised behaviours such as might occur in the general population, or is there still a perception and enactment of 'corporate witness'? If 'normative standards' are not significant for Quakers, how are these testimonies construed?

Study Findings in Brief

One hundred and fifty-nine Quakers co-operated with the study, of which 57 were members of Young Friends General Meeting, and therefore predominantly in the under-30 age group. The results indicate that Friends are mainly abstinent from gambling and are generally moderate in their use of substances. However, some gambling did occur among a minority, as did some non-moderate substance use. Where gambling did occur it was spread fairly evenly throughout the age-groups, while higher substance use was found more commonly in younger people – though not exclusively so in the case of alcohol. The results indicate a profile that does differ from what might be expected in the general population, and notably so in the case of gambling. This profile is consistent with a Liberal Protestant sect as regards substance use, and a broadly proscriptive sect for gambling. However, there were many commonalities in attitude in the way Quakers approached the two testimonies.

Significant Elements in Relation to These Testimonies

The Behavioural Creed

The testimony of abstinence and moderation is embodied in the fact that Meeting Houses are traditionally substance-free – as are some other Quaker establishments and some Quaker gatherings, particularly for young Friends. Responses within the study suggest that this practice has various kinds of significance, particularly in being embodied in the 'narratives of Meetings' and the 'habitus' to which Collins refers (this volume, Chapter 2). In Preparative Meetings, respondents described discussions about whether any events or gatherings of other groups who used the building could be allowed to include alcohol: one warden, for example, stated: 'The Premises committee had a heated debate about alcohol on the premises…' These discussions tended to be general rather than personal, and to focus on the nature of Quaker space, including in relation to the needs of other groups using the building. The concept of 'Quaker time,' which Dandelion defines as 'the time spent as a Quaker with other Quakers' (1996: xxvi), was similarly relevant, being considered both practically and in terms of what substance use in Quaker time would 'mean' in individual and group terms.

Within Young Friends General Meeting the issue has a more direct and pervasive significance, since gatherings are mainly held in Meeting Houses and the substance-free setting is a relevant consideration to non-timetabled time. Meeting House practice thus it has a defining significance as regards Quaker time and space: 'We're on Meeting House premises and [substance use] is very much not allowed - and people respect that...' Although there may be some discrepancies between private behaviour and the behavioural creed, the Quaker 'normative standard' is embodied. Another effect is to bring private behaviour into the Quaker realm: 'You're not allowed alcohol in the building, but you're allowed to bring it back inside you. But at least they're willing to talk it through with me when I speak to them...'

A further effect within Preparative Meetings and YFGM is at the more general level identified by Scully (this volume, Chapter 6). She suggests that moral frameworks are less about articulated codes than 'socially embodied, largely unspoken rules about what constitutes a good life for community members.' Several Friends construed Meeting House practice in relation to substances as having a significance mainly in terms of what it symbolises about the Quaker community – and on an individual level, this confirms the 'coming home' or 'at home' feeling of being a Quaker: 'I like being part of a community in which it's acceptable not to drink,' as one Friend put it. The testimony's embodiment in narrative and structure thus has significance in construing Quaker identity (both individual and communal) in the way that Scully suggests (even though individuals may critique the narrative or privately depart from perceived group norms when outside the limits of the behavioural creed.)

Pilgrim comments on the creation of heterotopic space in the enactment of testimony by early Friends, and the search for heterotopic sites for modern Quakers (Pilgrim this volume, Chapter 3). Substance-free Meeting House practice does not take over a 'worldly' space and re-order it (in the way that Pilgrim describes the seventeenth century courtroom), but nevertheless it does retain some heterotopic characteristics in being – and conveying – that the Quaker Meeting House space is a place of spiritually-based 'alternate ordering.'

There was no direct analogue in terms of place as regards the testimony on gambling and speculation. However, I do suggest that there is some parallel in considering Quaker space as 'gambling-free' in relation to the National Lottery, and in the decision of Quakers corporately not to apply for National Lottery funding (in contrast with other Protestant churches that have done so). A survey conducted by Quaker Peace and Social Witness in 2002[1] investigated how Quakers who are employed or volunteer in charitable projects eligible for National Lottery funding are responding to the challenges of this position. Because such work involves the addressing of social disadvantage, Quakers working as individuals in non-Quaker bodies did not feel they could make a stand against a source of funds when alternative resources were unlikely to be forthcoming. They did not find it tenable to treat these situations as heterotopic sites (as in Pilgrim's 'courtroom' example) – or to withdraw, as George Fox did from the drinking situation. The expression of testimony has therefore been made by Quakers corporately and by Quaker charities, rather than by Quakers as individuals.

Thus, Meeting House practice as regards substances and Quaker corporate policy on gambling could both be described as retaining some aspect of the heterotopic - but within internal Quaker space only. Pilgrim's analysis of different spiritual understandings – and therefore 'alternate *orderings*' (rather than ordering: Pilgrim this volume, Chapter 3) does have relevance to this study's findings, as I will explain below. In more general terms, however, the embodiment of these testimonies in the behavioural creed works at several levels in rooting them in Quaker narratives. The normative standard is asserted and enacted, a sense of Quaker identity and relationships is confirmed, and this is done in a way that juxtaposes them with wider society.

The Liberal Belief Culture

The liberal belief culture would suggest that attitudes to these testimonies might be non-credal, and therefore may not be approached as normative standards. Questions were asked about Quaker guidelines and their influence on personal conduct as regards substances. There was a spread of attitudes, with about 10 – 15% expressing a non-normative view. Responses in this group could be strongly individualistic: 'I hope not!' for example. Others could fit into what has been described as 'market-place': 'I pick and choose.' At the other end of the spectrum, there was a smaller minority of under 5%, who expressed strongly pro-normative views implying that the standard could and should influence behaviour: 'sometimes I wonder if a more robust discouragement might be helpful,' for example.

About three-quarters of those responding said they did consider Quaker guidelines of abstinence and moderation and the behaviour of other Quakers within their own decisions. The predominant view was one of active personal consideration of the written testimony and the behaviour of other Quakers – but not in the spirit of what could be described as conformity. 'They prompt me to make a well thought-out choice;' 'taken into account' were examples of this range of responses.

It is interesting to note that these proportions in response to the idea of 'guidelines' for substance use roughly equate to those Pilgrim suggests for the three groups within contemporary Quakerism (Syncretists, Exclusivists, and Inclusivists). However, a paradox that also relates to Pilgrim's observations, is that those who reject the idea of normative standards perceive this to be a Quakerly stance[2] – just as those who relate to the idea of normative standards also feel *this* to be Quakerly. On one level this could be considered as an example of an 'internally contested' heterotopic stance (Pilgrim this volume, Chapter 3) but the potential for a contested space is little realised in practice – partly because the study also reveals that responses to the idea of 'guidelines' are not consistently related to personal *behaviour* as regards substance use or gambling. Interview responses illuminated why this might be so.

Some who took a strongly non-normative stance were low users of substances or non-gamblers, who simply took this position in relation to the idea of 'rule-based' behaviour. For example, one such respondent commented in relation to gambling, 'It's is so against what I think Quakerism is about...' At the other end of the spectrum of behaviour, some with higher levels of use (in comparative terms) did not reject a normative approach, but simply were not always successful in acting on it: 'I try to follow the "in moderation" guidelines, but have difficulty' being one such response in relation to substance use. Although there was some evidence of 'market-place' approaches among this latter group, it was not the dominant pattern.

A further finding, particularly in the case of gambling, is that Quaker testimony and the approach of other Friends were described as reinforcing an existing disposition. As regards gambling, most respondents cited Quaker testimony as a secondary, rather than a primary reason for desisting from it: 'I don't think I'm directly influenced by Quakerism as such – just much more naturally aligned with the Quaker position,' as one Friend said. (However, as has already been described, this sense confirms personal narratives and identities as Quaker.)

So, in summary, for the strong majority of Quakers in the study these testimonies have some normative functions – including a confirmatory role – and this is reflected in the broad findings of abstinence and moderation. While this study confirms the suggestion that there is a plurality of responses to the idea of testimony as a Quaker normative standard, perspectives are not reflected in any particular configuration of behaviour. Differences in behaviour and in approaches to testimony are therefore not generally apparent or contested. Indeed, in a paradoxical manifestation of Quaker double-culture, those with a wide range of responses to the idea of Quaker testimony as normative find their Quaker identities variously confirmed – either by their freedom to interpret them within the liberal belief culture, or by the nature of the testimonies themselves.

Spiritual Journey

The general approach of Quakers in this study thus manifests Scully's formulation that 'Liberal Quakerdom' is resistant to deontological ethics that put 'rule' or text 'over the authority of individual experience and conviction' (Scully this volume, Chapter 6) – albeit that these testimonies also function normatively in the ways that have already been outlined. It has been suggested that the stress away from 'rule' is related to the primacy given by Quakers to individual spiritual experience, and this link was attested to in the present study. Friends were asked to select from a list of ten items the aspect of Quakerism that they found most fulfilling. Over 40% of those surveyed selected 'a concentration on spiritual journey rather than fixed doctrine' either as first or second choice (22.5% selecting it first).

Whilst this study confirmed the plurality of understandings of spirituality within Quakerism, gambling and certain kinds of substance use were widely regarded as unhelpful to spiritual life, and this was expressed in congruent terms. For example, A Christian theist commented, 'The clearer my consciousness, the more alive I feel and receptive to God's wisdom,' while a non-theist stated: 'I think it would affect one's thinking, reasoning, discernment and thus one's spiritual life.' Behaviourally, those who felt spiritual life (however construed) was a significant feature in their daily lives were also likely to undertake lighter levels of substance use. As regards gambling, a view that gambling is unhelpful to spiritual life because it encourages materialism was widely shared among Quakers, and spiritual considerations were stated as a motive for non-engagement in gambling activities. In general terms, then, notwithstanding the different perspectives on spirituality, its prime role for Quakers had a unifying effect in relation to these testimonies, both as regards how substance use and gambling are construed as spiritual matters, and in underpinning moderate or abstinent behaviours.

One exception to this general pattern appears to correspond roughly to the 'amorphous' group of 'Syncretists' as described by Pilgrim (this volume, Chapter 3) – or rather, to individuals who could be numbered within it. This small group considered it possible that some substance use could be spiritually enhancing in certain circumstances, and were more likely to have experience of cannabis (though not any other substance or gambling activity). This outlook was allied with a feeling of God's immanence in nature, and matches the group Vincett has described as Quagans, including Goddess Feminists – as this quotation illustrates:

> So it's not that particularly that God judges me and my smoking (of cannabis).... It's much more that I judge myself, and I think God just folds arms and says, "next time.".... ...it's about God and because my spiritual God-life has always been part and parcel of being a Quaker... It's very much about the relationship with God and feeling that – it goes back to that body as temple thing. How can I be fully related to God if in some ways I am escaping by smoking?

Consistent with Vincett's analysis, this conception of the Divine is of 'power with' rather than 'power over' (Vincett this volume, Chapter 10) – and this is associated with a non-judgemental, but not a permissive theology, which is not perceived as inconsistent with Quakerism. However, the internal dialogue, which is described as taking place over time and includes Quakerism as an integral component, results in a reduction of substance use.   Vincett's description of those who are 'essentially Goddess Feminists in belief, but their Quakerism shapes their praxis' (Vincett this volume, Chapter 10) seems to encapsulate this approach, while her analysis of a type of syncretism that is not 'superficial' or 'lacking in coherence' is also apposite. While there was some evidence of an individualised 'Quagan' spirituality associated with this behaviour, this perspective - in which understandings that are perceived as specifically Quaker are incorporated into personal deliberations - was more common.

Virtue Ethics and Phronesis

The internal dialogue taken by the last respondent was reflected in others that took place at all levels of substance use and gambling, and of abstinence.   The character of these, which tended to work from the perspective of the moral agent rather than from rules of behaviour or abstract general principle, was generally consistent with Scully's view that virtue ethics tend to be favoured by Quakers, and are particularly suited to the concept of testimony.   Scully's observations regarding virtue ethics and moral reasoning are further illustrated by the following quotation from a Friend, who describes his/her deliberations about when and where to drink alcohol:

> I do have a struggle with this one, because I do think there is a value in setting an example along with most other Friends, and I just feel very ambivalent about it to be quite honest...I would be most likely to drink with...[fairly close relatives], who might be drinking half a bottle between them with a meal and say - "would I like a glass?"- and I would probably say - "yes." - but I think that a large mixed party, with some vulnerable youngsters, I'd be far more likely to say no.   Which is, as I say, inconsistent and hypocritical. I haven't resolved that one...but it goes back to the time of George Fox and "wear your sword as long as you can." [3] Goes right back to the beginning, that you allow people to think about these things, rather than saying you should do this and you shouldn't do that... We do say "consider", so having considered, if you've decided what your doing is O.K. for the reasons that you're doing it, sometimes perhaps friendship is more important than witness.   Sometimes witness is more important than friendship. I like the word "consider".

This also illustrates what Scully describes as 'moral collage,' which seeks to 'articulate with integrity' the ethical understanding of the individual. The deliberation provides an example of *phronesis* in practice – the 'how to do it' process of enacting moral ethics and awareness. This Friend works through the difficulties (and inadequacies) of selecting a dominant deontological principle that should be followed in all situations. The importance of virtue ethics is apparent in the centring on the moral agent (as potentially 'hypocritical'). The result of the moral process is that the tensions and inconsistencies involved in sometimes working from one principle, sometimes from another, are acknowledged and held rather than neatly resolved – and this is done in a way that the speaker ultimately feels expresses Quaker advice to 'consider' one's use of substances in relation to the 'harms done' by them.

The study as a whole supports Scully's view that virtue ethics, which 'unite interior belief with external behaviours,' express the Quaker concept of testimony. However, as Scully notes elsewhere, 'Virtue ethics can produce a highly individualised morality' (Scully 2002, 219) and, as has been noted, the effect is potentially diversifying. My observation is that this potential diversity in terms of behaviour is offset by a number of unifying factors that work in terms of process.

Unifying Quaker Values

The potential for fragmenting diversity is partly contained by the expression and moral terms of the written testimonies in *Quaker Faith and Practice*. These have an impact on the terms and nature of the moral reasoning that takes place. So, for example, in relation to the testimony on abstinence and moderation, many Quakers (like the one in the foregoing quotation) stressed the power of example and the need to assess the general impact of their substance use on others, particularly children. This relates closely to the wording: 'consider whether you should avoid these products altogether, discourage their use in others, especially young people...' (*Quaker Faith and Practice* 1995, 20.40). Similarly, responses in relation to gambling reflected the sense in the written testimony, often stressing social justice, or the spiritually 'clogging' risks of greed. The ethical orientation of these written testimonies consistently showed a discernible relationship with the *nature* of the moral reasoning that was undertaken, even though behaviour varied.

Another significant counter-balance to the diversifying effects of virtue ethics is provided by certain key Quaker values, which were frequently activated in moral reasoning: these acted in a binding way in terms of process, and had strong deontological aspects in their functioning. The first of these values, cited by the last respondent and considered in a more deontological way than circumstantial specifics of testimony, is 'as long as thou canst.' This was consistently used as a touchstone value by Friends in this study – often as a way of reminding oneself not to be judgemental of others: 'I wouldn't dream of saying this is the only right way; do it "as long as thou canst." ' It was also used as a way of mitigating harsh judgements of the self - as in the case of a Friend who described a process of substance reduction: 'It's..."wear thy sword/smoke thy spliff as long as thou canst."'

The second value that was frequently utilised in the process of *phronesis* is 'that of God in everyone.' Dandelion (1996) and Scully (2002) have both noted its centrality in Quaker moral discourse in other contexts. [4] This was replicated in the present study, where, when Friends were asked to rank aspects of Quakerism they found most fulfilling (as described in section 3.3) 'that of God in everyone' was the second most frequently. The use of this value in practice was widespread, particularly in mitigating harsh or censorious judgements of others whose substance use or gambling diverted from Quaker testimony.

The importance of these key values not only relates to the way in which these testimonies were directly construed, but was also apparent in relation to the influence of asceticism. It has been suggested in previous research (notably Orford 1985) that the origin of low substance use and gambling in some religious people may be due to ascetic attitudes. This theory was upheld within the Quaker group, in that these attitudes were shared by about two-thirds of respondents, and those who endorsed them were lighter in their substance use and gambling behaviours. For example, those who agreed with the statement 'I would have reservations about using a substance just for pleasure' were less likely to use alcohol at all levels of consumption. However, within a Quaker context it is also particularly helpful to consider ascetic attitudes in relation to Collins' observations about 'plaining' and his suggestion that this undergirds all the testimonies (1996, and this volume, Chapter 2). The responses within the study about both testimonies are consistent with this formulation. 'Moderation, respect for self and others, simple life-style: these things not needed,' is a response from the study that succinctly summarises the 'will to plain' in the context of substance use and gambling.

Research in other Protestant denominations has found that these non-hedonistic attitudes, which I have described as 'personal ascetic,' are linked with an outlook that 'moral people' do not behave in such ways, and that members of their religion are unlikely to experience substance or gambling problems (Jolly and Orford 1983). However, most Quakers in the study did not feel that these behaviours would not be undertaken by moral people, nor that Quakers would be unlikely to develop problems. I suggest that dominance of personal ascetic attitudes underlie the abstinence and moderation of the majority, but also that these Quaker values mitigate 'moral ascetic' attitudes - and that their recessiveness has further individual and community effects.

This significance relates to Robson's observation that 'among Quakers I found that the thread of relationship exerts more pull than the thread of right outcome or justice.' (Robson this volume, Chapter 8) and to her view that the 'aspiration to unity' tends to be dominant. She comments on the concept of shame in a Quaker context, and on Scheff's formulation that this is proportional to the perceived amount of non-conformity with the community ideal (or 'espoused theory', as it could also be expressed). All of this can helpfully be applied to the psychological, spiritual and emotional reflections that Friends describe when relating their personal experiences with substance use and gambling. Robson's observation of Pinthus' dictum that 'what Quakers call "being human" other denominations call "sin".' (Robson this volume, Chapter 8) is particularly relevant to explaining the generally non-judgemental way in which Quakers tend to construe their own and others behaviour in relation to gambling and substance use.

My observation is that this nexus of interconnecting Quaker values – 'a concentration on spiritual journey rather than fixed doctrine,' 'as long as thou canst', and 'that of God in everyone' – undertaken through common processes of virtue ethics, and within a community that emphasises relationship over 'right outcome' - work together to mitigate (but not remove) the emotional discomfort that arises in individuals when their behaviour departs from these testimonies. The descriptions of Friends with a range of substance using or gambling behaviour was consistent with this formulation. One Friend with higher (but reducing) levels of substance use commented: 'I remind myself Quakerism's not about guilt...but it does help keep me in control sometimes.'

The accounts of some Friends with higher levels of consumption also provided examples of what Scully describes when she states 'the testimonies, unlike virtues, are not themselves the dispositions: rather they are moral claims or principles, articulated by the Society throughout history, that guide the personal and collective choices made by Friends, so that, in the end, appropriate dispositions are established.' (Scully, this volume, Chapter 6). The implicit relationship of virtue ethics to time, 'because the capacity for right judgement is acquired by training and practice' (Scully this volume, Chapter 6) is particularly apposite. Quakers who described reducing substance use or gambling patterns often framed their experiences in terms of a dialogue with Quakerism that took place over a period. Previous studies have tended to emphasise the stringency of the normative standard: whilst the current study upholds this factor – most obviously in the observed differences between substance use and gambling behaviours - it also suggests that time and process are deeply significant. For Quakers, the process of *phronesis,* crucially undertaken by Friends at *all* levels of gambling and substance use, appears to be a critical factor in individual and community functioning. It works against the individual who acts outside denominational norms being perceived as different or 'deviant,' and encourages a perspective of Quakers being involved in a common process, albeit at different behavioural levels.

My argument, then, is two-fold: firstly that this nexus of Quaker values have deontological and binding functions in the Quaker community - which balance the potentially fragmenting effects of virtue ethics and multiple, idiosyncratic, context-specific, individual formulations of testimony. Secondly, I believe the *content* of this balance accounts in large part for the denominational profile of Quakers as revealed by this study. That is, while behaviour is generally abstinent or moderate, some incongruent behaviour is able to be retained within the Society, because the values that have been described encourage inclusivity at a community level, and on an individual level they militate against mechanisms of shame/ cognitive dissonance becoming emotionally intolerable for the individual. Those departing from the letter of testimony are thus less likely to feel it necessary to leave the denomination, but the embedding of these testimonies in the behavioural creed and in the culture of the majority of Quakers means that the normative expression of testimony is retained – including in attracting 'recruits' of similar values and outlook.

Summary and Paradigm

My conclusion, therefore, is that Quakerism holds an unusual series of balances, which are represented in figure 5-1. This model outlines, with particular reference to Scully's idea of 'moral collage', the ethical terms and processes undertaken in the Quaker sample in relation to the testimonies of substances and gambling. The elements that foster a unified witness of abstinent/moderate behaviour, (embodied in the behavioural creed, the normative standard and the ascetic 'will to plain') are shown in the lower part of the circle. They are balanced and held in tension with the core Quaker values, which are shown in the upper half and tend to allow behavioural diversity in relation to the testimonies. However, these values are strongly unifying in providing a basis for community and individual identity (as Scully argues), and - since they are largely approached deontologically – they are also unifying in terms of process.

In terms of Quaker double-culture as outlined by Dandelion (1996, and this volume) it is interesting to note that these core values, while individually applied, are communally held - and their deontological treatment means that they carry a group binding/anchoring function. As Dandelion proposes, the letter of testimony is embodied in the Quaker behavioural creed, but it tends to be negotiated individually outside Quaker space and time. However, these negotiations are informed and – to a degree – unified by the values that have been discussed. Consistently with the double-culture model, it is the holding of the normative standard – *equally,* and in creative tension with – ethical and spiritually based negotiation that is the key to the Quaker balance that I have outlined. While Quaker double-culture presents problems to some in terms of diversity of belief, my thesis is that its operation in relation to these testimonies enables the retention of a meaningful standard without a loss of inclusivity.

The model represents the Quaker balance, and the factors that I believe enable Quakerism to present a profile of abstinence and moderation in relation to substances and the general eschewing of gambling – but with a minimised risk of 'losing' people, who, for whatever reason, behave differently. The effects of the balance are largely benign, in that low involvement in these behaviours is fostered, but, it seems, without discernible exclusion. For those who are adversely affected by dependency, this benefit is hard to underestimate. Holding the tensions – and sometimes the inconsistencies – of this balance is, I would suggest, a valuable modern Quaker testimony.

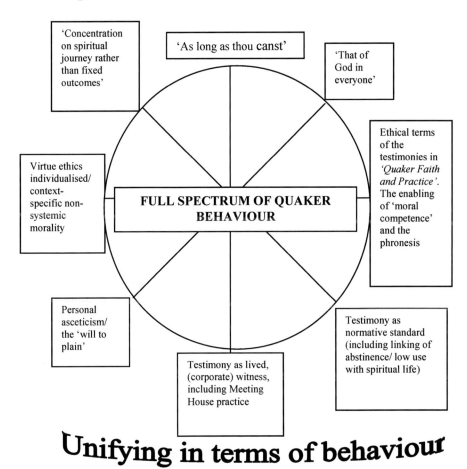

Figure 5-1. COLLAGE MODEL OF QUAKER TESTIMONY AND VALUES: diagrammatic representation of the ethical terms and processes undertaken in the Quaker study in relation to the testimonies of substances and gambling, based on Scully's concept of 'collage'.

Notes

1 And explored and described in the book *Role Over* (QPSW publications 2004).

2 With implicit or explicit reference to the passage: 'Dearly beloved Friends, these things we do not lay upon you as a rule or form to walk by, but that all, with the measure of light which is pure and holy, may be guided; and so in the light walking and abiding, these may be fulfilled in the Spirit, not from the letter, for the letter killeth, but the Spirit giveth life' (Postscript to an epistle to the 'brethren in the north' issued by a Meeting of Elders of Balby, 1656. *Quaker Faith and Practice* 1995, 1.01).

3 William Penn asked George Fox's advice about wearing his sword to a Quaker Meeting (given the Quaker testimony on peace and non-violence). Fox said, 'I advise thee to wear it as long as thou canst.' The passage in '*Quaker Faith and Practice* continues 'Not long after this they met again, when William had no sword, and George said to him, "William, where is thy sword?" "Oh!" said he, "I have taken thy advice; I wore it as long as I could."' '*Quaker Faith and Practice* 1995, 19.47.

4 Dandelion comments 'The only item of belief which was held by all respondents was the idea of "that of God in everyone"'(Dandelion 1996, 289), while Scully observes 'the absolute and equal moral reverence for every individual remained non-negotiable' (Scully 2002, 217).

CHAPTER SIX

VIRTUOUS FRIENDS: MORALITY AND QUAKER IDENTITY

JACKIE LEACH SCULLY

Ethics must deal with being good as well as producing good
—May 1994, 75.

Introduction

Human beings evolved as group animals and, given the chance, most people still opt to live in collectives with others. An important part of what makes life in groups possible are the rules about how we ought to behave towards those others, rules that we call morality.[1] Although there is an assumption in modernist ethics that 'moral behaviour' is about the acts of individuals, the fact that people rarely live in isolation means moral behaviour is necessarily about individuals interacting in societies. Whatever function they serve for the individual, ethical statements are therefore also statements about the groups in which we live.[2] Descriptive ethics give more direct accounts, but even prescriptive ethics indirectly say a great deal about a society by presenting the kind of societal ideals, priorities and values it encourages, who the prescriptions are intended to cover, and who has the authority to make them.

Recent work in moral philosophy and psychology has foregrounded the idea that questions of morality are inescapably also questions about *identities*. Charles Taylor and other philosophers argue that to understand oneself *as* a self entails alignment to the moral framework of one's community (Taylor 1995). These theorists are not making the obvious statement that moral choices contribute to a person's *moral* identity, but that orientation to a moral framework, provided through the practices and discourses of the community, is a major part of knowing *in general* who we are. These scholars are saying that the stance we adopt to beliefs about right forms of living not only shapes our personal moral worlds, but makes statements, to ourselves as much as to others, about the nature of the various social groupings to which we belong. The moral frameworks to which we align ourselves are not clearly articulated codes or guidelines - these come later, when moral beliefs are justified or defended. Rather, they are the backgrounds of belief generated by the practices of the community. These practices constitute socially embodied, largely unspoken statements about what constitutes a good life for the community and its members. They describe basic values, and prescribe modes of living that reflect those values adequately in the eyes of the community. They also define procedures for making judgements in situations of difficulty - for example, they indicate how to identify the sources of moral authority. For the most part we are not conscious of the background of rules and values with which we work, especially when all the intersecting groups to which we belong are compatible. But because many people in contemporary society participate in a large number of interlocking and nested groups, and these groups will often have their own, subtly distinct pictures of the good life, the contribution of morality to identity becomes complicated. Conscious negotiation may be necessary when what is taken for granted is suddenly exposed as open to question, for example if a new social situation makes the differences between groups more apparent; or if the mores of one group change faster than another; or if someone joins a new group that has radically different moral expectations.

In this chapter I argue that contemporary Liberal Quakers in Britain use moral judgement to reinforce their social identity as Quakers. They do this through the ethical framework and the sources of authority they use, more than the substantive content of those judgments. Based on empirical observation of Friends' moral evaluations, I have previously suggested that Liberal Quakers today use a 'collage' approach, with the tradition known as virtue ethics having an especially prominent (but not exclusive) place (Scully 2002). Here I explore further links between virtue ethics and key features of Quaker faith and practice that make the virtue approach so appealing to Friends.

Moral Evaluation in Britain Yearly Meeting

Between 1995 and 1997 I undertook a project within Britain Yearly Meeting, as Quaker Fellow funded by the Joseph Rowntree Charitable Trust, focusing on the ethical issues raised by advances in gene technology. Through this I was also able to make systematic observations of British Quakers' processes of ethical evaluation: how they identify situations of moral difficulty, describe and structure them, the precedents and values that inform their deliberations, and so on. Although the project was formally about genetic ethical dilemmas, the key observations seem applicable to ethical issues more broadly, as indicated by Helena Chambers' chapter in this volume.

A fuller account of the results is available elsewhere (Scully 2002). Two of the central conclusions were unexpected, at least to me. The first was to do with the *method of evaluation* that Friends used. Religious groups generally have a deontological bias to their ethics: they tend to organise their thinking around principles whose moral authority derives from their theological basis. Ethical commandments are accepted by the group because they are the word of God, for example. In the Christian tradition the Ten Commandments and the commandment of Jesus are often taken as the primary set of ethical principles; and orders like, 'Thou shalt not kill', or 'you must love your neighbour as yourself' become moral imperatives because of their perceived status as articulations of what God wants. I had anticipated that as a religious group, Quakers' moral evaluations would be consistently deontological. This turned out to be wrong. Friends did show one distinctive deontological trait (and I will return to that later), but other, non-deontological approaches were equally or more popular.

By far the most consistent feature was that when faced with a moral problem, the study participants constructed what I call a *moral collage*. By collage I mean that they did not use the theoretically consistent, logically coherent form of argumentation that professional philosophers are obliged to generate. Their disinclination to do so might have been predicted by their lack of philosophical training. However, from the comments that participants made it was also clear that, on the whole, whether they *could* do it or not was beside the point, because constructing a consistent and coherent argument was not their real aim. What mattered was not theoretical consistency nor the construction of what philosophers are fond of calling a 'killer argument', but whether participants could adequately articulate their interpretation of the morally difficult situation at each stage in the process of understanding it and reaching a conclusion about the best way forward. Fidelity to what was discerned was more important than consistency to an analytic framework. From a philosophical point of view, using more than one school of argument at a time shows incoherence. From the users' point of view, however, it could equally well suggest that real problems are not in fact best tackled by sticking to any one style of argument; that doing so might be inadequate to provide workable solutions, and moreover that pushing one theoretical approach to its limits is guaranteed (as philosophers know only too well) to reveal its weaknesses.

Hence Friends were willing to pick up and put down analytic methods as 'seemed right'. In the art of collage, diverse media are combined to give an expressive whole that makes sense in its entirety, even though made up of elements that would not normally be found together. By analogy, Friends selected elements from the ethical traditions available to them that seemed most appropriate at any given point. Coherence was maintained not by sticking strictly to the parameters of a theory, but by using concepts and symbols that unite Friends' moral understanding with elements from their religious lives. Among these, as I shall discuss later, are concepts associated with the testimonies.

Making a 'moral collage' therefore does not imply that participants invent ethical elements wholesale. Just as in a real collage it is possible to identify the square of purple velvet or the end of cornflake packet, moral collages also contain patterns of argumentation that could be mapped onto standard ethical theories. It was possible to identify statements that fit comfortably within a consequentialist argument, a casuist formulation, or a deontological justification, for example. Some participants may have been drawing on an academic knowledge of utilitarianism or of Kant, but in fact the arrow of cause and effect is likely to point in the opposite direction. That is, the fragmentary resemblances reflect the origins of all ethical models and theories: however technically sophisticated, they originate in and are elaborated from features of the everyday approaches people bring to their real-life moral quandaries.

Since carrying out this project, other research (Scully *et al* 2006 a, b; Banks *et al* 2006) suggest that the use of moral collage is in fact characteristic of secular lay moral discourse. The way in which academic moral philosophers go about ethical analysis is not how most people do so. In fact an increasing amount of evidence from moral psychology and cognitive science suggests that people tend to form moral intuitions rather rapidly, which they then back up with compelling (to them) arguments (see e.g. Haidt 2001). The moral collage would then be used to articulate and refine, and must be congruent with, these intuitions.

Use of something like moral collage is so widespread it cannot be considered distinctive of Quakers. Nor can it be assigned to one or other groups within liberal-Liberal Quakerism. Both Pilgrim's Inclusivists and Syncretists (this volume, Chapter 3) would, I think, use the collage approach. (Exclusivists might not, for the same reason that non-secular lay discourse can deviate from the moral collage model: the preferred use of strongly deontological, scripturally based argument.) What is particular to Liberal Quakers, and might vary between subgroups of Liberal Quakers, is the pattern of which ethical elements are prioritised and which left aside. Although the moral evaluations of these Quaker participants were, as one might say, *collaginous*, not all ethical theories or analytic frameworks were equally popular, just as collage makers might not find themselves drawn towards cardboard, preferring the purple velvet. Although consequentialist reasoning was common, for example, utilitarian thinking was less so, and contractarian approaches were notably absent. By contrast, one approach turned up repeatedly: a mode of thinking that relied on a model of the person who *could do no other* than act in accordance with the good. The closest parallel to this in standard ethical theory is virtue ethics.

Virtue Ethics

Virtue ethics is one of the three main strands of contemporary ethics, along with Kantian deontology and consequentialist approaches. For the sake of simplicity, I am limiting my comparison of virtue ethics with these two theoretical frameworks, a focus that necessarily means ignoring significant but less high profile ethical theories, including communitarian ethics, feminist ethics, discourse ethics, and the principlism favoured by medical and bioethics.

Originating in Greek moral and civic philosophy, and known especially from the surviving writings of Aristotle, versions of virtue theory dominated western morality [3] until being effectively displaced by the post-Enlightenment philosophies of Mill and Bentham on one side of the channel, and of Kant and his successors on the other. Since the late 1950s, however, virtue ethics has undergone a renaissance in academic philosophy (Hursthouse 1999; Crisp and Slote 2000). To a large extent this reflects dissatisfaction with the inability of the other frameworks to answer the most pressing moral questions of modernity, or to give a satisfactory description of moral personhood or the ethical life.

All forms of virtue ethics prioritise moral character over moral behaviour. This does not mean that virtue ethicists think that behaviour is irrelevant, or that a bad act becomes good if done by a good person. But virtue ethics does hold that the right act is not found by following a defined rule or algorithm - the utilitarian calculus, for example - but by identifying what the act of the virtuous person in that situation would be. This contrasts with the other major theories which prioritise evaluating the *act* itself. The precise criteria for evaluation of an act depend on the theory concerned: where Kantian ethics would ask whether it accords with the categorical imperative, utilitarianism looks for the maximisation of happiness (or, strictly speaking, of utility. Utilitarianism continues to argue about exactly what utility is, and what relation it bears to different understandings of happiness). Virtue ethics, on the other hand, tries first to give an account of the features, traditionally called virtues or excellences, that would be expected of a person leading a morally admirable life. Such a person, according to the theory, would be able to identify and carry out the ethically correct act in situations of moral difficulty. It is important to the plausibility of the theory that virtues are understood as more than desirable quirks making a person more likely to be, say, honest or generous. Virtues are better imagined as enduring, mutually reinforcing dispositions, similar in many ways to the dispositions of the Bourdieusian habitus discussed by Collins in this volume. Moreover they are not exercised as isolated characteristics, but result from mobilising multiple interlocking attitudes, understandings and expectations.

Virtue ethics' focus on agent as opposed to act does not mean that other moral theories ignore the prospect of the good person disposed to do what ought to be done. Any agent's readiness to commit herself to obeying a moral duty or to an ethical principle, such as maximisation of happiness, must indicate something about that agent's inward nature. Furthermore, even diehard deontological and utilitarian theorists will acknowledge that rules or principles cannot be applied without exercising a degree of ethical sensitivity informed by experience. But as May notes, this perspective still subordinates being to doing, and 'fails sufficiently to deal with a range of moral life that does not conveniently organise itself into deeds we can *perform*, issues about which we can make *decisions* or problems which we can *solve*' (May 1994, 78). This is the central criticism levied at act-centred ethical theories.

Giving an account of the enduring dispositions of a good person is only one part of virtue ethics. The second pillar of virtue theory is a person's ability to implement the virtues through making the right decisions. This is described in the Aristotelian concept of *phronesis*, or practical wisdom, the art of knowing what to do, and when and how to do it, and is the key to understanding how virtues are put into operation in real life. A virtue is a disposition, but not a mindless reflex response to a stimulus. Although the basic disposition to act in a particular way has prereflexive, emotional roots, it needs to be consciously exercised through the reason of the agent. To a moral psychologist, the idea of phronesis includes many of the features associated with normative moral competence, including the ability to grasp the relevant features of a situation, identify priorities, and have a realistic idea of whether and how to intervene and what the consequences are likely to be. The combination of character trait and ability to make correct choices means that, while a virtuous person can be relied upon to be truthful (for example), she can also perceive salient differences between situations in which honesty is called for, and will know how to respond to them most appropriately. Phronesis, moreover, is acquired over time, as dispositions are laid down through the choices made, and then exercised in making further choices based on a gradually accumulating grasp of the values at stake.

A well recognised practical problem of virtue ethics is that they are generally less helpful than rival frameworks when deciding between conflicting options. Acting in accordance with two different virtues (generosity vs. justice, for example, or honesty vs. compassion) may lead to opposing conclusions about the right course of action. In such cases, which one should take priority? Both utilitarianism and deontological approaches may offer clearer resolutions here. On the other hand, as Stohr puts it, 'virtue ethicists are not rushing to defend the idea that virtue ethics can supply a complete decision procedure' (Stohr 2006, 25). For a virtue ethicist, phronesis may manifest itself in knowing when to draw on other procedural or substantive resources, to resolve issues of priority between virtues.

Virtue ethics are also distinguished by the rich background picture of the good life they offer. Other ethical theories necessarily also contain normative ideas of how people ought to live in order to live well, but their focus on acts rather than agents means that the conceptualisation of 'living well' is secondary and sketchy. Virtue ethics distinctively prioritises the account of the morally excellent life, as the prerequisite for morally excellent action. However, there is more than one contemporary version of virtue ethics and while they all agree that the virtues are constitutive of the good life, they disagree on the reason(s) why. For some, virtues are the traits that enable a person to *respond* optimally to the moral demands of life. Ethical naturalists consider that to live virtuously is to live a life that, for biological or other non-moral reasons, is fitting for a human being (Stohr 2006, 24). Others, taking the concept of *eudaimonia*[4] as the way of life that is morally good for people, say that the virtues are those traits the exercise of which enables a person to flourish, not just as a human being but in the way that a *eudaimon* life requires.

Virtue Ethics and Quakers

There are straightforward reasons why deontological or utilitarian approaches may not hold much appeal for Liberal Friends. A central one is Quaker belief about the source of moral authority, which is connected to the rejection of written creeds. Quakerism gives primary authority to personal experience - of life in general, and more specifically to personal experience of the Light. This authority, common to all branches of Quakerism, is most explicit and defended most strongly in Liberal Quakerism. Deontological ethics, by contrast, is effectively creedal. It emphasises the obligation to sign up to a rule, whether religious or other, and in general Liberal Quakerdom resists appeals to the status of a text or figure over the authority given to individual conviction. Hence in the making of British Friends' moral collage in the study described earlier, the driving force behind the construction of the collage was the need to articulate with integrity each individual's *own understanding* of the situation, not whether that understanding was in conformity with scripture or even with Quaker precedent. Turning next to utilitarianism, it may be that what has been described as the 'utilitarian calculus', the maximisation of benefit for the greatest number of people, could never hope to be popular in a group that has rejected voting as a decision-making tool. The value Quakers place on social justice is also likely to sit uneasily with utilitarianism's inevitable tendency, as a quantitative system of sorts, to disadvantage minorities.

I want to suggest however that there are more structural reasons why British Friends favour a form of virtue ethics. There are features of virtue ethics which parallel beliefs and practices of the Religious Society of Friends in such a way that not only are they intrinsically appealing to Friends; they also reinforce the identity of the Society of Friends as a social group. These reasons are therefore more sociological than they are to do with tenets of Quaker belief. I outline some of these below. (For the purposes of this analysis I am not going to explore further how Quaker theology, or the lack of it, has itself determined how the Society is structured and functions.)

The absolute perhaps: Several contributions to this book acknowledge the cluster of ideas present in contemporary liberal-Liberal Quakerism indicative of a Quaker epistemology of the 'absolute perhaps' (Dandelion, this volume, Chapter 1): truth is partial, revelation is contextual and limited, spiritual life is a journey, the spiritual path involves seeking rather than finding. Quaker epistemology and Quaker ethics are deeply historical, contextual and nonidealistic. By contrast, deontological frameworks are in principle none of these; and although utilitarianism can be contextual and pragmatic, both deontological and utilitarian frameworks operate around an assumption of *epistemological closure* - the right answer can be known, by following the commandment or by undertaking the evaluation that produces an irrefutable conclusion. (I recognise of course that these are highly simplified versions of the forms of ethical analysis these frameworks offer. My point is about the response of a lay group to exactly those fragmentary versions of these approaches available in lay moral discourse.) An ethical framework based on interior character, on the other hand, presents as more contextual and emergent, necessarily contingent on the moral 'revelation' available at a particular place and time.

Linkage of virtue ethics to testimony: Virtue ethics are agent-centred because they make the statement 'I am this kind of person' rather than 'I think this is the kind of principle to follow'. Moral philosophers may dispute the idea of virtue ethics as always and entirely agent-based, and deontological or consequentialist approaches as always and entirely act-based. As I mentioned earlier, even in virtue ethics acts are not irrelevant, while act-based approaches acknowledge to a limited extent the actor's motivations. Nevertheless, it is broadly true that virtue ethics distinctively prioritise what it is about a *person* that leads her to choose one course of action, while the other two prioritise what it is about the *act* that leads a person to choose it. Virtue ethics therefore makes a distinctive type of connection between the inward nature of the person and her outward behaviour. The idea of an action being performed 'from virtue' entails a particular causality between the action and the agent's beliefs and desires. In virtue ethics outward acts are not simply *expressive* of the agent's interior moral nature; they are *generated* by it, and considerable attention is given to how that internal moral structure is developed.

Continuity of inner and outer life is also central to the Quaker concept of *testimony*, one of the cornerstones of living as a Quaker. As Dandelion argued (1996), religious self-identification for Quakers is in terms of behaviour more than through statements of belief. It accords with a model of religious commitment that sees the mode of life as the outward evidence of the inner orientation to God, as testimony, so that *what Friends do*[5] becomes a more convincing statement of faith than any words. In Quaker thinking, testimony relates both to the pattern of life to which Friends should adhere, and to the rationale behind that way of life. The global term (testimony) is often broken down into discrete aspects ('the testimonies') that are more easily used as guidelines in everyday life. At the start of the 21st century these are generally held to include the peace testimony (probably the best known outside the Society), and testimonies to justice, to simplicity, to equality, to integrity/truth, to community, and latterly what has been described as an 'emerging testimony' to the environment. Not only has the number of separate testimonies varied through the Society's history, but their sociological function has changed as well. Until around the middle of the 20th century they served to mark the separate identity of the group *against* that of the non-Quaker world, while the testimonies that are maintained today are more concerned with structuring the Quaker role *in* the world (Dandelion 1996, 121).

A few of the testimonies as given could map directly onto a list of virtues. Honesty, simplicity, or integrity would be among these. Others might be better understood as the *enactment* of particular virtues: equality, for instance, might express the virtue of giving the same respect to all people. To view the testimonies as unproblematically equivalent either to the virtues themselves or to their enactment, however, is a major oversimplification. For one thing, not all of the traditional virtues could be extracted from the testimonies without some strained reformulation, because - unlike the virtues - the testimonies are not intended primarily as a guide to ethical living. According to *Quaker Faith and Practice* the testimonies are 'not abstract qualities, but vital principles of life', derived from the 'experience of Friends ... that the Light led them into an understanding of the Christian life and the way it was to be lived' (1995, 19.33). Thus testimony is simultaneously an ethical statement (about the right way to live), an anthropological statement (about the nature of human beings), a sociological one (about the ordering of the Society) and a theological one (about Quakers' relationship with God). Moreover the testimonies, unlike virtues, are not *themselves* the dispositions to act in good ways: rather, they are the moral principles, articulated by the Society throughout history, that guide the choices made by Friends so that, in the end, the appropriate dispositions are laid down.

Although the virtues cannot be equated straightforwardly with the testimonies, there is nevertheless a significant structural parallel. If the virtues are seen as enduring dispositions towards actions that reflect a background commitment to the *eudaimon* life, this is echoed in a view of the testimonies as setting up analogous enduring dispositions towards actions that reflect a background commitment to the Quaker ideal, the Peaceable Kingdom. The model of right living given by testimony certainly has more in common with the virtue approach than it has with those ethical theories that evaluate the outward act, more or less detached from the inner life of the agent. The right act in utilitarian and deontological theories need not say anything about the moral identity of the actor; but for virtue ethics, it is *necessarily* a reflection of the actor's moral commitments, especially if it is part of a consistent pattern of right actions.

If morality and ethics are essentially about how people behave towards each other, as I suggested earlier, then to position an individual's behaviour as equivalent to her statement of faith is to connect moral life with religious identity in an unusually direct way. Obviously, this does not mean that other denominations or faith groups exclude moral behaviour from their visions of religious life. It is hard to imagine a faith group that would not expect spiritual commitment to be evidenced outwardly in the believer's actions. But a religious identity primarily defined through belief statements such as 'accepting Jesus Christ as my lord and saviour' does not depend on particular behaviours, and hence a gap is inserted between moral life and religious commitment. This cannot be the case for a Friend claiming to be a 'good Quaker' in any sense that the Religious Society of Friends would find meaningful.

Discernment: Virtue ethics also differ from the other major theories in that *discernment*, based on experience, is an integral part. It is not enough to have a characteristic such as generosity or compassion, or a theoretical grasp of what being generous or compassionate means: you have to know how to do it. Knowing how to do it is phronesis, the wisdom acquired through experience and practice. For the other major ethical theories, discernment is not essential, although some degree of wisdom in the exercise of ethical judgment will be desirable in practice. In theory, and unlike acting from virtue, all you need is to grasp the central rule by which one is bound by obligation, or that lies behind the version of utilitarianism you prefer, in order to exercise adequate moral behaviour.

The requirement for phronesis also explains why virtue approaches use a model of a *socially embedded* moral agent. The development of the virtuous person is dependent on human interactions: the accumulation of experience in making wise judgements about problematic interpersonal situations cannot happen outside a social world in which we learn how to do so. Virtue ethics therefore places weight on ethical formation in the family and school, through mentors, role models and so on, in a way that neither utilitarian nor deontological theories do.

Liberal Quakers will spot an overlap here between the concept of phronesis and the Quaker understanding of spiritual discernment. In lay terms the word discernment tends to be understood rather passively, as relating to how things are perceived. In contemporary Liberal Quaker thinking, however, discernment is a skill the rudiments of which are present in each of us, but which can be actively developed in spiritual life. Moreover, in Quaker thinking discernment usually means identifying the right course of action: according to *Quaker Faith and Practice*, 'Throughout the discernment process there should be one overriding principle before the hearts and minds of all: is this individual or group right to believe this *action* or *service* has been "laid upon them" by God? (1995, 13.06, my italics). Finally, like phronesis, discernment is tied to the model of a collectively embedded moral agent. It is not anticipated that a Friend will be able to exercise discernment without guidance from the Quaker tradition, as practised in the 'collective phronesis' of discernment during Meeting for Worship for Business and similar problem-focused gatherings (Scully 2007).

I have downplayed one essential difference between phronesis understood in the context of secular virtue ethics, and Quaker discernment. This is the *source* of the expertise. Skills of discernment and practical wisdom are both acquired through the combination of experience, practice, and internalization of the traditions of the moral community. However, Quakers (and other religious groups that use the concept) would claim that although discernment requires all, it is not a cognitive skill. It has a spiritual source: it requires input from/access to God. Discernment for a Quaker is less about the cognitive skills of perception or assessment than about the ability to attend to 'the promptings of love and truth in our hearts' (*Quaker Faith and Practice* 1995, 1.02).

The virtue of care: In Susan Robson's discussion of internal Quaker conflict (this volume, Chapter 8) she identifies in passing several characteristics that Friends value, i.e. Quaker virtues. Among the expected virtues (honesty, quietness) this empirical observation finds that value is placed on self-control and restraint, with a corresponding dislike of vehemence and any expression of strong feeling. In the context of internal disagreement, Robson finds that 'the thread of relationship exerts more pull than the thread of right outcome or justice' (this volume, Chapter 8). What makes this interesting in terms of virtue ethics here is the identification of a strong *care ethic* among Friends. The ethic of care is defined as an orientation that prioritises relationality and empathy, rather than rights and autonomy, and there is ongoing academic debate about whether care ethics is a subspecies of virtue ethics (McLaren 2001) or a broader concept that has a place in other ethical theories and approaches as well (Baier 1985; Held 2005). Without getting into that debate, it does seem that Robson has identified the existence (and drawbacks) of a bias towards care-related virtues in the ethical economy of Quakers. Although care ethics was initially associated with feminist ethics (Carol Gilligan's original work described a gendered bias towards the use of justice or care concepts in moral evaluation; see Gilligan 1982) recent work suggests that relationality is morally prioritised in many socially marginalised groups, including women and ethnic minorities (Stack 1979; Cortese 1990; Tronto 1993). The implication is that while socially dominant groups can afford to trust in existing frameworks of justice, since their experience shows it works for them, marginalised groups must prioritise (or feel they must prioritise) mutual support of their members over the formal implementation of justice. Seeing the Religious Society of Friends apparently operating in the same way therefore raises some intriguing questions about Quakers' perception of themselves in relation to dominant social organisations.

Quaker Identity and the Deontological Tether

British Friends have compelling sociological, as well as theological and ethical, reasons for taking an approach to moral problems that resembles a virtue ethical theory. This does not mean that all Liberal Quakers use virtue ethics in a form that moral philosophy would endorse: moral philosophers will find my account of virtue ethics, and its use by Friends, sketchy. Nor does it mean that Friends are *only* virtue ethicists; their strategy is an eclectic one of moral collage, but with more reference made to the motivations of the good Quaker than to any other style of ethical thought.

One of the theoretical limitations of virtue ethics is that it only 'works' as an ethical system in the context of a common ideal of the good or excellent or virtuous person. Virtue theorists are divided on whether there are universal virtues that cut across all cultures or if some, at least, are culture-specific. Some virtues seem to go out of date: a common example in the literature is how meekness and servility are no longer (universally) taken as the markers of the virtuous woman. As Martha Nussbaum points out, 'Past writers on virtue, including Aristotle himself, have lacked sensitivity to the ways in which different traditions of discourse, different conceptual schemes, articulate the world.' (Nussbaum 2000, 175). Like other faith groups, the Religious Society of Friends today is engaged in ongoing discussion about the shared identity, or loss of identity, of post-war British Quakers. Several observers have diagnosed the disappearance of a predominantly Christian framework of belief and its replacement by multiple, often less clearly defined positions (see Pilgrim and Vincett, this volume), although this has been challenged (Mellor, also this volume).

Dandelion (1996, and this volume) has identified strategies that enable British Friends to accommodate an ongoing diversification of belief by (i) making epistemological uncertainty prescriptive: the 'absolute perhaps', and (ii) retaining a collective identity through a Quaker double-culture in which a behavioural creed conserves patterns of outward practice as inward belief diversifies.

Dandelion (1996) applied the model of double-culture to behaviours within Quaker time, e.g. the format in which Meeting for Worship is held, or the retention of archaic terminology. It may also be fruitful to look at it in a more general form, less as a separation of the domains of belief and practice and more as a means to spiritualise the performance of religious identity. To an extent all religious groups use behaviours and practices to carry their religious self-conceptualisation, since meaning is embodied (as Collins' discussion of habitus shows, see this volume, Chapter 2). In sociological terms, this is the function of Quakerism's theology of testimony. Part of the appeal of the virtue ethical framework, then, is that its emphasis on an inner nature generating certain acts makes it entirely congruent with the Quaker theology of testimony, and through such congruence virtue ethics consolidates Quaker identity in a way that other ethical frameworks cannot.

Within the Religious Society of Friends, a shared understanding of what being a 'good Quaker' involves is generated by a number of routes. The testimonies provide not merely the theological rationale for a way of life, but some indication of what that way of life should look like. Knowing that 'a testimony to simplicity' is part of Quaker orthodoxy indicates that the virtuous Quaker is supposed to lead a simple lifestyle, although the details of what constitutes simplicity (or equality, or peace, or any other aspect of testimony) in a given context are always up for discussion (see Chambers this volume for one example of how interpretation of testimony is negotiated). Other models for the good Quaker life are provided by the written obituaries, known as 'Testimonies to the grace of God as shown in the life of' a deceased Friend. These are produced by local Meetings and sent to Friends House, the central administrative body of Britain Yearly Meeting, to be published at the time of the annual Yearly Meeting gathering. They are distinct in form and content, and convey to successive generations a clear sense of the kind of Quaker life that is admirable. In these and other ways, a felt sense of a good Quaker life is inculcated.

Common visions of good Quaker life are generated at various locations and structural levels that differ subtly in which community they represent. The Religious Society of Friends as a whole, local and regional

Meetings, the numerous specialised groups within the Society such as Quaker Action on Alcohol and Drugs (QAAD) or the Quaker Lesbian and Gay Fellowship (QLGF), even short events at places like Woodbrooke and Swarthmoor Hall,[6] are all instances of what Pilgrim calls 'heterotopia' - real or conceptual spaces that offer the conditions of possibility to be other. These are spaces the feminist theologian Sharon Welch referred to as 'communities of resistance and solidarity' (Welch 1985), and the ethicist Cheshire Calhoun as 'abnormal moral communities' (Calhoun 1989); within them heterodox opinions can be invoked and counterstories (Lindemann Nelson 2001) crafted, with the aim of articulating and presenting the meaning of virtuous identity for that particular community. It needs to be noted here, however, that 'abnormal' and 'dissident' and 'hetero-' are always terms relating to a tacit standard. While I argue that the Religious Society of Friends offers alternative moral discursive/physical/temporal/cognitive space to be 'other' to the wider society, at other times we need to recognise the groups within Quakerdom, such as Quaker Pagans (see Vincett this volume, Chapter 10), the Experiment with Light (Meads, this volume), and adolescent Friends (Best this volume, Chapter 11) that bear the same relationship of otherness to the Religious Society of Friends itself. In terms of virtue ethics, they are all engaged in the task of providing visions of eudaimonia, the excellent life that is their moral goal.

There is more work to be done here to clarify what makes visions of the good life, and certain moral collages of justification, compelling to Quakers while other visions and justifications are not. Although there is considerable potential for diversity in the understanding of what a 'good Quaker' is, some options are clearly excluded (the good Quaker arms dealer is a near impossibility). Some kind of centrifugal core of moral value is present, and it sets the parameters for multiple interpretations of the good life to be produced. This is why at the same time as inclining towards a virtue ethical approach, British liberal-Liberal Friends also make use of one outstanding deontological 'tether', and this is George Fox's injunction that Quakers must recognise 'that of God in everyone', the phrase that some writers identify (Dandelion 1996, 289; Scully 2002, 217) as the bare minimum left which all Friends can still sign up to. Whatever its theological interpretation, it sets the normative standard demanded of Friends in their dealings with others. The good Quaker not only responds to that of God within herself but recognises and responds to it in others. Like 'love your neighbour as yourself', or Kant's categorical imperative that people be treated as belonging to the realm of ends, with all the respect and care that entails, this Quaker categorical imperative provides the minimum normative core around which the virtues of Quakers cohere. The deontological statement that I was at first unable to find in this religious group's ethics is present not as a set of commandments, but as the heart of the Religious Society of Friend's vision of how best to live, through which contemporary Quaker identity is operationalised in the individual and collective acts of virtuous Friends.

Notes

[1] The debate over whether these 'oughts' derive primarily from the *non-moral* realm of society or biology (for example, that we ought not to kill each other because doing so produces unstable societies) or whether they are primarily rooted in some kind of *ethical* statement (such as, that killing others is wrong because it fails to show proper respect for them as persons) is not one I want to enter into here.

[2] The terms 'moral' and 'ethical' are variously defined. In this chapter I take moral to refer to patterns of how people live, ethical to the systematic reflection on it.

[3] Although I refer to western virtue ethics here, some comparative philosophers consider Chinese Confucianism to be a school of virtue ethics.

[4] *Eudaimonia* is a notoriously hard concept to translate, but in Aristotelian virtue ethics it connotes a broad idea of happiness in the sense of flourishing and doing well.

[5] I mean this in terms of how they behave in the world rather than 'how they go about being religious', that is, not the behavioural forms that Dandelion claims are the social glue for British Liberal Quakers, but everyday ethical and social choices.

[6] Woodbrooke is the Quaker study centre near Birmingham, Swarthmoor Hall is a building in Cumbria of major significance in Quaker history. Both run courses and events, often residential, for Quakers or other interested people.

PART III:

MEETING CULTURE

CHAPTER SEVEN

CONGREGATIONAL CULTURE AND VARIATIONS IN 'GOSPEL ORDER'

DERRICK WHITEHOUSE

Introduction

The usual ways of measuring the performance of a congregation are not so easily applied to Quaker Meetings. Quaker worship is based on stillness and silence and participants vary widely in their beliefs and with competing theologies. No two Quaker Meetings are the same. This chapter outlines the elements of Quaker congregational culture[1] and depicts how they vary in 'health'. Historically, Quakers have used the concept of 'gospel order' to describe the 'right ordering' of Meeting life and this concept is adapted for sociological use in depicting the Quaker ideal.

Gospel Order

When gospel order is mentioned amongst British Quakers many, even birthright and 'seasoned', i.e. experienced Members, glaze over or ask what is meant by the term. Usually when it is referred to it is in relation to the conventions and regulation set out in *Quaker Faith and Practice* (*Quaker Faith and Practice* 1995) [hereafter *QFP*] also referred to as the 'Book of Discipline'.[2] What I do is take the notion 'gospel order' from the theological ideal that is rendered in the 'book of discipline' and relate this to the cultural reality of local Quaker Meetings.

Gospel order was developed in the 17th Century as a tool to reinforce the discipline and the authority of this new religious body. *The Testimony from the Brethren* (1666), which was one of the earliest forms of discipline and formed the basis for gospel order (Moore 2000, 227). This was particularly aimed at re-establishing regulation of business affairs as well as setting out guidelines for personal conduct and is still conceived as conforming to what is disseminated in the Quaker book of discipline.

George Fox said a good deal about gospel order with a Christian vision of the way Quakers need to function. In his epistle 313, Fox pledged himself to the 'new covenant order of the church under the headship of Christ' (Jones 1989, 312). Fox suggested that it is the responsibility of Christians 'to live in this gospel order, both out of a desire to do God's will, and as a testimony to the rest of the world about the gospel or 'good news' (Wilson 2001, 5).

I maintain all Quaker congregations are striving to accomplish gospel order, even if not recognised by the participants in those terms, but implementation differs from one Meeting to another, which has a profound influence on congregational culture and spiritual nurture.

Revisiting Gospel Order

Some Quaker writers have enlarged on the rudimentary interpretation of gospel order, most notably three American Friends: Lloyd Lee Wilson (2001), Patricia Loring (1999) and Sandra Cronk (1991), as well as British Friend Janet Scott (2002). Each one has taken the understanding of the term to be much more than just the functional correctness of the Quaker congregation.

Cronk argues that Friends have attempted to preserve an understanding of gospel order.

> Gospel order is the term, which has historically been used to gather together many of the most significant elements of Friends' understanding of the church-community. George Fox made use of the phrase when he began to describe more fully the practices of worship, decision-making, and daily living in Friends Meetings. His writings indicate that his interest in this topic grew as the Society of Friends, created initially in a period of spiritual upheaval and ferment, began to take shape as an ongoing movement, living out the implications of being led into God's new order (Cronk 1991, 3).

Often in Quaker Meetings today, particularly in business Meetings, reference is made to check that a particular practice 'is in right ordering'; does it conform to what is understood by gospel order? In other words is what is being proposed congruent with the guidance that comes from *QFP*.

Janet Scott provides a contemporary interpretation of gospel order:

> The Quaker concept of gospel order is a way of describing the nature, organisation and work of the visible church. The invisible church consists of all those who have been reached by and who have responded to the

Light, whilst the visible church has the task of being a sign and witness to
the nature and life within the kingdom of God (Scott 2002).

I argue that gospel order represents the 'ideal aspiration' that is talked
about and permeates the culture of the Quaker congregation, which may be
realised in a variety of ways (Whitehouse 2005, Chapters 1 and 6).

Collins is helpful in clarifying the nature of congregational culture
when he contends that Quaker Meetings operate as 'habitus' providing
several scales from which individuals construct or improvise their own
score. He reminds us that individuals comprise multiple selves, which they
articulate to promote a measure of coherence, of unity and harmony. He
admits that this may not be a neat process but suggests this to be a
pervasive dynamic in identity formation for religious faith and practice
(Collins 2002a, 147-61).

Sandra Cronk argued that no part of the individual's life or that of the
faith community should be separate from their vision of gospel order. She
wrote, bringing the essential areas of the life of a Quaker congregation into
focus:

> The content of gospel order (as it relates to church-community concerned)
> falls into three general areas: the inward life of worship and discernment,
> the interior functioning of the church-community (and the Quaker home
> which, in some ways, is seen as a smaller version of the Meeting
> community) and the social testimonies of Friends. (Cronk 1991, 9)

She qualified this statement by adding that: 'These categories are
simply helpful ways to cluster the patterns of faithful living for the
purposes of discussion' (Cronk 1991, 46). Cronk summarised the spiritual
aspirations of Quaker Meetings through the term 'gospel order' and
divided it into three components, which I term worship, witness, and
community.

Wilson supports Cronk's view that witness and Quaker testimonies are
inextricably connected as a feature of gospel order (2001, 147-89). British
Friends, in *Faith in Action: Quaker social testimony,* amplify this concept
by showing how the Quaker testimonies can be incorporated into
individual Quaker support and attesting to each other as well as the
witness of the congregation to the world beyond the Meeting (Cave 2000).

Janet Scott is clear on the parameters of gospel order implicitly
supporting Cronk's perception and elaborating the scope of the concept as
follows:

a)   To describe the relationship of Meetings to each other; (Monthly Meeting, General Meeting, Yearly Meeting)
b)   To describe the way in which the business is conducted; (Worship / Discernment)
c)   To describe the business with which the Meeting deals (Worship, Community, Social Witness). (Scott 2002).

Gospel order also describes the relationship of a Meeting's participants to the life of the congregation as a whole. Scott continues:

The business with which a Meeting deals is that of the visible church and includes:
• Maintaining relationships with God (e.g. worship, education);
• Maintaining and strengthening the Meeting community (e.g. outreach, oversight, provision of resources for these tasks such as buildings);
• Maintaining witness in and service to, the world (e.g. prison ministry, peace vigils, relief work) (Scott 2002).

When I asked Meetings what they considered to be the fundamentals of Quaker spirituality,[3] how it could be recognised and what was necessary to bring about the well rounded Quaker Meeting, they all came up with equivalent proposals (Whitehouse 2005, Chapters 2 and 3).   Research carried out on other faith communities produced findings that parallel what Quakers are advocating for their own faith communities (e.g. Ammerman 1997; Becker 1999).

All list three common elements of the ideal congregational culture *worship and discernment* (this includes how Quakers process decision making), *covenanted community* (where individuals are at ease with each other and claim to be led by God) and *social witness* (many individuals and Meetings take communal action to be at the heart of their spiritual quest by embracing the Quaker social testimonies – see Testimonies Committee 2003). Participants claimed all three elements ideally have equal status, which, when braided together, interact as one to form a pattern for the congregational spiritual culture and the pervading form of gospel order.

Exploring the Elements of Gospel Order

'Functional style' is the generic term I use to describe the range and nature of expression within the three elements of the congregational culture. In some instances the adjectival descriptions used appear to be quasi-hierarchical. However, the subtle nuances, I contend, best describe the functioning of particular elements. In some instances the descriptions reflect a rudimentary trend towards either a dysfunctional or non-functional spiritual culture. The inter-relationship between the functional styles provides an overall portrayal of a 'congregational cultural profile'. The way these elements are manifest in Quaker Meetings varies and this has a profound effect on the culture of gospel order.

The result of variations in functional styles has an influence on the characteristics of the 'behavioural creed' (Dandelion 1996, 100-10 and this volume, Chapter 1). However, from my participant observation and what Friends have told me of their personal faith and practice, I add a further category to the double-culture, namely that of the function of the *'activist'*. Activists are Friends who concentrate on 'social witness' in one form or other with motivation from a moral and ethical point of view rather than a spiritual perspective. Such a stance implies that they are apt to distance themselves both from the mores of Dandelion's *liberal belief culture* as well as the *behavioural creed*. However, as Members, they wish to be identified with heart of the life and witness of the local Meeting and the Religious Society of Friends.

In a similar manner Simon Best (this volume, Chapter 11), in his conclusions describing a triple culture for the adolescent Quaker group, presents three characteristics that are congruent with the elements of gospel order (bracketed below) outlined by my own research, namely:

- 'Ritual – the culture of contribution' (Worship and Discernment).
- 'Networked Community' (Covenanted Community)
- 'Narrative and Behaviour' (Social Witness).

Pilgrim (this volume, Chapter 3) perceives contemporary Friends as falling into three groups, namely 'exclusivists', 'inclusivists' and 'syncretists' all influencing the diversity of Quaker thinking and action in the expression of a Meeting's culture.

Worship and Discernment

The culture of 'worship and discernment' (Gorman 1973, Sheeran 1996) embraces both the formal and informal acts of worship and decision making that take place within the conventions of the tradition as well as at other times connecting with the functioning of the congregation, e.g. Meetings for Worship for business, social witness, special events, healing groups and study sessions. It also reflects the place of worship in the everyday lives of members of the congregation and the range of faith perspectives amongst participants.

Some Meetings have a dynamic where there may not be a consensus of beliefs amongst the Members and Attenders. However, if there is a trusting sense of community it is likely to give rise to a functional style of *exploration*. Sometimes this is controversial and challenging and needs good humour and careful handling. It is likely that personal progress and growth results from this dynamic although not always by the same route for every individual.

A *steadfast* functional style comes about when a large number of the Members have a similar spiritual outlook. In this climate there is not the same need to grapple with basic perceptions as there will be a sense of common bond on spiritual leanings. This is likely to be manifested in a stable and 'steadfast' approach to the life of the Meeting generally.

A Meeting realises a *drifting* functional style when there is no clear lead or direction towards a culture of discussion or sharing of spiritual matters. This could emerge when 'cultural architects' (see below) are unsure of their own stance on spiritual perspectives or possibly there could be a feeling abroad amongst Members that they do not wish to express or share their views with others. This may come about when there is not the bond between participants, which comes from a flawed sense of 'covenanted community' (see below).

Covenanted Community

'Covenanted Community' describes the manner in which those in the congregation relate to one another. Having a strong sense and practice of an energetic community is a critical and integral aspect of congregational culture if spiritual nurture, learning and growth are to be effective. Involvement with the local community beyond the congregation is also a consideration.

When writing on gospel order, Lloyd Lee Wilson describes the Quaker Meeting as a 'covenant community'. Wilson perceives the covenant between Quakers and God and each other reflected in the faith and practice of a Quaker community. The Quaker concept of community should not in Wilson's terms be simply about caring and sharing but overtly embraces the spiritual dimension as an integral constituent of all aspects of congregational life (Wilson 2001, 61-72). The informed ideal is that Quakers are zealous to 'seek to know one another in the things that are eternal' (*QFP* 1995, 1.02.17).

The evidence from my research suggests that spirituality and a sense of community is interlinked in the minds of most Quakers. Patricia Loring explains how a 'covenanted' notion of community can have meaning.

These are some of the major, human ways that modern Friends seek to bond with one another in spiritual community to affirm and reinforce their spiritual stance over and against a society rooted in something other than unity in the Love of God. As may be seen, the ways of modern Friends focus primarily on fellowship within the community. This is very important in a culture that fragments relationships and even our contacts with one another. However, the forms of our fellowship that overtly reinforce the sense of the ground of our community in a listening spirituality are in a distinct minority. Most of our modes of fellowship owe more to purely human 'community building' techniques that evolved in the seventh decade of this century, a decade through which most of the present generation of Friends has lived. Many of us were actively formed socially through that period. It is a discipline to yield the techniques of that time to the less organized nudges and movements of the Spirit (Loring 1999, 246).

For example consuming food together has been a major way of bonding in most cultures and many religious groups from earliest times (Loring 1999, 241).

Where there is conviviality between participants one is aware of an energetic and outgoing friendliness towards one another. Sometimes this is strong and *demonstrative* whilst in other Meetings there is a calm but pleasing *collective* atmosphere. In some Meetings there is often an ambience of simply being affable with no sense of sincere engagement with one another or enquirers, which becomes manifest as a *reserved* functional style.

Social Witness

Although individual Quakers are moved to demonstrate through personal action, 'social witness' as a category here is concerned with the combined stance and achievement of the congregation. This means involvement both in the local and wider community on matters relating to social and community concerns including inter-faith activities, political, moral and spiritual interests. Social witness for many traditions and individuals is perceived as an integral component of their spiritual life. The concept of gospel order interacts with the Quaker testimonies and many Friends claim that their social witness, whatever the concern, is an integral component of their spiritual quest (Whitehouse 2005, Chapter 3).

There are Quaker Meetings where there is a strong commitment to action on the testimonies in one area of disquiet or another. Friends regularly bring their concerns to the Meeting and gain support. This may be in the form of taking action perhaps locally in some cases whilst in another it might be to engage in a cause needing wider consideration of possibly 'speaking truth to power' . When this happens on a regular basis it is manifest as a pivotal component of the Meeting's culture. A *fervent* functional style would be an appropriate description for this forceful attitude towards collective concerns and action.

A more typical description of what happens in Meetings is that the congregation will feel *moved* to engage in concerns as they arise. Often this is likely to be brought about as a result of one or more Friends being roused and bringing the 'concern' to the attention of the Meeting resulting in carrying certain others along to engage in subsequent action.

Frequently Friends claim they feel bombarded with details of distressing situations occurring at local, national and international level. Within this climate of 'compassion fatigue' a Meeting will often feel concerned yet helpless and therefore, the functional style is best described as *touched*. It is always possible that a Meeting may be grappling with its own problems or has a long-term commitment to a specific project, which may not come directly under the heading of Quaker testimonies or concerns. Consequently, though touched, action will not ensue or commitment may only be limited as far as the congregation is concerned and becomes a marginal element of gospel order in the congregational culture.

Supporting Elements of Gospel Order

For spiritual elements of gospel order to flourish supporting elements are required. I have described the characteristics and functional styles for the supporting components (Whitehouse 2005, 148-84) as *Cultural Architects, Functional Participation, Management Style* and *Resource Availability*:

Cultural Architects

Cultural architects refer to those who influence and have or assume various responsibilities for the effective working of a Meeting. Cultural architects play a crucial part in the life of the Meeting and the creation of the culture. Certain cultural architects will have designated management roles such as clerks, treasurers, elders or overseers. Others may be Members of the Meeting who have served in these capacities but for a while are 'resting' but nevertheless exert influence. One of the features of Quaker life is that everyone is seen to be able to bear the role of elder / overseer if willing and appropriate (*QFP* 1995, 12.15-19). There may be other people, not necessarily Members, in the Meeting who by virtue of their personality, skills and training are capable and articulate enough to exert a strong sway at certain times (Dandelion 1996, 237-81).

The size and nature of this collective group varies from Meeting to Meeting. It can be a force that exerts a profound effect on the spiritual life and culture of the congregation. The facilitating ability of cultural architects, which may not always be categorised as either management or influence, is manifested in a range of guises, even in modest form, such as managing the coffee rota, organising walks or caring for the garden.

When people find themselves in a position to influence others they can present themselves as either 'controlling' or 'nurturing'. Observation of Quaker Meetings bear this out. Many of those who control seem to be those Friends who are well organised in their own minds and able to express themselves readily. However, one can sometimes detect that controlling individuals can use their skills to avoid getting on with the task in hand, particularly if the implication is that more work or involvement might be a possible outcome. In some instances, during research workshops certain individuals acting as clerk who had a controlling disposition presented a minute that was accepted, which reflected much of their own opinion rather than a consensus of the group. This was due to the strength of personality of such individuals, which persuade the group to unite with their own version of what has taken place. Controlling Friends frequently bring out a 'dependence' feature in others. Often more than one controlling individual in a congregation will embrace this characteristic leading to a cultural style I describe as *interactive.* This category summarises the tensions existing between people, which, depending on the pervading circumstances, could lead either to difficulty or positive outcomes for the Meeting.

Those who want to influence by *nurturing* appear to be much more compatible with the development of an inclusive Meeting culture. These people have the gift of spotting potential in others and drawing them out to the point that a Meeting can progress on a much broader front. These individuals attempt to provide clarification and guidance in order to help the group move forward. Sometimes their voice is not heard and efforts fail if there are interactive / controlling Friends in the same group.

Difficulties arise when cultural architects are either not plentiful (this is often a problem encountered by the small Meeting but not necessarily so) and / or those placed in the role are *limited* in their own understanding of the needs of individuals and the nature and ways of managing the Quaker culture. Should this be the prevailing position then there is a risk that the Meeting will not be served adequately and could go into decline.

One style is not better than any other, just dissimilar. Each has a contribution to make to the life of the Meeting when every individual could be well versed in the 'way of Friends'. However, interpretations may differ. What is required is balance. Sometimes this is not possible and can be particularly disturbing and disruptive to a Meeting if interactive Friends attempt to impose their strongly held views and opinions on a particular issue.

Functional Participation

Central to the life of a congregation is the proportion of committed Members whether this is in formal worship and business or activities concerned with community and / or social witness. The Quaker Meetings studied suggest a correlation between the proportion of committed core participants who actively supported the life of the Meeting and the 'health' of the Meeting. This concept of a committed core was supported in casual conversation with the Meetings studied by way of comments about those who were either 'never seen' or seemingly had lost interest and moved.

The reason for adding 'functional' to 'participation' is to emphasise the active dimension of the term and to facilitate understanding of the four functional styles identified. Functional participation is concerned with individual responses that collectively lead to the fashioning of the culture of a congregation. The four functional styles identified describing *'Functional Participation'* are:

Committed –where a high proportion (up to 50-60 %) of the membership is regularly involved for the most part in the activities of the Meeting.

Restrained – describes regular participation by up to 40% of Members in Meetings for worship but who hold back from involvement in other activities in the life of the Meeting.

Variable – where the membership support fluctuates towards activities in the life of the Meeting. As a consequence it will appear that congregational life, including Meetings for worship, is supported scantily.

Detached – describes a congregation where up to 70-80% of the formal membership is not participating in the life of the Meeting.

Management Style

Management style refers to the administrative and organisational qualities vested in those who have the responsibility for and have influence over the life and culture. These are in the main designated Friends, namely, Clerks, Elders, Overseers, Treasurers.

Although all who participate in the life of a Quaker Meeting have a responsibility for how the Meeting functions, in practical terms it is most likely that the functional climate and culture is in the hands of designated cultural architects. From experience and observation the one key person in this equation will be the clerk of the Meeting. The interaction between the clerk and the Meeting is a two way process. A charismatic and efficient clerk along with a good team of cultural architects interacting well is a key facilitating factor of a healthy gospel order / congregational culture.

When a Meeting engages the majority with a sense of belonging plus feelings of collective ownership, it could be described as *progressive* in terms of its functioning style. Although the overall membership feels responsible for the life of the Meeting, it could be said that it also has much to do with the direction forthcoming from the cultural architects inspiring the Meeting.

A Meeting is *comfortable* when there is a climate where the clerk and other cultural architects are working well together but the Meeting is not stretched in exploring new ways of being or initiating development. For some, coming into this type of Meeting can be cause for discomfort. Sometimes such individuals will attempt to influence the Meeting towards progress and if this fails they may decide they no longer wish to worship with Quakers or seek a Meeting with a progressive functional style.

Where a Meeting lacks positive management and displays a *relaxed* functioning style, there is a risk that the congregation could be 'receding' both in management style and more than likely numerically. This may not be conspicuous, as the trend is subtle and difficult to pinpoint. However, if a Meeting is to change this trend then at some point it could look closely at the symptoms leading to a relaxed functional mode.

Resource Availability

Resource Availability influences many aspects of congregational life ranging from the condition of the building and fabric through to support for those in distress or having other needs as well as the maintenance and development of training and study programmes. If an energetic spiritual culture is to be nurtured it is largely dependent on having the resources (plant, fabric, human and financial) to develop and sustain such refinement.

Wealth had always been unevenly distributed among us and it was recognised that those Friends or Meetings who had access to substantial wealth, were able to follow their concerns more easily than others, and to exercise power and influence over other concerns they chose to support (Heathfield 1994, 73).

Broadly the resource availability of a Meeting can be described as:

plentiful – where there is confidence in the fact that the congregation has financial and human resource in relative abundance enabling it to carry out all that is required to maintain and develop the culture of gospel order at an ample and even generous level.

comfortable – where the financial position allows the congregation not to have too many anxieties about fulfilling its obligations and maintaining standards of gospel order without feeling stretched.

stretched – where the active membership is likely to be numerically weak and those handling resource matters may lack the knowledge and skills to develop a healthier economic standing.

Finance may relate to the size of the Meeting in terms of the number of Members in relation to the proportion of Attenders (who will or may not contribute to the income of the Meeting). There could also be a reference to the degree of affluence amongst the Members and whether there is income from property or reserve funds through trusts or money (sometimes substantial) received through legacies. Where there is money available, a Meeting is enabled to support Members who wish to attend courses and conferences, which will in turn assist in the spiritual learning, nurture and development of gospel order in the Meeting.

The Transforming Trend and Quaker Congregations

With every Quaker congregation there is an ambience that reflects the disposition of the culture and the 'will of the people'. I term this the *transforming trend*, which reflects the directional impulse of the spiritual culture of the Meeting. During research fieldwork, there were pervading impressions of the way a particular Meeting functioned along with a sense of the direction in which the congregation might be heading in terms of its spiritual nurture and practice.

I am defining 'transforming trend' as a form of assessment that appraises the disposition of a congregation towards gospel order and development of cultural change. The extent of desire to transform ranges from healthy congregations wanting a metamorphosis upwards in form and appearance, through faith communities resolved to maintain the *status quo,* to congregations so impotent that to make an effort of any kind to advance would be unworkable. In addition, there are groups wishing to make an effort to develop but have embarked on the assignment from flimsy starting points. The transforming trend is vital to understanding both the functional processes.

The transforming trend describes the disposition towards change, which is evident in every congregation / Meeting. One could refer to the functional style invoked as having either an optimistic or pessimistic outlook or maybe simply wanting to be stable and untroubled. Transformation is not just about 'aspiration' but is concerned with the 'possible' and both these frameworks need to be reflected in the functional styles.

Thus, the direction in which the congregation is travelling relates to the collective disposition of the participants. This could be an *energetic* path where the aspiration is to develop and progress. Then there is the congregation that senses that things could be much better and is *striving* to make progress, possibly against the odds. On the other hand a Meeting could convey the impression that it is happy with its present *stable* culture and would wish to maintain that stance. Another mode is less easily detected, certainly by the Meeting itself, which is when there is a pervasive mood of a *diffident* transforming culture. When this situation exists it could be perceived that a congregation is ushering in a state of steady decline.[4]

Defining a Cultural Profile

From the range of functional styles it is possible to construct a profile of how gospel order is operating in a Meeting (see Figure 7-1). Congregational profiles tend to embrace gospel order as a group of styles at a similar functional level. In other words a lively Meeting could have a gospel order that is *exploring, demonstrative* and *fervent*. Whereas, a more stable cautious Meeting appears as *steadfast, collective* and *moved*. Meetings that are in poor health will appear as *drifting, reserved* and *touched*. Each may be striving towards attaining the ideal of gospel order but it is obvious that in some instances the reality can be some distance away from the ideal. This will for the most part depend on the *transforming trend* and degree of *functional participation*. Merton suggests that functional unity, whereby change in part of an organisation brings about another change elsewhere in the organisation, is a matter of degree (Merton 1968).

'Functional unity' is somewhat protean in nature. I believe 'unity' exists in a paradoxical form in a congregation where there is often a movement towards a quasi-unity without necessarily achieving the full effect. This is particularly relevant when considering that change materialises at a different rate within each element of every congregational culture.

There is a 'catch up' process, which eventually works towards 'functional unity' be it at either a higher or lower functional level depending on the nature of the 'transforming trend'. My research found that in most case studies there were matching levels in 'functional style' across the profile of each element describing the Quaker Meeting under investigation. However, this represents an observational descriptive form, which does not reflect the precise dynamic and perception about 'functional unity' being experienced within the membership of the congregation. Consequently, the most that can be claimed for designing a 'cultural profile' is that it presents an indication in graphic terms that is a useful aid to improve understanding of a congregation and the pervading culture.

The choice of the constituent criteria depicting the functional style for each element in the cultural profile is based largely on outcomes from participant observation when working with Meetings plus the synthesis of responses by Members. There are some factors that are assessed by perceptible facts given by individuals and groups whilst others are based on participant observation and comparison from a range of Quaker congregations. In some instances understanding is based on confirming evidence from other sources such as observation of Quaker gatherings outside the research and documentary evidence from Quaker literature and written reports.

How can a congregation that is having drawbacks in attaining effective gospel order, develop so as to cope with the diversity of personalities and perspectives and nurture the spiritual needs present amongst Members and Attenders? In theory, everyone participating in the life and witness of the Meeting should be aware of their personal responsibility to make things happen to bring this about in a 'church' that professes a 'priesthood of all believers'. In other words, everyone should strive to be a *cultural architect*. In order to achieve a state where spiritual nurture flourishes, Quakers need to be better informed, sensitive and skilled in the art of fostering gospel order. This is about convivial human relationships facilitating the distribution and exchange of effective spiritual nourishment in order for the entire congregation to be able to grow in their personal and corporate faith. Then worship and discernment will flourish along with fostering a covenanted community with aspirations for meaningful social witness, all of which interconnect to sustain an authentic and inspired Meeting culture.

It is anticipated that this form of investigation will contribute not only to a more informed and better nuanced understanding of Quaker Meetings, but also to the wider and growing field of congregational studies as described, for example, by Ammerman 1997, Guest *et al* 2004. The form of analysis outlined allows Quaker Meetings and / or academics to undertake an audit of congregational life.

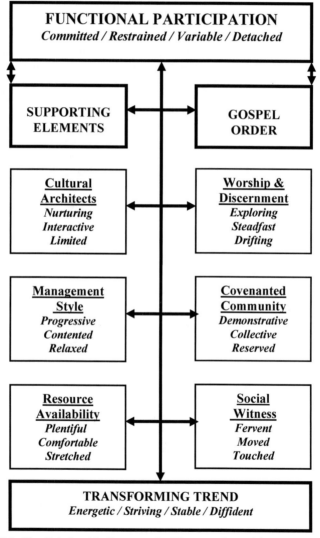

Figure 7-1: The Relationship Between the Elements Comprising Congregational Culture.

Notes

[1] 'Congregational' is used here to refer to the local community of believers, not refer to any ecclesiological style.

[2] The book of discipline is a regularly revised anthology of extracts designed to maintain and nurture Quaker faith. The current edition is called *Quaker Faith and Practice* (1995).

[3] This chapter is based on fieldwork with nineteen Meetings in Britain, one in each General Meeting area.

[4] In assessing the transforming trend, there has to be confidence to make some subjective judgements, which means that the researcher / assessor needs to make personal judgements based possibly on 'hunch' or retrospective interpretation. Objective criteria are compelling and crucial, and need to be drawn up to assess the transforming trend and its consequences on progress or otherwise in feedback, subsequent action and change (see Whitehouse 2005, 175-84, 228-36).

CHAPTER EIGHT

GRASPING THE NETTLE:
CONFLICT AND THE QUAKER CONDITION

SUSAN ROBSON

Introduction

'Conflict' was the flavour of the year among British Quakers in 2000. Perhaps the advent of the millennium prompted a resolve to tackle this difficult subject anew, with sessions on the topic at Yearly Meeting, in Quaker Life Representative Council, at Woodbrooke Quaker Study Centre and with the publication of a new book of guidance 'Conflict in Meetings'.[1] It was at this time that I started my research into conflict handling among Quakers, the story of which was told in 2005 (Robson 2005, 214-27; Gabriel 2000). However, conflict is not a discrete entity, either in time or human space. It is always expressed and engaged in by people; they are embedded in their own particular social contexts, and positioned by the discourses in those contexts and communities (Winslade, 2003). Therefore my study of conflict among Quakers was also a study of the organizational culture, of the community narratives, and of the tension between the collective and the individual in Quaker life. Conflict is but one thread in a loosely woven cloth of many threads, where the links and the tensions between the threads are fluid and changeable. With that assertion, I first outline my findings about conflict among Quakers and then explore the links with other elements in the Quaker condition, Dandelion's 'absolute perhaps' (this volume, Chapter 1) and Scully's Quaker virtue ethics outline (this volume, Chapter 6).

Conflict among Quakers is unexpected; the espoused image of the Quaker community is peaceful and tranquil. In the community narrative, commitment to 'mend the world' is undoubted but conflict within the community is handled with aversion, not articulated, and harmony is privileged above justice. The 'theory in use' is 'don't ask, don't tell, don't even think about it'. Quaker identity is cherished and challenges to it provide the rationale for intractable conflict sagas. The hesitation of the 'absolute perhaps' (this volume, Chapter 1) is visible in unwillingness to appear authoritative about tackling conflict. (Robson 2005, 124) A different account is reported from Ireland Yearly Meeting where Friends appear to be able to grasp the nettle of conflict and remain friends.

Positioned as Researcher

Other writers (Dandelion 1996; Collins 2002b; Nesbitt 2002) have explored the position of the Quaker insider researcher. The most meaningful description of my own position came from organizational studies with Torbert's 'observing participation' (1991) which features a continuing relationship with the organization studied, with interaction and influence between the research process and the participatory role within the organization. In my case there were several roles, as I was carrying a great deal of Quaker responsibility, or even power.[2] I was positioned by at least two discourses (Harré 1999), the research discourse and the Quaker discourse. Sometimes these seemed to be separated by invisible but ethically significant boundaries, sometimes the doors were open between the two. However, this was only one aspect of data gathering. I also undertook 39 semi-structured interviews[3] and a workshop and follow up with 20 self-selected Quakers. These people gave me my primary sources of data. Responses to presentations of my work continue to add data and develop my learning.

The Intriguing Question, an Uneasy Juxtaposition

The question at the heart of my research was one which both disturbed and disquieted me. It was expressed most neatly in a Fat Cat cartoon in *The Friend.* [4]

Here Fat Cat, as the Clerk of the Preparative Meeting, sitting under the clock, says 'If we cannot agree to alterations to the Meeting House shall we turn to ideas for peace in Kosovo?' This uneasy juxtaposition of enthusiastic grandiosity in the public sphere with inadequacy in dealing with more personal distress nearer home recurred in my own experience. I was embarrassed by what seemed like inappropriate smugness among Friends and wanted to know how it came about. I must also admit to a desire to change it.

Figure 8-1: Fat Cat

An example of the imbalance of attention given to the wider world and domestic responsibilities occurred at Yorkshire General Meeting in October 2002. Several of the contributors to the research had already told me of the Yorkshire Conciliation Committee which existed to resolve disputes among Friends, blissfully unaware that it had been disbanded for lack of business some ten years previously. At this General Meeting there was an item on the agenda concerning the replacement arrangements for the Conciliation Committee. The Clerks felt ill-equipped to implement these. In a five minute item, an offer from the Finance and Trusts Committee to take on this role was accepted.[5] The Meeting then devoted its two main sessions to speakers on conflict handling in the wider world. The first was about the Quaker-originated Oxford Research Group, and the second from the armed forces about their increasing responsibility as peacekeepers. This imbalance between the attention given to the wider world and the attention given to the workings of the Quaker community struck me most forcibly.

The Quaker Construction of Conflict

An English teacher friend said 'Quaker Conflict, that's an oxymoron', 'a pointed conjunction of seeming contradictories'. A colleague, embedded in another denomination, asked of my research 'what do you have to do, go round stirring up all those peaceful Quaker Meetings?' It is not generally expected that Quakers fight even without outward weapons, and Quakers themselves share this expectation. Many Quakers experience the Meeting as a haven: 'a balm... a healing place, a privatised place' (Robson 2005, 95) [6] in which they will not be challenged. Thus, 'it was a big shock when conflict finally burst among us' (Wrench 2006), as it has in most Meetings. Though the 1994 *Advices and Queries*[7] enjoin Quakers to 'bring into God's light the emotions, attitudes, and prejudices which lie at the root of destructive conflict' (*Advices and Queries* 1995, Para. 32) this is connected with public, community and international conflict. Within the Meeting caution and self control is advised to 'avoid hurtful criticism and provocative language': 'think it possible you may be mistaken' (*Advices and Queries* 1995, Para. 17). I would be glad to be directed to Quaker extracts which encourage one to be brave, strong, or courageous.

The expectation regarding Quaker response to conflict in the wider world is much more easily observed. A participant in a conference spoke of the overload of exhortation to work for social justice which is apparent on any Quaker Meeting House notice board, with flyers for demonstrations, requests for volunteers and money, and news of projects across the world. Nevertheless the contributors and many other Quaker individuals and groups are very clear that it is an important Quaker task to 'mend the world'. This phrase comes from a well known extract from William Penn (Quaker Faith and Practice 23.02[8] written in 1682). The phrase is now the title of a book explaining the current work and thinking by British Quakers for social justice in the world (Phillips and Lampen 2006). The short quotation also contains the notion that true godliness enables men to live better within the world. Penn was concerned to assist this process and set out a template of guidance about how to handle conflict within the Quaker community (Hartshorne 1993; Robson 2006). Interestingly, this has almost faded from contemporary knowledge. In contrast, mending the world in the wider sense is almost a buzzphrase.

Quakers Engaging in Conflict

Despite the fact that it is unexpected, conflict is endemic in Britain Yearly Meeting, as in all communities. Many people started their interviews saying something like 'I'm not quite sure what you mean by conflict, but I've written down several things in my notebook which I want to talk about'. These examples were nearly always events which were known in the Meeting community and had at least in part been played out in the forums of Quaker business Meetings. I was only offered one example of a personal disagreement between two people, which was resolved by prayer and dialogue. In the main conflict was experienced and navigated in the 'Quaker time' aspect of the double-culture. (Dandelion 1996). This is congruent with Kline's (2002) findings about conflict among Scottish Quakers. His analysis uses Goffman's distinction between 'on-stage' and 'off-stage' behaviour, but also includes 'out of theatre' behaviour, which takes place where there are not strong Quaker constraints. 'On stage' conflict in worshipful settings is usually denied or controlled, 'off-stage' accounts of conflict at social or informal events are more expressive, but 'out of theatre', where Quaker rules do not apply, conflict behaviour is unpredictable.

Aversion

A distinctive pattern of Quaker conflict handling emerged from the data. The first characteristic was the difficulty in recognising and acknowledging the existence of conflict. The contributors were well aware that they, individually and collectively, often 'avoided' conflict, using a term from the 'dual concern model' of conflict analysis (Thomas 1988).[9] However, it seemed to me that they went further than this; they failed to recognise conflict, and failed to bring it into public view, because they were afraid of living with it and ashamed of its existence. When conflict erupted or refused to be denied they failed to explore the reasons for it, circumnavigating the real issues and painful feelings in the urgent need for resolution. I described this as 'aversion' rather than avoidance, turning the eyes and the mind away from conflict, with a concomitant sense of distaste.

Harmony or Justice?

The second characteristic is the privileging of relationship over outcome; the need for community harmony is more important than the right decision. The dual-concern model of conflict resolution proposes two sets of interests or concerns, concern for the outcome of the conflict and concern for the relationship of the actors, which are in tension. The diagrammatic expression of this model suggests that these pull in opposite directions, however this can rarely be the case and I see these two concerns more as two threads which are spun together in one strand with different tensions. However, among Quakers I found that the thread of relationship exerts more pull than the thread of right outcome or justice. It is usually a more important aim that the group retains its members than that a searching process finds a right way forward even at the expense of disagreement and loss. This aspiration to unity is of course built into the Quaker method of decision-making,[10] which in turn influences all Quaker communications. There is sometimes confusion between decision-making and conflict handling; they are related but they are not the same, and may require different methods of communication.

Morgan[11] expressed provocative views on the relationship between the substance of justice and the outward form of harmony among Quakers. She devised an orthogonal model (see Figure 8-2) which includes attention both to the specific context, the Quaker culture and the way it construes conflict, and the individual and the strategy or style they adopt. It contrasts values commended in the Quaker context, honesty and restraint, with qualities which are unacceptable to Quakers, vehemence and mendacity. In non-Quaker society, honesty and mendacity are constructed as a dichotomy of good and bad, but restraint and vehemence are not. Their opposition is a particularly Quaker polar construction. Morgan's model points to a clear strategy for achieving success in Quaker disagreement in Quaker terms, to adopt restrained honesty. However, her own experience was that this resulted in more concern about the outward form of harmony than the substance of justice. The Quaker collective turned in on itself and presented a solid front which excluded the aggrieved person and did not accommodate their needs. Therefore Morgan herself chose to adopt the course of vehement honesty. She deliberately expressed her view in language which was strikingly different from restrained Quaker language.[12] Unfortunately this was probably not effective in achieving justice either.

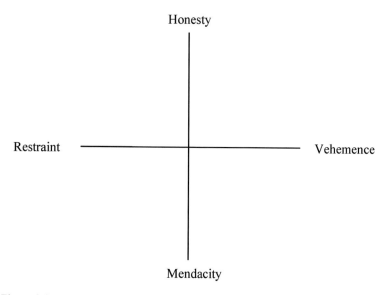

Figure 8-2: Morgan's Model for Quaker Conflict

Non-Articulation

The third characteristic of Quaker conflict clearly has some connection with the previous characteristic relating to strategic Quaker style. I describe it as non-articulation, which may be translated as not speaking out. This is not to say that Quakers are inarticulate, far from it, but they are constrained by the organizational culture into not speaking out on many subjects and in many settings.[13] The silence of worship which underlies Meetings for business makes quietness a commended default option in all circumstances (*Quaker Faith and Practice* 1995, 2.12-17, 3.09-3.12) In conflict a strategy which Quakers often commend is listening, but only one contributor specified that this should be active listening which offers a response. For most people listening was not differentiated from being 'like a sponge and soak(ing) it all up' (Robson 2005, 99).

The lack of human verbal exchange in the accounts of conflict was striking. Questions were not asked, emotions were not named or expressed, issues were not explored in detail, people were not to be upset by the use of words. They were aware of the tradition of Quaker plain speaking, but there was little evidence that it happened now. One participant at the end of six months reflection asked where were the 'Quakers [who] can seem rather brusque; without the conventions of flattery and half truths' (Quaker Faith and Practice 12.01) He pined for their presence but observed instead a level of shrinking sensitivity which could not tolerate this style.

It was 'unQuakerly' to show strong feelings, especially anger. One contributor summed it up: 'it's even fine to say that you're angry, but it's not fine.....in the sense that people won't like it or won't like you, if you exhibit anger' (Robson 2005, 137).

Therefore very few people ever stay to articulate their anger with a tirade in a Meeting. It is much more common to leave the room, the Meeting or the Society, or to stay away when a potentially divisive subject is discussed These are all very powerful moves in preserving Quaker 'broiges'.[14]

Causes of Quaker Conflict

There were several common causes for conflict. It was practical questions which forced conflict onto local Quakers, where dates and figures had to be decided and agreed to. Fat Cat's example, the failure to 'agree on alterations to the Meeting House', showed acute observation. Developing the Meeting House was often the reason for discord, sometimes of major proportions. Employment, particularly the employment of Wardens or Resident Friends, was almost equally fractious. Other recurring causes of conflict were children in Meeting (felt keenly by parents, but irritation not admitted by others), break up of relationships (disappointment with the reaction of the Meeting), and Quaker education.[15]

Interestingly, in my data, theological difference was not acknowledged as a cause for conflict[16] (Dandelion this volume, Chapter 1; Best this volume, Chapter 11). Diversity of belief was recognised but largely practiced in private, with a carefully constructed zone of tolerance. However, this may overlap with what was called 'unacceptable ministry'. Many Meetings struggled with this, often as an unresolved conflict, where particular vocal ministry annoyed the Meeting. This was rarely explained in terms of the theological flavour of the ministry, but usually focused on the form 'too often, too long, always the same thing'. Elders were not seen as able to constrain this ministry, often because they could not agree on what, if anything, to do.

Despite the Quaker urge to resolve conflict quickly, even without exploration, it did persist in many cases, and was resolved in some. In the course of the study the conflict that appeared intractable in year one was sometimes constructively resolved by year four or five. However, a long lasting conflict is usually played out in terms of identity conflict, which may long outlast the original occasion of difference. Identity conflict is relatively intangible and based in the history, psychology, culture, values, and beliefs of the group with which one identifies. Methods of conflict resolution most effective with this intractable kind of conflict (Rothman 1997; Winslade 2001) require demanding reflexive exploration of all these issues.

> Identity issues frequently arise as a result of insensitive behaviour during conflict that unwittingly challenges the individual's cherished self-identity and that of his cherished group(s). (Sandy *et al* 2000, 310)

Many issues which started out as a difference on a practical matter soon change into exchanges about what a 'proper' Quaker[17] should do, often focused on procedural matters in the collective method of discernment and decision making rather than the justice or compassion of the decision itself. An example of this was the decision about the future use of the Quaker International Centre[18] in 2004. Some were in favour of it being used to obtain rent, others in favour of it being used by a Quaker group for a Quaker purpose. The latter faction, which was unsuccessful, felt that debate had been stifled, but then continued a long campaign of criticism about the way in which Meeting for Sufferings, specifically the Clerks, had handled the matter, asserting that this was not the proper Quaker way to do things.[19] The claim that we are Quakers and we should do it the proper way, not your way, recurs at all levels of Britain Yearly Meeting. Quaker identity is cherished and defended above all else.

Quaker Identity and Conflict

Personal construct psychology (Kelly 1963) asserts that humans construe the meaning of their current experience based on the way they have interpreted their previous experience. Using this framework Bannister (1985) explores the experience of identity, of self, of belonging. He notes two ways in which identity is formed. Firstly identity is found by focusing on the common shared experiences in a collective. This is taken from Kelly's 'commonality corollary' which proposes that 'each person employs a construction of experience which is similar to that employed by other persons, and therefore his or her psychological processes are similar to other persons' (Kelly 1963, 90). The point here is that not only do several people undergo a common experience, but they also interpret it in the same way; for them the meaning is common. If there is a lively argument and someone says 'We need a little silence', the Quakers will know what is happening and probably react with some commonality. A non-Quaker will think 'What are we waiting for? When do we take the vote?' The shared understanding creates the common identity.

The second method of constructing identity is by focusing on the differences between people[20], the attributes and experiences which make them distinct from each other. This is based on Kelly's 'sociality corollary' which proposes 'the ability to play a social role with another is dependent on the extent to which a person can construe the construction processes of another' (Kelly 1963, 95). This is often put more memorably as the ability to walk in someone else's shoes, or to feel what their experience is like. The emphasis here is not on a role prescribed by the organization or society in which the actor lives but on a social process about how they understand and then interact with someone else. To quote Bannister, 'we may seek to inspire them, confuse them, amuse them, change them, win their affection, help them to pass the time of day, or defeat them' (1966, 22). In all these ways the actor is taking part or playing a role in a social process, but it is not a role that has a specific name. It is sociality and it requires open-minded attention and responsiveness to the experience of the other. This may be another way of describing Buber's 'I-Thou' relationship.

The co-existence of commonality and sociality poses a problem for Quakers. With limited Quaker time individual Quakers are less interested in individual differences than in having the common Quaker experience. They want to practice being Quakerly, that is why they are there. So it is not surprising that commonality is privileged above sociality and the comfort of the 'proper Quaker' way is sought. However for conflict resolution, sociality, or the ability to walk in another's shoes, is needed, which may be less comfortable. If Quakers have not practised this they may feel at a loss to know the 'proper Quaker' way to do it. They are used to knowing how they expect other Quakers to behave, but they have little experience of focusing on themselves and creating a new interactive pattern in conflict. Also sociality requires reflection on the self before reflection on the other (Lederach, 1999, 123). This is not always an appealing process for Quakers, as Meads (this volume, Chapter 12) indicates in her accounts of ambivalence and apprehension about the setting up of 'Experiment with Light' groups.

Self Examination

Though the Queries have always asked Quakers to examine and connect their inner experience with its effect on action the contributors to the study gave little account of this. Whatever happens in Quaker silence came over as a blankness or emptiness. There were a notable few who had learnt the skill of self examination in another context, either in counselling or therapy or in another religious setting. They saw this as adding depth and richness to their approach to conflict, giving them courage to face it and engage with it. But for most it was as if they did not want to find out the difference between what they themselves experienced and what the 'proper Quaker' experience was. Particularly with regard to conflict they did not want to become aware of their own difference from the idealised stereotype. The whole ethos of Quaker culture in which the individual submits their concern or idea to the group for testing works against the idea that the individual is important. To focus on the self in conflict even in private is uncomfortable. One contributor making an anonymous written record of her reactions to conflict in her Meeting said:

> It also makes me feel very uncomfortable to write so critically because though my head tells me to get a grip on this for goodness sake, my 'gut' hints that I am a very bad Quaker for saying such nasty things.....Oh dear! (Robson 2005, 203)

This is a good example of 'shame', a concept which Scheff (2000) argues is at the root of all conflict, on intimate or international scale. Shame occurs when one feels negatively evaluated by oneself or others. In my account I used terms like embarrassment or discomfort to describe the awareness of discrepancy between personal behaviour and the ideal. Scheff says discomfort deserves the stronger name of shame. This is not a word much used among Quakers; it was only after finishing my thesis that a non-Quaker asked me where shame featured in my thinking. Quakers use less emotive words if they do consider the less serene activities and emotions. Several times in my data a phrase like 'we are of course human' occurs. This was a puzzle to my secular academic supervisors. To solve it Eva Pinthus, Quaker theologian and ecumenicist, suggested that what Quakers call 'being human' other denominations call 'sin'. For Scheff shame (or its obverse, pride) is the marker of the state of the social bond between the individual and other individuals which form the collectivity. The amount of shame experienced by an individual indicates the perceived amount of conformity or non conformity with the community ideal, and unrecognised and unarticulated shame is one of the triggers of conflict.

Shame and sin do not feature in the Quaker community narrative. There are historical reasons for this from the start (Dandelion *et al* 1998, 110, 154, 207), but also sociological and psychological reasons. The utopian community of Levana,[21] which was understood to be the Religious Society of Friends after nuclear catastrophe, had no experience of power politics, distress and disease, or sex and showing off to offer its young people. They had to go out into other provinces to learn about these. This fictional sanitised version of Quakerism is also the real experience of others; Kirkby (2001) and Steer (2001) are both highly critical of a community which suppresses knowledge of the 'warring, partying, deal making, cheating, divorcing bit' (Steer 2001), and hopes that all is sweetness and light.

Quakers are fond of the Jungian idea of the shadow (Wallis 1999) which places the primitive, unadapted and awkward qualities in a separate part of collective experience bounded by the conventions. This enables them to preserve the illusion of the peaceable kingdom from which occasional safaris may be made to look at the wild animals of human experience.

Pilgrim (2004, and this volume, Chapter 3) describes the heterotopic process convincingly. The metaphor of the individual spiritual journey is inherent in the community narratives of Quakerism, explored in detail by Kline (2002). Though in theory the journey does not stop with the entrance into the Quaker community, many people regard that community and its practices as sanctuary or a haven, or a 'neverland to escape to' (Francis 2006, 113). But it is definitely a distinctive other place perceived as different from all other religious communities, so they expect that distinctiveness to be expressed and exhibited by all the members. If it is found that they are either not distinctive at all, or distinctive in different ways from the weary traveller, the whole of the sometimes uncomfortable journey is called into question.

The Community Narrative

The stories told by all the contributors produced a shared image of their collective experience. This could be described as the dominant community narrative (Salzer 1998). It is the story Quakers accept which explains their history, purpose and heterotopic understanding to themselves. Firstly there was no doubt among my contributors that Quakers would not be Quakers if they did not attempt to improve the world in which they live: 'I do feel we should be up there with what's being decided behind closed doors' (Robson 2005, 133).

This was far more than 'love thy neighbour', it meant that wherever there was difficulty and distress Quakers: 'are very deeply concerned about what is happening, and nearly always attempt to do something about it' (Robson 2005, 132).

As above, this responsibility to 'mend the world' has been characteristic of Quakers at least since William Penn. The Quaker organization which sets out to mend the wider world may also perceive itself as already in a mended state.[22] The idea that the Quaker organization is a 'peaceable kingdom' (Isa 11:6-9) has many strands. The American Quaker artist Edward Hicks painted several versions of this peaceable kingdom where the lion and the lamb lie down together. Scott (2003)[23] suggests that animals acting in this unnatural way are meant to symbolise the transformation which takes place when the kingdom exists. The animals in their wild state represent the faults found in humanity; these faults have to be tamed if people are to live together peacefully, not banished to the safari park of 'the shadow'.

By the late 20th century the Quaker Peace Testimony had obtained a special status as the most unifying testimony, although Francis (2006, 107) argues that for newcomers it may now seem an optional extra or a stumbling block. Quaker witness against fighting with outward weapons has varied in interpretation and emphasis since the seventeenth century, and has not been as monolithic throughout the whole Society as the current dominant narrative suggests (Phillips 1989; Ceadel 2002). After world war twice in the twentieth century which challenged individual young Quakers to place their lives and their integrity at risk, the pressure is much relaxed and rigorous self scrutiny is less required. The surrounding society is also less in favour of military *bragadoccio*. New Quakers are therefore able to see the society as peaceful rather than suffering or waging peace.

Scully's virtue ethics model (this volume, Chapter 6), in which she also identifies the dominant community narrative as the 'peaceable kingdom' is extremely useful in explaining the process by which the collective vision is translated into individual action. Fuller exploration of how this model illuminates Quaker conflict, and indeed many other aspects of the 'double-culture' (this volume, Chapter 1) is awaited eagerly.

Theories of Action in the Quaker Organization

These two strands of 'mending the world' and living in 'the peaceable kingdom', form part of the dominant community narrative, but would also be described by Argyris and Schön (1996) as the 'espoused theory'. Espoused theories are the values on which people believe their behaviour is based, to which the organization has made a public commitment. They are usually fairly easily discovered, in authoritative resources and in overheard conversation and are keenly defended.

However, the espoused theory is only half of Argyris and Schön's analytic scheme of theories of action, which is applicable to all organizations. Co-existing with the espoused theory is the 'theory in use', which is not so easily discovered. Theories in use are the notional maps which guide action in the organization on a day to day basis. They may differ from the espoused theories but people in the organization may not be aware of this difference, and may not be aware of the messages in the theories in use which guide their action. Theories in use can often only be discovered by inference from behaviour, including speech. What people actually do often reveals the theory in use more clearly than what they say, or what they say they should do. These values are not necessarily explicitly in awareness and the dangerous prospect of exploring them is often defensively resisted. I explored the term 'unQuakerly' with the interview contributors, and listened to and observed the responses in and after the workshop. I learnt that it is unQuakerly to be immoderate, to show strong emotion, particularly anger. I also learnt that talking about conflict among Quakers requires the coaxing which Plummer (1995, Chapter 2) describes as necessary to bring stories of sexual variation into public view. Conflict is a subject which is constrained by many invisible injunctions, often rationalised as a need for confidentiality to protect the participants. These two threads wove together to suggest to me that for many Quakers the injunction in the theory in use about conflict is 'don't ask, don't tell, don't even think about it'. It was common for questions not to be asked, especially to the main actors, for accounts to be limited by the need for confidentiality (or saving face?), and for people to feel bad if they think about conflict in a Quaker setting.

To continue Plummer's coaxing metaphor about sexual stories, I realised early in my research that I felt like a voyeur observing Quaker conflict, and am now cheerfully resigned to this. As spreading the counter narrative about Quaker conflict is so uncomfortable I can at least get some enjoyment from the early stages of the process in collecting data.

Non-Assertiveness, Non-Conviction

Those I interviewed surprised me with another aspect of non-articulation. When asked to give hypothetical advice to a new Quaker about conducting a personal conflict, drawing on any resources they chose, they were largely flummoxed. Most of them were uncertain, unable to draw on either the Bible or Quaker Faith and Practice with precision, or at best: 'they will find a paragraph which tells them what to do' (Robson 2005, 98).[24]

They seemed unaware of useful strategies (except unspecific listening) and did not wish to appear confident or capable in handling conflict. Indeed for some confidence seemed unappealing, one said : 'I think I'd be allergic to someone who thought they could [advise on conflict]' (Robson 2005, 123).

The only person who cheerfully embarked on a simple one paragraph description of what a Quaker, or anybody else, should do when they find themselves in conflict rather wryly described himself as considered to be slightly belligerent. In fact on this occasion he was merely well grounded and confident, not uncertain and hesitant. Lack of hierarchy was often stressed as a valued Quaker characteristic, and it seemed another expression of this could be lack of authority. The contributors did not want to appear authoritative, perhaps they were aware that if they made assertive statements about how a Quaker should conduct themselves in conflict they exposed themselves to attack from other Quakers. They did not even include 'think it possible you may be mistaken' (*Advices and Queries* 1995, Para. 17) as part of a recommended process, though it clearly positioned them in a comfortable place.

This connects with the 'absolute perhaps' (Dandelion 2004b, and this volume, Chapter 1), where it is more comfortable for a Quaker to construct a personal narrative which depicts him or herself as a seeker who has not yet found and who obdurately remains open to new light, without having any firm criteria about what is light and what is darkness. Personal narratives are tentative rather than assertive, re-adjusted in private. Counter narratives which are assertive and authoritative may be ignored,[25] or may encourage assertiveness in others, which might turn into conflict, which is unpleasant, unQuakerly and might result in exclusion. This appears to be a process in which the aversion to conflict and the unwillingness to be certain both reinforce the other.

Grasping the Nettle

Some months after completing the thesis I presented a version of this analysis to the Hardshaw East (Manchester) Peace Group. Among the audience was a Friend from Ireland Yearly Meeting who said that her experience in Ireland was different. There Friends did not avoid conflict, they engaged in it with conviction. They were not uncertain, but asserted different certainties within the community. She was aware of two difficult issues which were on the agenda for the next Ireland Yearly Meeting, the substance of Quaker belief and the Yearly Meeting's response to homosexuality. In Britain Yearly Meeting diversity is espoused as a positive value in both these matters and they are rarely argued on the public stage. However, the epistle from Ireland Yearly Meeting ('Epistle from Ireland Yearly Meeting 2006) showed that there had been 'forthright exchanges' on both these topics with a range of views, but also recognition that 'different views can exist within a fellowship of love under the governance of the spirit of Christ'. This Christian language would be unlikely to appear in contemporaneous Britain Yearly Meeting: the tone is not sufficiently 'liberal' or 'perhapsish'. The condition of Ireland Yearly Meeting would appear to be different from that of Britain Yearly Meeting, as the condition of Ireland is different from that of Britain. In Ireland religion is still embedded in public and political life; the wider context for Quakers in Ireland is sectarian affiliation which engenders deep animosity and tragedy. In contrast Quaker disputes must appear mild. Britain has succumbed to post modernity in which religion occupies a much smaller importance in the public consciousness, and where its reputation is often judged by the ability of the church to present a united front on contemporary issues.

The heterotopic boundary between Quakers and the wider society is differently placed in Ireland Yearly Meeting and Britain Yearly Meeting. The degree of difference between the surrounding society and the small Quaker group varies on different topics in the two settings. Regarding conflict both Quaker groups reflect the society round them. Britain Yearly Meeting reflects the polite and restrained tradition of not talking about religion or politics with its theory in use not to talk about such topics; in a tradition riven by religious affiliation enacted in politics Ireland Yearly Meeting is robust enough to grasp the nettle of conflict with firmness.

Notes

---

[1] These were a two day workshop at Woodbrooke Quaker Study Centre in February, a session of Britain Yearly Meeting in May coinciding with the publication of the book *Conflict in Meetings* (2000) and a session of Quaker Life Representative Council in October. The Tuke Centre, attached to The Retreat, York also ran a three day course on conflict for Quakers in June.

[2] For most of the time of the study I was serving as Clerk to Brighouse Monthly Meeting , and as Clerk of Quaker Outreach in Yorkshire with associated responsibilities in Yorkshire General Meeting.

[3] These were in sequences with 7 Key Informants, 25 Grassroots or 'conscientious core' Quakers from across the north of the UK, and 8 'Edge Quakers'.

[4] The cartoon appeared in *The Friend* of June 4 1999. It is reproduced here with permission of the Barnes family.

[5] By 2005 there had been no referrals to the Finance and Trusts Committee, though there were unresolved conflicts in the General Meeting area.

[6] These and other phrases and sentences are from contributors quoted in Robson, 2005.

[7] Advices and Queries are a 'reminder of the insights of the Society', which are supposed to be read regularly in Quaker Meetings. They are found at the start of *Quaker Faith and Practice* and also published as a separate pamphlet.

[8] 'True Godliness don't turn men out of the world but enables them to live better in it and excites their endeavours to mend it' 1682 William Penn in *No Cross, No Crown* cited in *Quaker Faith and Practice* 1995, 23.02

[9] This model is used in a popularised version in *Conflict in Meetings*: Quaker Home Service, 2000, in which the different conflict handling strategies are likened to animals. See also Wrench 2006 and Robson 2006.

[10] For a thorough, though transatlantic, analysis of this decision making process see Sheeran 1983.

[11] Personal communication with Olwen Morgan, 2004, following exchanges on Quaker-B asynchronous message board.

[12] For instance, she referred to her opponents as 'arseholes'.

[13] Early in the study a Quaker who was a local councillor commented on his different experience in local politics and Quaker community. In the former he relished the rough and tumble of slanging matches, but he found contention among Quakers very upsetting because he did not expect it in that setting.

[14] 'Broiges' is a Jewish term indicating an ongoing, but fully savoured, resentment or grudge. This was explained to me by Judy, a fellow student at Sheffield, and confirmed by Maureen Lipman (*The Guardian* February 10 2006 and July 17 2006 via www.guardian.co.uk, accessed 2.7.2007). One of the most experienced contributors had already commented 'there is for some [Quakers] a strong resistance to letting go which I would like to explore'.

[15] The ethics of fee paying education provided by the seven 'Quaker Schools' are often fiercely debated. One view sees this as a means of spreading the Quaker message and providing a protected educational experience, the other sees the financial barriers as immoral.

[16] Later experience in my own Monthly Meeting suggests that tensions on such issues exist but are rarely explored. (See Mellor this volume, Chapter Four)

[17] See Collins' version of the prototypical Quaker (Collins 1994, 19)

[18] Quaker International Centre was a property in central London, close to Friends House, which had been used by Quakers as a centre for international hospitality since the 1950s. Changing social needs had made it economically unviable by the 1990s.

[19] See data from Workshop 2 (Robson 2005), reports of Meeting for Sufferings and letters in *The Friend* throughout late 2004 and early 2005, *Quaker Work in 2006,* 17-47

[20] This does of course depend on the person having achieved some sense of their own uniqueness. See Kelly's individuality corollary (1963, 55).

[21] See Davison 1982, a drama presented to the Yearly Meeting by the Quaker Youth Theatre. The actors are now in their forties.

[22] For a full discussion of the theological grounding of this belief see Dandelion *et al* 1998

[23] In her introduction to the *Proceedings of the Quaker Theology Seminar 2002-3*

[24] Compare this with Scully (Chapter 6, this volume) on the lack of theological framework.

[25] See Shellens'(2004) account of the fate of the Quaker Women's Group's Swarthmore Lecture.

CHAPTER NINE

THE TEMPORAL COLLAGE: HOW BRITISH QUAKERS MAKE CHOICES ABOUT TIME

JUDY FRITH

Introduction

In this chapter I explore the complexity of decisions about time that Friends face at the beginning of the twenty first century. As the Religious Society of Friends has no paid clergy it relies heavily on time given voluntarily as service to the Society by the membership, but its membership, in common with other Christian churches in Britain, is in decline. The number of members and adult attenders was 26,310 in 1965, falling to 23279 in 2006 (*Proceedings of Britain Yearly Meeting* 2006). In a similar period, average weekly attendance in the Church of England fell from 1.6 million in 1968 to under 1.2 million in 2003 (Gedhill 2005). Friends perceive themselves as 'overstretched' and 'juggling too many responsibilities' (The Meeting of Friends in Wales 2003). A minute from Britain Yearly Meeting 2001 read:

> Many Friends have been expressing concern at the over-fullness of our lives. Conflicting calls upon our time can result in stress and not doing anything well. We are called to 'life in all its fullness', but are our lives too full? (*Proceedings of Britain Yearly Meeting* 2001, minute 13).

This chapter shows that Friends' lives are indeed full, but that they make choices about time and build temporal collages of faith, busyness and community.

In contradistinction to other studies on busyness (Fenn 1997; Osborn and Osborn 1993), I describe time as polychronic rather than linear, because interviews and group work with Friends reveal time that has varied qualities. Linear time is the time of clocks, calendars, and diaries, with specific beginnings and ends, but polychronic time is heterogeneous. Sometimes time is paradoxical, cyclical, juxtaposed and interconnected as well as linear, and describing time as polychronic permits the either/orism, paradox and contradiction (Phipps 2004, 147) that emerges from Friends' descriptions of their use of time. Here, polychronic time comprises diverse elements drawn upon to build individualised and flexible constructs with priorities that vary from person to person and are adjusted throughout each lifetime.

For the purposes of this chapter I take the elements of personal polychronic time and add threads of a 'networked community' enriched with both 'bonding' and 'bridging' social capital to illustrate a 'temporal collage' stitched upon an ill-defined but persistently pervading spiritual fabric. I draw upon Scully's use of 'collage' (2002, 212 and this volume, Chapter 6) to describe how Friends make ethical choices as there are similarities in the ways in which Friends make choices about time. For instance, individual collages are creatively compiled, but need not share a common language. Choice about time is perplexing for individuals, as there is a lack of consistency or coherence between different life stages, and between the way they perceive and describe time in conversation with others. Further, the outcome of collage decisions is not necessarily predictable, especially in areas of service, paid work and relationships.

Temporal collage is a descriptive tool for the compiled, interwoven elements of an individual's time that accommodates the complexities and paradoxes brought about by choice. Although temporal collages are individualised, I show they operate for both the individual and the Religious Society of Friends through the web of social capital they both create and draw upon. Each temporal collage reflects how an individual's time is assembled and its threads drawn together to form the whole. Within the collage, time is polychronic rather than linear, and as time is shaped to fit the individual's needs the collage reflects choice, variation in texture, interweaving and interconnectedness. Linear 'clock time' is included in the collage, but usually overlaps other elements. Components of the collage may remain with the individual throughout life, but reshape or reposition in adjustment to responsibilities and commitments, whist others may come and go.

For the purposes of this chapter, I distribute the collage elements between three layers. The first is a foundation layer, taken here to be Friend's spirituality. The second layer is built with the practical elements of work, relationships, service and volunteering. Finally, there is an overlaying mesh of time spent in the networked Quaker community and Quaker social capital to which Friends contribute and from which they draw benefit.

The First Layer: the spiritual foundation of Quaker polychronicity

Although the greater part of the lives of Friends who took part in the interviews and group work is spent in the secular world, Friends consistently declined to distinguish any part of their life as free from the spiritual. Friends were not asked to describe what they understood by spiritual, but whether or not they distinguished between the secular, the spiritual and the religious life, and to give examples of activities they would assign to each. In common with Scully's research groups, respondents were hesitant (Scully 2002, 213), and descriptive language was inconsistent (Scully 2002, 224). Dandelion (2005, 124) claims that 'liberal- Liberal Quakers have lost their sense of working in God's time' and that 'The 'Now' is all. Everyday is equivalent rather than special'. For this chapter, that equivalence permits spiritual, religious and secular tasks to be melded together under a spiritual heading. By this I do not intend to undermine the integrity of the belief that all activities are spiritual, but to suggest this belief 'works' (Scully 2002, 212) for Friends as they build their collage.

That the spiritual underpinning fabric is itself flimsy, unstructured, ill-defined and lacking in clarity is unsurprising. Hay (2003, 2) found distinctions between spirituality and religion blurred. Wildwood (1999, 87) describes the variety of spiritualities upon which people draw (including himself) as living 'between stories', that is, between the time when the Christian church held a hegemonic monopoly on spirituality in Britain and now, when organised religion is irrelevant to the majority. Many who come to the Society are unchurched or combine religions. Friends lack a common story (Wildwood 1999, 4) and vocabulary, but creatively build their temporal collage in the absence of a single theological metanarrative.

When asked about how they made decisions, only a few described religious or spiritual practices such as prayer, retreat or clearness groups, but for those few Friends, these practices were a significant part of their discernment processes. Retreat or a request for a clearness group (*Quaker Faith and Practice* 1995, 1.02.27) was largely reserved for difficult times or decisions such as whether or not to take early retirement, or move home or take a particular job.

A spiritual perspective on time takes a long-term view of time (Brand 1999, 9). It reflects the slower process used for making choices, including prayerful discernment, listening, retreat, reflection and seeking clearness. It is qualitatively different from other elements because it is permanent, eternal and unhurried, always there as a resource.

The Second Layer: finding a place for practical matters on the temporal collage

Overlaying the spiritual foundation of Quaker polychronic time are the practical elements of life which most Friends have to balance, and which are at the forethought of those who speak of Quaker busyness. Often, and in contrast with the spiritual layer, choices about time in this layer take a short term view, are pressured, opportune and individualised or secularised. The temporal collage is a better tool than a linear sequential model of time to interpret these paradoxes. Understanding choices about time in terms of temporal collage does not overcome the social and institutional demands on an individual's time (Fenn 1997, 38), but it offers a model that accommodates inconsistency and incongruity in people's busyness.

This part of the collage comprises clock time, Quaker time, 'holy busyness', 'faith in action' and relationships, each of which is described separately, but the boundaries between these elements are not always clearly distinguished, and fragments of each may be found in some or all of the others. Thus Quaker time contains aspects of holy busyness and relationships are found in, or vie for, clock time with each of them.

Clock Time

Clock time was introduced to meet the needs of modernity, which required machines to be kept working and employees who arrived at work on time (Toffler 1980, 115). Now, clock time permeates all of the practical elements of Friends' lives, especially most working lives, where Friends have to meet deadlines and prioritise. Fenn (1997) claims that some of the features of modern societies that expand time pressures for state and corporations are passed on to individuals as increased demands for skills and productivity. He claims that time pressures which increase the rationalisation of time into 'schedules, quarterly objectives, time values and response times, and minimal times-out for individuals under stress' urge a search for spiritual resources in order to ease the adverse effects of busyness (Fenn 1997, 38).

For Friends in full time employment (and, sometimes, self-employment), balancing the demands of deadlines, diaried time and time tables with life outside of the workplace is often difficult. Making time for life beyond the workplace requires assertiveness to withstand a long-hours and work-focussed culture embraced by colleagues who work beyond their ascribed working hours. The pressure of planning and controlling work is often difficult, especially for parents. Particularly heavy workloads meant the forfeit of leisure activities and, sometimes, Meeting for Worship. Others Friends work part time or become self-employed to free time in order not to be 'inordinately active' or 'to make a virtue of "being in the world"' (Wildwood 1999, 92).

Clock time is linear and monochronic. Viewed as an asset akin to money it can be allocated, spent, commodotised and therefore it is potentially scarce. It can be divided into functions (Csikszentmihalyi 1997) or compartments (Jönsson 2003) for different types of activity, for example, money generation, family and friends, maintenance activities (such as cooking or laundry) and leisure. Yet, whether full time or part time, employed or self-employed, the thread of Friends' Quakerism runs through work for most. Either the work itself is service for them, or the work generates the spirit within those with whom they work, or some draw upon skills acquired through their Quakerism (mediation, for instance) or affirmed by it, such as paid work in the voluntary sector, social care or teaching.

Quaker Time

According to Dandelion (1996, xviii) 'Quaker time' distinguishes itself from other time in the lives of Quakers as their lives outside of the Meeting became privatised at the end of the nineteenth century and during the twentieth century. Dandelion describes Quaker time as 'the time spent as a Quaker with other Quakers' (Dandelion 1996, xxvi), and within a Quaker's temporal collage, 'Quaker time' includes Meeting for Worship and participation in the structure of the Society, special interest groups and learning opportunities. The ending of endogamy in 1859 and the required use of plain dress and speech initiated a removal of the 'hedge' between Quakers and the world (Dandelion 1996, xxv). By the end of the twentieth century Friends decided for themselves when and with whom they shared aspects of their life outside of the Meeting (Dandelion 2005, 68). Within the temporal collage, Quaker time is placed as a separate element, but the work it generates is described as a further element, 'holy busyness'. For very committed Friends, Quaker time occupies most of their time, and other parts of the collage are placed within it, but for others, Quaker time is confined to Meeting for Worship and a few related events.

A remaining peculiarity distinguishes the time Quaker's give to the Society from volunteering in the community. As a 'priesthood of all believers', Quaker volunteering within the Society is described as in this chapter as 'service' and takes place in Quaker time. The Society's membership was set up as a 'priesthood of all believers' as part of the disdain for the intervention of priests between the individual and God. All members of the Society are part of the clergy and have responsibility for the Meeting and for the community (*Quaker Faith and Practice* 1995, 11.01).

Holy Busyness

Holy busyness is time given for or out of faith, usually driven by clock time but enfolded by spirituality, or God's time (Dandelion 1998, 148). As an element of the temporal collage it is not inviolable, and may be infringed or embraced by paid and unpaid work in Quaker time or in the wider community. Where employment is seen as service, or as God's work, or to have a spiritual aspect, then that too would be holy busyness, as would the love and care given to family and friends.

Most of the work that Friends undertake for the Society comes to them via nominations committees whose stated purpose is to wait on God and find names for service within the Society, and each of the Meetings for business is managed by Friends in nominated roles. *Quaker Faith and Practice* (1995, 3.22) confirms, 'the responsibility of a Christian community to enable its members to discover what their gifts are and to develop and exercise them to the glory of God', and it falls to nominations committees to 'discern' those gifts in others. Nominations committees do not make the appointment, but put forward names for service. In best practice, the nominees have been asked if they would agree to serve (*Quaker Faith and Practice* 1995, 3.24 f.). This practice distinguishes Quakers from the voluntary sector, where individuals can put themselves forward for office, or be openly nominated prior to a vote, as Quakers do not vote. Nevertheless, as it emerges in the paragraphs that follow, some Friends position themselves for nomination to office or otherwise.

How Friends decide whether or not to accept a nomination is described in Figure 9-1. The process has become individualised and is largely privatised. The table is divided into four quartiles, the top two describing acceptance or involvement and the lower two indicating refusal or withdrawal. Either can be tinged with guilt or a sense of duty. Each choice can be actively or passively invoked, and Friends are often ambivalent or hesitant about positioning themselves. Positioning is not a permanent, now and forever and for all requests statement, and Friends 'pick and mix' from the quartiles according to their life stage, busyness, level of current involvement, the perceived value of the opportunity or the priority given to the nominating group by the Friend.

Friends like to balance their roles according to the time they have available, or to have a variety of interests, or because they like to work both in the Quaker community and in the wider community. They are careful in their discernment processes, seeking clearness, learning about the role and speaking to others about it. Usually, the nominee knows the group where the role is available, and knowledge of the amount of support available helps the decision. Friends also consider whether or not they have the skills for the role, and what they might learn, but even experienced Friends can be surprised either at how they develop within the role or by the amount of work involved. For a few Friends, the skills are sought as part of their continuing professional development.

Some Friends claim they find it difficult to say 'no' to nominations committees, especially when they suspect there is no-one else to do the work, but they also know their capabilities and limitations and decline tasks they feel unable to do. Most Quaker roles are time limited (*Quaker Faith and Practice* 1995, 3.23) giving incumbents a chance to declare their non-availability when their service is finished should they want to. Friends use several ploys to avoid nomination. Some claim they are not approached if they are known to be busy either in their paid work or in a Quaker job that might be difficult to fill, and others take a less demanding job in the hope their name is not put forward for a bigger one.

Acceptance/ involvement			
Active	▪ Express an interest ▪ Complete a Britain Yearly Meeting form ▪ Seek clearness ▪ Use discernment process (enquire, discuss, attend, read, thresh) ▪ Seek balance ▪ Seek rewards (training, travel, variety) ▪ Ask family or Friends whether or not to accept ▪ Enthuse in a role	▪ Be active in a Quaker community ▪ For those with many roles, know which will be resigned first in order to accept a more favourable one ▪ Be aware of rewards in a role ▪ Be flattered when asked ▪ Be aware of support in the community ▪ Know the time is available ▪ Aware no-one else has said 'yes'	**Passive**
	▪ Seek clearness ▪ Use discernment process (enquire, discuss, attend, read, thresh) ▪ Declare non-availability when a time limited role has finished ▪ Accept a role in order to be unavailable for more demanding ones ▪ State a lack of available time ▪ Resignation	▪ Non-attendance at a level of the structure or a type of Meeting ▪ Deflect requests ▪ Recognise own lack of skill or inclination ▪ Be sure to be known by nominations to be busy ▪ A dislike of bureaucracy ▪ Aware of own need for rest or reflection	
Refusal and/or withdrawal			

Figure 9-1: Reasons as to Whether or not to Accept Nomination

Faith in Action

Although some Friends prefer to keep their holy busyness within the Society because of the high level of time and commitment involved, most also volunteer within the wider community. Friends do not necessarily express their Quakerism when they volunteer in the wider community, and for this reason, I describe such volunteering as 'discreet witness'. This also applies when the activity has a link with Quakerism, either because it meets in the Meeting House or because it was started by local Quakers or local churches. Non-proselytising is not necessarily down to societal taboo or funding obligations. Many Quakers uphold the taboo according to Dandelion (1996, 305), who states 'Proselytising is illegitimate among Quakers in social and theological terms'. Friends' reticence about their Quakerism is not wholly due to Quaker culture, but to a taboo on mentioning religion in some workplaces (paid or voluntary). Indeed, when external funding is sought, overt proselytising risks breach of an organisation's funding criteria and its equal opportunities terms. To some extent, and in some places, Quaker time is defined for Quakers by the secular world.

Nevertheless, it is not unusual for volunteering to be informed by Quakerism. In the much-valued local Meeting Friends learn about causes and issues not necessarily spoken of in their day to day life. They can go on courses or to workshops or read literature in support of their ideals. Punshon (1990, 176) places activity at the heart of religion, say, 'a religion which consists of an obsession with beliefs is not in the life'. Religion includes 'our ethical commitments, the controversies we are involved in, the nature of our discipleship and the way we understand God'. As a result, Friends volunteering is diverse. They include peace and mediation, human rights, criminal justice, health, homelessness, advice work, the arts and political work.

Relationships

Family life is in transition and British Quakers have not been immune from these changes. Quaker family relationships are now privatised and beyond the authority of Quaker faith and practice when once they were endogamous. Only 13.8% of Quakers have experience of Quakerism from childhood (Rutherford 2003), but any current Quaker families are as likely as any other to be caught up in the transitional changes affecting families in Britain. Families today are formed in many variations from the traditional mother, father and children living in close proximity to an extended family network. Over a lifetime, a person may live alone, cohabit, marry, divorce, parent together or alone or any or all of these things (Williams 2004, 6). Families are getting smaller as women have fewer or no children, or choose to have them later (Inman 2005, 2). A child's life may be formed by its parents, step parents, step brothers and sisters, close friends, same sex partners or ex-partners. At the axis of these families there is often a 'kin-keeper' (Williams 2004, 17), who help them stay in touch.

The diversity of living arrangements and family form or groupings has largely gained acceptance both in the wider community and within the Religious Society of Friends. Other economic, social, cultural and demographic changes have shaped family life and key personal relationships. More women are working (either full or part time), there is an increasing older population and a global society brings together people from different parts of the world, and sends others elsewhere to live.

Whether Friends are married, partnered or single, family and friendship jostle for space on the temporal collage, demanding clock time and challenging Quaker time. For the majority, regardless of whether or not other members of the family are Quakers, clock time is required for immediate family, for kin-keeping and for intergenerational care. Most Friends now come to Quakerism in adulthood, and live their lives in a secular world in which the remainder of their family and friends may be unchurched and unsympathetic to the demands of Quaker time or holy busyness.

Both optimistic and pessimistic outcomes from family change emerge. A pessimistic view includes threats from individualism, secularisation, and generational decline in religiosity, and Quaker families are no longer the main transmission route for the Quaker tradition which was previously passed from one generation to another. The dilemma for Quakers (and for other Christian churches in Britain) is to understand how the Quaker story is to be transmitted, when it cannot reliably be passed from one generation to the next, yet optimistic possibilities emerge from this research. For the optimists, that same individualism frees people from fixed conventions and restraints leaving them able to shape their own lives and relationships. Given that family life is beyond a return to traditional family patterns, the implications for time available to support the work of the Religious Society of Friends are considered here in a similar light.

Giddens (1994, 4) claims commitment and intimacy have shifted from marriage to sexual love relations, parent child relations and friendship which are replacing the economic contract that once bound the marriage partnership. Relationships have become democratised, and communication and intimacy are prioritised over and above blood ties. Friendships have acquired a significant importance. The democratic and communicative structures of family life enable negotiation of autonomous and equal decision-making (Giddens 1998, 93) by Quaker family members, freeing them for participation in Quaker life.

Roseneil's (2004, 12) work on networks of intimacy, formed by people in her study who were without partners, signals possibilities for the preservation of autonomy, independence and connectedness to others that are echoed by Friends. Friendships with other Quakers are highly valued by Friends, as Best found in his work with young Friends, but most people are embedded in a complex set of intergenerational familial and chosen relationships (see Best this volume, Chapter 11). The old is in with the new (Williams 2004, 24), at times preferring friendship over family and conversely. Whether married, partnered, widowed, divorced or single, Friends commit both time and energy to friendship networks both in Quaker time and with other Quakers outside of it.

Greater longevity, relationship breakdown and a longer period of delay before marriage or partnership, if it is a chosen life route, has resulted in 6.5 million people in Britain living on their own (Inman 2005, 2). It is clear from Roseneil's research and from the degree of involvement identified by single Friends in interview that living alone does not necessarily equate to being alone. Most Quakers have close friends in the Society, and these friendships roll from one life stage to another.

The Religious Society of Friends is a network of interlinked communities. Most Friends attend Meeting for Worship at the their local Meeting, but they may well be involved in other parts of the structure. The 'gospel order' established by George Fox in the 1660s to reinforce discipline and authority (see Whitehouse this volume, Chapter 7) now comprises local, Monthly and Yearly Meeting. It absorbs time, but also provides a place to meet old friends and make new ones. There are residential events, including courses, for Friends to attend if they wish, and special interest groups. Thus friendships often extend beyond the local Quaker community into the network of Quaker communities which can be accessed at any stage in life.

The Third Layer: Quaker threads of social capital and networked community

This section considers the overlaying threads of networked Quaker communities that add additional texture to the collage, stitching other elements with bonding and bridging social capital. Threads for this layer comprise multiple strands spun together which both tie other elements one with the other and which carry the social capital of the Religious Society of Friends. For British Quakers, the elements of their collage include temporal strands of the networked Quaker community. These strands carry the social capital that holds the Society together as a distinctive organisation. Two types of social capital, bonding and bridging, are particularly important for this function. Putnam distinguishes between the two thus: 'Bonding social capital constitutes a kind of sociological superglue, whereas bridging social capital provides a sociological WD-40' (2000, 23). In other words, bonding social capital holds the group together and reinforces its particular identity, but bridging social capital is inclusive and generates a broader identity. Putnam acknowledges that there is not always a clear distinction between the two, as some organisations might 'simultaneously bond along some dimensions and bridge across others' (Putnam 2000, 23). In the same way, the temporal collages of some individuals vary, and some may contribute more to and gain more from one type of social capital than the other, or may have involvement with both. Social capital is brought about by connections among individuals that build trust and reciprocity (Putnam 2000, 19). Thus the time people give to those connections, that is, the more they 'stitch' into each of the other Quaker elements of their temporal collage, is upheld by the time given by others, benefiting the Society and deepening the individual's commitment.

Quaker networks thrive within the structure, but also in places where groups meet for learning, committee meetings, conferences, special interest groups or for any of the many other reasons that Friends come together. Each group, however small, partakes in bonding activities that reinforce an exclusively Quaker identity and encourages homogeneity in what are often disparate groups in terms of belief (Dandelion this volume, Chapter 1) and interest. Bonding social capital can be fostered in small acts, such as making coffee (Amit and Rapport 2002, 165) as well as more active ones, for instance in a Quaker nominated role. Bourdieu (1997, 52) confirms the need for continued effort as networked connections are not naturally or socially given, and, once acquired, they need constant renewal and regular review.

Some Friends restrict their activity to their local group, perhaps including their Monthly Meeting or any special events it arranges, but they still contribute, sometimes considerably, to the bonding social capital in the area. Success in accessing community is not necessarily easy, especially for the newcomer (Heeks 1994, 18) and some people remain at its edge for some time. Responsibility for engagement lies both with the community and with the individual. Bourdieu (1997, 57) speaks of 'institution rites' that mark the essential moments necessary to produce and reproduce the relationships that permit access to the benefits of the community's social capital. Newcomers to the Religious Society of Friends need a degree of assertiveness and robustness to access the rites, as some, such as silence and ministry, are subtle and nuanced.

Both bonding and bridging social capital transmit the faith story and reinforce the social memory for the group and its members (Hervieu-Léger 2000, 141). The nature of each Friend's involvement with the Society governs the nature of the social capital within the temporal strands of their collage. Those whose service and interests lie largely beyond the local Meeting, with Britain Yearly Meeting committees, or with special interest groups, for instance, contribute to and gain most from the bridging social capital. Despite the threats of secularisation, liberalisation and social change, those committed to the Society yield a high level of activity and strong statements of belonging as conduits for social capital. In order to show the reliability of the networks of belonging, I draw on two contrasting examples of networked community, Young Friends General Meeting and Woodbrooke Quaker Study Centre. In each of these, despite declining and thinly spread numbers, communities of British Quakers continue to build the social capital of trust, co-operation, learning and information transmission.

Young Friends General Meeting (YFGM) is the national organisation for Young Friends in Britain. It follows the structural rules of the Religious Society of Friends and is beset with the same problems of finding people to fill nominations as Britain Yearly Meeting. Young Friends meet three times a year to conduct their business at a residential weekend and create a distinctive, if temporary, space for themselves, as Best (this volume, Chapter 11) found in his work with younger Quaker groups. They have nominated roles within the group, nominate young people to roles within the Society and to representation outside of it if required, but nominees are not required to be in formal membership, as they are elsewhere in the Society. YFGM actively promotes the use of the Quaker business method in its meetings, encourages the right holding of meetings and appoints elders and overseers (YFGM 2003). This careful structure inducts young Friends into the rites of institution by example.

Woodbrooke is a Quaker Study Centre in Birmingham that provides educational opportunities to explore Quakerism. It is also a conference centre for Quakers and other groups. Some Friends use and support the centre repeatedly and for a number of purposes, and it thus fosters community in networks of belonging, some of which are very temporary (its weekend courses, for instance) and others which are recurring. As a place of temporary but repeated and varied community, Woodbrooke reinforces the 'resources' or 'credit' (Bourdieu 1997, 51).

The networks in each of these examples build durable social capital in temporary settings which is fungible throughout the Society, though there is no clear evidence of bridging from these activities to the local Meeting. Both YFGM and Woodbrooke offer opportunities for learning about Quakerism, either in courses, or workshops, from guest speakers, in special interest groups and a range of other settings. Woodbrooke offers specific courses as preparation for Quaker roles, and a long-term 'Equipping For Ministry' course for those who want to deepen their faith and Quaker education over a two year period. It is also used as a venue for conferences (Quaker and for other organisations which sometimes include Quakers), events, meetings and Quaker special interest groups. There are, in addition, opportunities for chance meetings with old friends met in other areas of service or interest, or planned meetings with current friends.

Each of these examples offer conduits for social capital despite their very different natures:
1) each provides learning opportunities
2) friendships are built and endure
3) friendship networks develop in the intimacy of sessions at courses, meetings or conferences, or, less formally in the shared necessary activities which make these things happen
4) each offers the experience of Meeting for Worship and Meetings for business
5) each offers either experience or understanding of trusteeship.

There are residential opportunities in each, including service as Friends in Residence at Woodbrooke, a role undertaken by a few interviewees, where the experience of Quaker community can be reciprocally shared. Young Friends cater for themselves, and sleep on the Meeting House floor, lending repeated opportunities for forming fellowship (Amit and Rapport 2002, 165). In each, friendships are made and renewed, and Young Friends interviewed told how these endure, often extending beyond the age at which they moved on from YFGM.

These two examples are not alone in the Society as places of temporary meeting, friendship renewal and brief but reinforcing events. Local and Monthly Meetings hold events and invite speakers either for a day or an evening, and sometimes at residential venues, which bring together both Attenders and Members. Planning for these evolves from small committees who are not always known to one another before the event, again reinforcing the networked social capital. There are centres other than Woodbrooke holding residential weekends (for example, Charney Manor in Oxfordshire and Claridge House in Surrey). Meeting Houses host events for special interest groups, such as Quaker Green Concern and Quaker Women's Group and many committee groups meet at Friends House in London.

Thus, networked community has aspects that are spiritual, are governed by clock time, and are influenced by the nature of their own holy busyness, service, friendships or the witness. The mesh of networked community both overlies the temporal collage and is stitched within it, and, in common with the layers beneath, it changes and shifts throughout the lifetime of an individual.

Summary

This chapter has illustrated a Quaker temporal collage constructed with elements of time about which Quakers make choices in keeping with their faith. Within the collage, polychronic time is shaped by choice and circumstance to fit an individual's needs throughout their lifetime. As the collages are polychronic they can accommodate the long-term, on-going elements of time, including a spiritual and family life, as well as the short-term demands that arise, for instance in paid work or volunteering.

Using collage as an interpretative tool offers an imaginative and creative approach to understanding choices about time in a changing and fragmented world. Collage is a better tool for understanding the paradoxes presented by time that have to be faced by individual Friends as it provides a framework for analysing the variations of texture with interwoven and interconnected components. Thus linear clock time can interweave or pressure other elements of the collage and invoke a sense of busyness. When a great deal of a person's time is pre-set either by others, or by fulfilment of their core needs, then the variety of elements in their collage is likely to be limited, but their time remains polychronic. Temporal collage represents the outcomes of choices about time that everyone faces. In terms of the sociology of Quakerism, temporal collage offers not only a model of how time and choices about time are utilised by participants, but an analytic tool for better understanding the way an organisation dependent on high levels of time given by individuals actually works in practice.

PART IV:

DIVERSE FORMS

CHAPTER TEN

QUAGANS: FUSING QUAKERISM
WITH CONTEMPORARY PAGANISM

GISELLE VINCETT

There is a vital and growing practice of Quaker Pagans made up of Pagans of various traditions who have found a second home within the Religious Society of Friends, and of Quakers who have found the same within the Pagan movement. Because those who are drawn to Quaker Paganism tend to be drawn to simplicity and silence in their spiritual practices, their presence in both the Pagan and Quaker community can be overlooked. (Cat Chapin-Bishop www.quakerpagan.org, accessed 20.07.2006).[1]

Introduction

The Quaker dislike of creeds and formal doctrine have opened the door, in the Liberal Quaker tradition (both in North America and in Britain), to the fusing of contemporary paganism with Quakerism. Though there are no formal statistics, my own research based upon interviews and observation of web-based resources is that Quaker Pagans or *Quagans*[2] as they sometimes (tongue-in-cheek) call themselves are a growing phenomenon. In this paper I situate Quaker Pagans in the context of British Quakerism and contemporary paganism,[3] I extend Pink Dandelion's theory of a Quaker 'behavioural creed' (1996), and I outline how my Quaker Pagan informants creatively hold together their two religious identities, particularly looking at the Quagan use of story, metaphor, and ritual.

My research is based upon 50 semi-structured interviews with Christian and pagan women (specifically, Goddess Feminists[4]), as well as participant observation of two ritual groups (one Christian, one Goddess Feminist), participant observation of feminist Christian and Goddess activities (conferences, festivals, and public rituals), and monitoring of the literatures associated with both these groups (insider generated and academic). Participants were scattered throughout England, Wales, and the

Isle of Man.[5] During interviews and fieldwork it became clear that the Christian and pagan groups were not discrete and that there were a significant portion of participants who to a greater or lesser degree straddled the boundaries between groups.[6] This group of people I call *Fusers*, and I subdivide them into *Fusers proper* and *Quagans*. This paper will deal solely with my Quagan findings. I interviewed four Quaker Pagans, and observed two Quaker Pagan email lists and several Quagan blogs. [7] The Quaker Pagans whom I interviewed were white women in their mid-40s to 60s with middle-class backgrounds, as such they fall into a category of people who whilst they are disaffected by traditional religion, are searching for spirituality and meaning, a category predominately female (Berger *et al* 1974, Roof 1993, Heelas *et al* 2005).[8]

Quagan Profile

Gay Pilgrim has written of three different types of British Quaker: Exclusivists, Inclusivists, and Syncretists (2003, 2004 and this volume). Pilgrim's description of Quaker Syncretists loosely fits Paul Heelas and Linda Woodhead's description of self or holistic spiritualites (Heelas *et al* 2005). She writes that Syncretists have a 'personal spiritual quest', are disconnected from 'traditional sources of meaning', 'sceptical about fixed systems of belief', and 'seek and value comfort, healing and hope' (2003:153).[9] Whilst my Quagan participants tended to seek these qualities, they were also emphatic that their Goddess Feminism was not 'just sweetness and light', but a spirituality that 'recognises the dark and the painful' (Elise).[10] Further, participants emphasised that Goddess Feminism was for them 'quite solid and grounded, and hard work, but very inspiring as well' (Alison).

The emphasis Pilgrim finds on 'healing' amongst Syncretists may partly be attributable to gender.[11] Susan Starr Sered found in her study of women's religions that healing was a key theme (1994). Linda Woodhead argues that women in holistic spiritualities search for healing as both a way of helping them cope with the stresses of life and in particular, the 'second shift' which many women find themselves working,[12] and as reflective of women's emphasis on relationality (healing always being part of the greater wholes of body, mind and spirit, *and* community and world) (2008). For example, consider what Alison said of what the goddess Aphrodite means to her. Aphrodite is love, but that

> is not some waffly thing that says 'oh I love you'. It is something very strong and basic and fundamental, and it is to do with sweat, and it is to do with dirt, and it is to do with the stuff of life that if you love your child you

wipe its snotty nose and you wipe its messy bum and this is love. This is
how love is.... So that Aphrodite is something very sort of basic, and
incredibly strong.

Whilst women in holistic and alternative spiritualities *may* be seeking
'escape' from 'the routines of everyday life' as Pilgrim suggests (this
volume, Chapter 3), Goddess Feminists tend to emphasise that their
spirituality empowers them to cope with and fight against that which is
'oppressive, soulless, ethically and morally unsatisfying' (Pilgrim this
volume, Chapter 3). Pilgrim suggests that Syncretists belong to what
Hamilton and others have characterised as 'pick-and-mix religion' (in
Pilgrim 2004, 222).[13] The 'dominant discourse' as Aupers and Houtman
call it (2006, 201), within the sociology of religion on 'self-spiritualites'
(Heelas 1996) is that they are so individualised that they lack any
coherency (Bruce 2002): 'Luckmann emphasises that such personal
meaning systems remain strictly private: by their very nature and unlike
church-based Christian religion in the past, they lack wider social
significance' (Aupers and Houtman 2006, 202). Several scholars have
begun to challenge these assumptions (Heelas 1996; Hanegraaf 1996;
Heelas *et al* 2005; Aupers and Houtman 2006 and 2008).

Quagans are, in Pilgrim's terms, syncretistic, but the supposition that
their syncretism is either superficial or without coherence is unfounded.
As one Quaker pagan blogger recently wrote online: 'I am syncretistic, not
because I'm picking and choosing from the smorgasboard of spirituality,
but because I'm *not*' (Cat Chapin-Bishop http://quakerpagan.blogspot.com
accessed 29.08.2006). That is, she has not consciously chosen two paths,
but feels she has been 'drawn' to each. As she wrote, 'Something without
a name called me so powerfully I could not do anything but follow'
http://quakerpagan.blogspot.com, accessed 29.08.2006. Chapin-Bishop
refers to an inward experience of an immanent divine which leads her. In
my observation of Quaker Pagan email lists and blogs, the use of Quaker
language and theology to authorise fusing is common.

There is a well known phrase which contemporary pagans use to
describe coming to paganism: 'coming home' (Eller 1993; Harvey 1997;
Rowntree 2004). It refers to the sense that participants have, not of
conversion, but of finding a name or group for what they always were. As
one pagan said to me, 'I think I was born this way'. Similarly, Alison said,
of both Quakerism and paganism, that she knew immediately 'this was my
stuff'. This recognition involves more than an attraction to 'lifestyle'
(Pilgrim 2004, 221), although the importance of that cannot be
underestimated, but also an attraction to ritual style, theo/thealogies,
symbolism, and other belief systems. Quagans demonstrate long-term

commitment to *both* Quakerism and paganism for all of these reasons; these are no passing fancies to be dropped in favour of something new tomorrow, nor are they identities which are picked up in a facile manner. If a substantial number of British Quakers are 'post-Christian' as Dandelion argues (1996), the two traditions being fused here (Quakerism and paganism) are not necessarily 'logically opposed to one another' (Pilgrim 2004, 222).

Pilgrim admits that there is some 'overlap' between Inclusivists and Syncretists, but argues that Inclusivists adhere to Dandelion's 'behavioural creed' (and that Syncretists, by implication, do *not*) (2004, 220, 221). By this definition, my Quaker Pagan informants would appear to be on the 'overlap' between types as it is quite clear from my data that Quagans take the behavioural creed very seriously, both as the term is used by Dandelion *and* as I extend it below.

Practical Belief

An email from one of my research participants announced the formation of the 'Quaker Goddess Network' in Britain: 'for people whose spiritual journeys overlap two paths: a love for goddess spirituality, stories and ritual, and the practice of silent Quaker worship together with the disciplined Quaker way of making decisions'.[14] The logo for this new network is revealing: a large *Q*, in the middle of which is a picture of the 'Venus of Laussel'.[15] In this logo, the *Q* of Quakerism surrounds a figure representative of my participants' Goddess Feminism. That is, their Goddess Feminism is shaped by and enclosed within their commitment to the Religious Society of Friends.

Pilgrim's claims Syncretists 'are drawn by a lifestyle but not a religion' (2004, 221), but it is clear to me that for Quaker Pagans, Quaker lifestyle cannot be separated out from religion. That is, Quaker practice *enacts* (often unexpressed) Quaker belief systems, including theology. Dandelion has demonstrated that what Quakers say they do *not* do, 'can also be a shorthand way of identifying features' (1996, 302). For example, the Quaker opposition to creeds is long-standing. When Quakers object to creeds, they do so often on theological grounds:[16] Friends object to the stasis of revelation implied by formal adoption of creeds (*Quaker Faith and Practice* 1995, 27.23). Divine revelation is on-going for Quakers and undergirds the unprogrammed liturgy of British Quakers who wait silently for the promptings of Spirit. On-going revelation is one reason Elise reported (unlike the Christian women in my research sample), 'I'm quite comfortable with the idea of ...a Goddess that is constantly changing'. It is also another reason why Quagans find it easy to exist in the Quaker context. As Alison said of Quaker Meeting for Worship:

> Out of the silence people speak when the spirit moves them. ...it is what the spirit is telling you *now*. And so if you have that basic frame of reference in relation to the worship of the divine, to your spiritual practice in relation to the divine, um then how the divine is going about its business of relating to *you* is really your own affair.

The emphasis Alison placed on 'now', which Molly also stressed ('the now is very important to me, the *power* of now'), also stems, I argue, from the Quaker concept of on-going revelation, and is indicative of Liberal Quaker belief in limited, contextual revelation. That is, the claim that the divine reveals itself in many ways to many people at different times. As Alison put it, 'we all need different things from our gods and goddesses. ...that is, different individuals need to relate to the divine in different ways'. As an entry in *Quaker Faith and Practice* (*QFP*) stresses, Quakers adopt 'not so much a set of propositions [as in a Creed], as the discipline of working out in one's life and experience the consequences of the truth one has espoused. The value of the beliefs lies solely in their outworking' (1995, 27.25).[17]

When Dandelion writes of a Quaker 'behavioural creed' (1996), he refers to the corporate form of Quaker Meeting for Worship and Quaker business Meetings. The quotation from *QFP* is very clear that the form of Quakerism extends to the whole fabric of one's life. My participants confirmed this. As Alison said, 'being a Quaker is really *how* you are, rather than what you believe in. Um...and I think that is pretty widely accepted'. As Dandelion relates in this volume, in the Swarthmore Lecture of 1980 given by Janet Scott, she answered the question ' 'Are Quakers Christian?' by saying that it does not matter. What matters to Quakers is not the label by which we are called or call ourselves, but the life' (Scott 1980, 70). The 'how' of Quakerism, insist my informants, extends to

- how Friends interact with others (which for Quaker Pagans includes other-than-human-beings[18]),
- the Quaker emphasis on 'justice' (Gwen),
- on 'being active' (Molly), by which she meant what would be called pastoral ministry in other contexts,
- social, eco-justice and peace 'activism' (Gwen).[19]

This way of life behavioural creed is informed by Quaker tradition, particularly the Testimonies which *QFP* states 'are not abstract qualities, but vital principles of life...[and] ways of action' (1995, 19: preamble)[20]. Thus what Quakers, and by extension Quaker Pagans, *do and do not do* are highly important to their belief systems.

This behavioural creed does not simply encode ideology (eg., pacificism), it encodes or *performs* theo/thealogy. [21] Participants repeatedly stated, 'Goddess is not into power over, but power with'. Quaker Pagan social and eco-justice activism, and their feminism reflects their notion of a divine that is non-hierarchical, shares creative and other powers, and is (self) limited in power. 'Power with' may also imply a divine which is revealed in on-going participation with Creation (although many of my informants would not use this particular word).

Peter Collins argues in this volume that there are certain 'narratives' canonical within Quakerism:

> [these narratives] were threads which no sooner were spun were woven into the social fabric of the meeting and of Quakerism more generally. They are woven...into the testimonies—those fundamental narratives which are grounded in the faith and practice of the first Quakers and rehearsed in innumerable ways since then throughout the Quaker movement (this volume, Chapter 2).

Collins points to 'plaining', which he argues undergirds all of these narratives, and which he says is ultimately 'a verb...a tendency to approach the world in a particular way' (this volume, Chapter 2). Similarly, Jackie Leach Scully (this volume, Chapter 6) uses virtue ethics to demonstrate how Friends perform through embodied behaviour their ethical beliefs and thus their Quakerism.

Edward Schieffelin points out that in the West, people tend to interpret *performance* to mean acting or illusion (2005, 131), with the implication that a performance is not *real* or *true*. As Schieffelin writes, performance 'embodies the expressive dimension of the strategic articulation of practice' (2005, 130, emphasis in original).[22] When Quaker Pagans attend Meeting for Worship or participate in social justice activism they *perform* Quakerism. When they participate in Goddess Feminist rituals, or tell Goddess story, they perform their Goddess Feminism and they create new meanings of and improvise female becoming. Performing Quakerism and Goddess Feminism for Quaker Pagans creates and reinforces certain 'embodied dispositions' (Coleman and Collins 2000, 318) or ways of being in the world.

Fusing Quakerism with Goddess Feminism

Coming to Goddess Feminism

All of my Quaker Pagan participants found a home in Quakerism but as Elise said, 'I don't find that Goddess Feminism is a rejection of Quakerism, but Quakerism cannot do everything, and I was searching for something that the Friends could not provide'. In the same way, Alison wrote, 'As a spiritual person I had found my spiritual community among the Quakers, but as a worshipful person I had nothing to worship' (Leonard 2003, 11). The paganism of participants thus specifically turns their Quaker way of life into a Quaker Pagan (enacted) thealogy.

The women's peace camp at Greenham Common during the 1980s was formative for several participants. For Molly, Greenham was an entrée into Quakerism, 'women's spirituality', and feminism. It was a powerful experience that changed her world:

> I can remember going up to women who were clearly not the little wife at home, who were in touch with much bigger things than the female space I'd squeezed myself into before. And they were talking about the feminine principle in the divine. I felt something was really moving for me. ...It was like a freeing up. ...After that I became *the* feminist at school—I taught for 13 years. My marriage was foundering then, everything was shifting.

Feminism, women's spirituality, and the introduction to new kinds of ritualising at Greenham were all confirmations that Quakerism could not provide informants' spiritual answers *in toto*. Below I explore some reasons why these particular issues shift everything for Quagan participants.

Though Quakers have traditionally rejected ritual as empty (Alison, Elise), Dandelion has argued eloquently that Meeting for Worship, though silent, is still ritual (2005). Further, while many Goddess Feminists of Christian backgrounds find Goddess Feminism affirming because it heals the pain of feeling other to the divine, Quakerism is founded on the notion of 'that of God in everyone'.[23] British Quakers have no priesthood, but practice (like most feminist Wicca or Goddess Feminism) a priesthood of all believers (Dandelion 2005, 28, 29; Starhawk 1999, 21; Alison). Indeed, as Elise related, 'I've found that questions are encouraged in Quakerism. And women are very present and strong in Quakerism'. That said, Molly implied that Goddess Feminism provides non-traditional models of being a woman which Quakerism does not necessarily model. Despite the egalitarianism of Quakerism, Goddess Feminism showed Molly new ways of enacting femaleness.

For Alison her attraction to Goddess Feminism came first through its bodiliness, its affirmation of embodied life (especially the *female* body) and its sensuality. As she has written, '...rediscovering the childish pleasure of skinny-dipping in lakes and streams, [I] found it was a spiritual pleasure too' (2003, 17). So despite the positive role for women in Quakerism, I read Alison's story as discovering that the emphasis on Spirit in the Friends meant a lack of celebration of embodiment, which she finds in Goddess Feminism and participation in Goddess Feminist rituals.

Quaker participants find in Goddess Feminism a religion which mirrors many of their ethics. First, Goddess Feminists and contemporary pagans are always keen to emphasise that there are many routes to the divine. Second, pagans would also generally ascribe to the idea of the divine in everyone (here this would extend beyond humans) (see for example the website of the UKs Pagan Federation, http://www.paganfed.org/paganism.php accessed 12.10.2007), which for Goddess Feminists is also based upon the broader feminist concern for social justice and egalitarian structures and methods (eg., in decision making or ritual). Third, the Wiccan teaching 'Do what you will, if it harms none'[24] has been read by many (the American activist feminist witch Starhawk being probably the most influential of these) as an injunction against violence, and a call to working for social and eco-justice.

Above I situated Quaker Pagans in the differing contexts of their dual identities; below I give a few examples of how Quagans explore Goddess Feminism in a particularly Quaker fashion.

Story and Metaphor

As a writer, Alison is drawn to story. Indeed, story for Alison is substantive. That is, story is a way of calling things into being. Story is thus *real* for Alison, and she spoke of 'the truth of story'.[25] In this she reflects the Quaker approach to the voicing of spirit in ministry during Meeting for Worship, and the way Quakers make real canonical narratives or practices through their enactment. However, it was the *many* stories of Goddess Feminism that was a big draw for Alison, as it was also for Elise. Dandelion has written that one consequence of the 'culture of silence' (1996, 238) that exists within the Religious Society of Friends is that Quakers rarely have opportunities to discuss with each other what they really believe. Alison said, '[in ministry] I might refer to something that has happened in my sort of—in the Goddess arena, but it is much more likely that it would come out in a way that didn't have any particular frame of reference at all'. The post-Christian context of Liberal British Quakerism is such that the stories which originally undergirded the group (i.e. the Bible) are rarely read in many Meetings for Worship now (Dandelion 1996 cites that 36.7% of his respondents never 'feel moved to pick up the Bible' during Meeting for Worship). Although Alison's approach to story reflected her Quakerism, Goddess Feminism provides a way to develop and celebrate story in a way not possible in the Friends. For example, Alison pointed to the 'fluidity' of goddess story, the 'magic' in them, and their use of symbolism.

Story also images—indeed it invokes and shapes images—and several Quagan informants pointed to the emphasis on (a diversity of) imagery as being an important attraction for them to Goddess Feminism and paganism. Quakerism has traditionally been anti-imagery (Elise),[26] not wanting to limit the divine in any way. But the open-ness of Liberal Quakerism, and the multiplicity of images of the divine in Goddess Feminism result in a similar acceptance of diversity.

In Goddess Feminism, there is considerable diversity between what is meant by the term *Goddess*(es) (Long 1997). The most important issue for this discussion is whether Goddess is metaphor or real. However, even for those for whom Goddess is metaphor point to the real effects that metaphor has on the lives of women (Culpepper 1987 and 1997, Morton 1989, Long 1997). Two Quaker Pagan informants (Alison and Molly) claimed that goddesses are 'metaphor' (Molly) for them, that they 'don't really experience them um as an active force in my life', but as 'powerful stories which influence my thinking' (Alison).[27] Molly and Alison's use of the word metaphor to describe goddesses reflected their Quaker dislike of anything which seems to *define* or limit the divine. However, both experience metaphor in a real way. For example, Molly's use of 'the void' as image and metaphor for the divine is lived and embodied; she experiences the void in meditation when the divine 'mystery' 'comes up through me'.

I asked Alison whether story and writing were invocation and ritual for her, and she said, 'I think it is becoming the case, and I think in some way it has always been the case without my recognising it'. I suggested above that story for Alison is a way of calling things into being, in this way Alison participates in the creative action of the divine, or rather, as she has written, 'It often seems to me that my job as a writer is not to 'create' as such. It's to keep that channel clean and clear.... If my channel is clear, then the mystery will flow through it and down it' (1995, 90). In Meeting for Worship she is aware of 'waiting in the void, waiting in the light' (1995, 88), and she writes that the *process* of beginning to write is also a process of 'wait[ing] patiently in discipline' (1995, 92). Alison then, has conflated the form of her Quakerism with the form of writing, and experiences the creative action of writing as the creativity of the divine working through her. That is, Alison experiences writing in charismatic Quaker terms. Story and metaphor become for Alison real expressions of the divine.

In this context, goddesses may be metaphor, but their stories are also channels for experience of the divine, and in that sense they are real. Like Molly's experience of the void, goddesses and their stories become lived and embodied. Story is not simply a mental experience for Alison, but is something she experiences in an embodied way. Furthermore, like the Quaker 'narratives' identified by Collins (this volume, Chapter 2), Goddess Feminist stories impel participants to live in a certain way.

Let me give an example. The cauldron of Cerridwen was referred to by all of the Quagan participants[28] and is an important lived metaphor for the divine. Alison described Cerridwen's cauldron as 'this great pot of life'. And participants emphasised that Cerridwen's cauldron contained 'everything stirred up together' (Molly), the hard parts of life included (Alison, Elise). Alison related the cauldron back to the earth by saying it is 'a symbol of this amazing sort of composting thing'. Cerridwen then is 'an agent of transformation' (Elise), and the cauldron her main *instrument* of transformation. It is a polyvalent metaphor because it represents the physical spaces of the earth and the ritual circle (in which Goddess Feminists ritualise transformation), and the mental or cognitive space of transformation or change. Participants embody and enact the metaphor of the cauldron by applying it to the life cycle of 'menopause', 'healing' (Elise[29]), and to the process of inspiration in writing (Alison).

Contact with the Divine

Molly suggested there is 'energy' in effective metaphors, and that Cerridwen's cauldron is 'about knowing the mystery'. 'Mystery' for Molly is a way of referring to the divine. The fundamental possibility that, as Molly put it, the divine can 'come up through me', of 'being a channel for the divine' (Molly) is something that is common to both Quakerism and Goddess Feminism. For example, some Goddess Feminists ritualise embodying the Goddess(es), though they would usually baulk at the word 'channelling' because of its implied passivity. [30] Gwen also said that one of the reasons she originally became a Quaker was that she was interested in 'the mystical aspect of Quakerism'.

Contemporary paganism is often described as a 'nature religion' because it places great stress on humanity being part of (and dependent upon) the natural world (Harvey 2007, 4). The earth, as well as elements of the natural world such as rocks and trees, is seen as sacred and often as a personal divinity.[31] This outlook was particularly evident during my interviews with Gwen and Molly, both of whom spoke of having communication with other-than-human-beings. For Gwen these contacts were relearned in adulthood, but experienced spontaneously in childhood. She recounted of her childhood in Australia,

> In the bush, there's a plant—it's like a tall tree fern with a large velvety spike, like a bulrush. ...And I remember one of those bowed to me, or waved, anyway it made contact with me. I assumed this kind of relationship with living things was normal at first. I also remember having contact with Golden Mimosa—it's the spirits of these plants that make contact with me.

I asked Gwen if these were 'simply spirits, or would you call them deities?' to which she replied, 'Yes, yes! All I know is that I have contact', but she later confirmed that she considered them 'divine'. Rather than define these spirits, Gwen was wanted to emphasise 'the inner transformations that result from making contact'. She stressed that contact with the sacred pushed her into 'activism' on the part of the natural world, but also that it brought her 'compassion, and clarity into my everyday life'. For Gwen, it was necessary to ground her experiences of the sacred in living them out and she pointed out that this active spirituality tied in with her Quakerism.

However, although the Quaker practice of waiting silently on the divine to speak through them places Friends (potentially) on the charismatic end of the religious spectrum, the 'culture of silence' militates against charismatic testimony such as is found in Pentecostal churches (Dandelion 1996). So while Gwen and Molly's experiences of communicating with nature spirits may be acceptable in Quaker terms as the divine speaking through them, these experiences are not likely to be vocalised in Meeting for Worship. As Pilgrim writes, 'those who [speak] of [unmediated experiences of God] as real [are] likely to be misheard and misunderstood, if not (politely) ignored' (2004, 206). The reticence I found amongst my Christian feminist participants toward this kind of religious experience (even, or especially, amongst those who had had such experiences whilst in charismatic denominations) is not present amongst Quagan participants for whom the practice of 'waiting upon God' is familiar.[32]

Ritual

Probably the most striking difference between unprogrammed Quakerism and (other) Christian churches, the silent Meeting for Worship, is also the most striking difference between Quagans and contemporary paganism. For whilst many Christians and pagans alike may practice silent worship individually (alternatively expressed as meditation, prayer, contemplative prayer, etc.), collective worship tends to be verbally expressed. The communal nature of the silent Meeting for Worship is emphasised by Dandelion: 'The silence is the very medium through which the group approaches God.... This emphasis on collectivity is critical to both orthodox Quaker theology and to the limitation of individualism within the worship process' (2005, 3). Silent worship is not simply an absence of words, but the silence is experienced as spatial and as a location of the divine. As Molly put it, 'God is 'I am', the void'. In the silent space of worship is the presence of the divine; silence for Friends facilitates experience of the divine presence (Dandelion 2005, 31). As Molly elaborated: 'Quakerism for me is about letting spirit speak to me, about being receptive, and about letting go of my expectations and getting in touch with the void'. The Quaker 'void' is communal: a space and a divine which are not static (participants several times referred to the Goddess chant 'She Changes'[33]), and though it is silent and empty, yet it is does not signal the absence of the divine, and it may be approached communally.

Dandelion writes, 'the theology behind [Friends] holding worship at any time and in any place is not about a constancy of sacramentality as much as a constant potential for it' (2005, 114). Such a viewpoint shifts the way an adherent sees and interacts with the world. The constant potential for unmediated experience of the divine potentially widens a participant's conception of what is, or might be a sacred place/being ('that of God in everyone'), and/or leads to a state of 'receptivity' (Molly) for experience of the divine. Perhaps this is why Quagans are drawn to and have various forms of direct experience of the divine (trance, dreams, visions, spirit communication).

Molly spoke of a Quagan ritual she had attended at an ancient stone circle. Ritualising in such a place is certainly not a traditionally Quaker thing to do, but her experience of the ritual was bound up with being a Quaker, and is revealing of Quaker sacred space, Quagan theology, and the Quaker sense of silent communal religious experience:

> I am particularly drawn to stones, like at Avebury. There's an energy that comes through them. Once with some friends of mine from the Quaker

women's group, and one man...we went to a stone circle and we stood inside the circle and held hands...and time shifted inside there. There's a real sense of energy and divine connection that they have. And there was a sense of something happening in the silence; it was to do with us as Quakers, but it was also about the stones. There was a sense of power, and energy. There were six of us, but it was really strange, when I shut my eyes, there was (sic) seven. I felt very 'in touch' and beyond space and time, or rather, it was all time and space in that circle. I think it is important that they are stone *circles*, because in a circle it is hard to find an end and a beginning. ...And Quakers sit in *circles*.

This notion that there are places where the divine is particularly easy to experience is a strong pagan belief. But as Alison put it, for Quakers 'the thought of [one place] being more sacred than anywhere else um is— is actually anathema to me. ...I don't have any time for--for that'. However, her pagan experience of sacred places modifies her Quaker belief in the sacred being accessible anywhere and everywhere: 'I mean clearly there are sacred places ... and you can feel a concentration of spiritual energy there, but there are many, many, many of them'. Like Alison, Molly stressed that stone circles are not more sacred than other places, but have a strong 'connection' with the divine. She equated Quaker Meeting for Worship with the liminality of the stone circles, suggesting that the same liminality is produced in both, and that it is partly the *communal* delineation of sacred space/time that is responsible for the possibility of experience of the divine within that space.

Many Quakers describe what they do in Meeting for Worship as 'listening'.[34] But as most Meetings only have a few short spoken contributions (Alison), what a Friend mainly listens to/for in ritual is the silence and silent presence of the divine. Such a regular practice helps to explain both why Gwen (who has always heard the voices of spirits in the natural world) was originally attracted to the Friends, and why in the Quagan ritual described above, Molly is sensitive to the 'energy' of the stones. It is the practice of and possibility of communication with/from the divine that is primary: silent worship 'is the means to the experience, central to the Liberal Quaker project' (Dandelion, this volume, Chapter 1).

Molly emphasised that it is important that this site is a stone circle, and she referred to Quakers sitting in circles during Meeting for Worship. This has not always been the case, but most Meetings for Worship now use chairs placed in a circle (Collins 1996, 320). This arrangement symbolically affirms various dominant Quaker beliefs: non-hierarchy, priesthood of all believers, etc. (1996, 320). Molly also pointed to circles having no beginning or end, which she related to the sense she got of being in a time out of time in the stone circle. She suggested that the ritual and symbolic space of a circle contains *and contributes to* the 'energy' of the ritual. This is consistent with contemporary pagan belief (see Salomonsen 2002, 177; Rowntree 2004, 149), the majority of whom also ritualise in a circle.

It is largely the potential for experience of the divine (and the lack of dogma) in the Friends and paganism that makes ritual central to both. For unprogrammed Friends, ritual may seem 'invisible' (Dandelion 2005, 2), but one thing that makes unprogrammed Quakers unique is their adherence to a ritual of silent (potential) communal experience of the divine.[35] The Quaker emphasis on experience means that Friends 'argue that the validity of worship lies not in its form but in its power' (Dandelion 2005, 71), a description which certainly fits the ritualisation of Goddess Feminists also. One reason the ritual which Molly related above was so affective, was 'the sense of power and energy' she had of it. In both cases, 'power' refers to what the participant experiences during ritual, in the ritual space, and what she carries with her from the ritual: deep experience of the divine, a divine which is active, relational and immanent, and communal connection.[36]

Listening to the Divine and Others

I am struck by the number of voices that are in the transcripts of my interviews with Quagan participants, and by the amount of listening implied for the hearers. These are the voices of the spirits which Gwen hears, but also the voice of the divine which spoke to Molly ('I am') which was a confirmation for her of the universal immanence of God, the 'voices' of the river and trees which Molly also hears, the 'voices' of the goddesses which Alison hears through their stories, and even the voices of the characters in her own stories. The emphasis here is on the hearer, or more accurately, on the hear*ing*: on listening as spiritual act and experience. Elise, for example, spoke of how 'listening to' (by which she means sensing) other peoples' needs was an act 'supported by Goddess', and how she 'couldn't hear the guidance [of the divine] in the Christian framework'. Elise also found it important to highlight that 'my prayer is usually a chat—I talk, but I also *listen*'. Goddess then, opens Elise up to hearing the divine, but I argue that it is the Quaker *framework* which has nourished both the prominence of Quagans listening for the divine and the notion that this is a spiritual act in itself.

The listening that Quagans do underlines the theme of relationality which runs throughout the spectrum of my participants. As Molly put it, 'the sacred is relational'. For Quagans, the relational implies the possibility of change. That is, in listening to the other, or in listening to the divine, one opens oneself up to the possibility that one's own beliefs/position may change through relation. Perhaps inevitably as Quagans fuse two spiritual traditions, this group of my participants spoke of their spirituality as a 'process', a 'journey' (Alison), or an 'exploration' (Gwen). Quaker Pagan personal spirituality cannot be divorced from relationality and indeed it is *because* Quagans listen to the Other (divine, human, other-than-human) that they must define their spirituality as a journey or process.

Conclusion

As academic study of Quaker Pagans is in its infancy,[37] my aim in this chapter has been to begin the process of situating and explicating what appears to be a rapidly growing segment of both Quakerism and paganism. Clearly, further work needs to be done and my hope is that larger scale studies of Quaker Pagans will deepen our understanding of this grouping in the near future. In this chapter I have shown that Pilgrim's category of Syncretist Quakers (2003, 2004, and this volume) is insufficient, and partly inaccurate, to describe Quaker Pagans. I have shown that certain 'canonical narratives' (Collins this volume, Chapter 2) in Quakerism, and particularly my notion of an extended behavioural creed, provide an underlying framework for Quaker Pagans as they develop the theo/thealogy and practice of their dual identity. I have emphasised that the syncretism of Quaker Pagans is based upon a behavioural creed that is a way of being in the world and a *performative* religiosity. As Molly put it, Quaker Paganism is about 'blurred boundaries'. Quagans thus inhabit an unusual space: a space that holds together difference, and the crossing-over point(s) between differences. My informants are not Quakers *and* pagans, as if the two identities could be held separate and the individual could oscillate between the two. Instead, they are Quaker Pagans, the identities cannot be separated out from each other but create something *sui generis*, a third thing entirely—Quagans.

Notes

[1] Although this website is an American, where the community of Quaker Pagans appears to be larger and longer established (personal communication with American Quagans), it is relevant for the growing community in Britain, especially as the bloggers are from the uprogrammed branch of U.S. Quakerism.

[2] I first heard this term in 2001 when it was used by a participant in my M.A. research, an American Quaker-Pagan.

[3] It is notoriously difficult to define contemporary paganism as the term itself is a catch-all phrase that includes many and varied traditions. Despite the diversity between pagans, several researchers have shown (for example, Harvey 1997 and 2007, Berger *et al* 2003) that paganism does have cohering themes and concerns some of which I will discuss below.

[4] Goddess Feminists are a subset of pagans who work primarily (but not necessarily exclusively) with the Goddess or goddesses. As with other contemporary pagans, there is no one form of Goddess Feminism nor is there a unifying institutional structure. That is not to say that one cannot speak meaningfully of Goddess Feminism as a coherent term.

[5] Except where participants are public figures already (for example, writers who have published work on their spirituality), all names have been changed and identifying details obscured.

[6] It is difficult to quantify this group as it depends on how one defines what constitutes 'fusing'. According to the way I have defined 'fusing' (see Vincett 2008), there are 12 interview participants who show evidence of fusing.

[7] Other web-based resources include: observations from other researchers on a Pagan scholars email list, Quagan generated on-line articles, and flyers and invitations circulated on the web. Taken together, the two Quagan email lists consist of over 100 members.

[8] As with other mainline liberal British churches, British Friends are predominantly white. Brierley (2007) includes the Religious Society of Friends in his 'smaller denominations' category, in which 6% are non-white (5.19). Goddess Feminists also tend to be mainly white. The ethnic profile of Goddess Feminism has been both criticised and rationalised by insiders and outsiders. Cynthia Eller (1993) presents some good reasons for why Goddess Feminism tends to be white. For example, a) in the US at least, the needs of women of colour may be being met elsewhere (for example, in the rise of voodoo and African traditional religions), and b) the different emphases between feminists, Mujeristas, and Womanists may mean that women of colour are not attracted to a religion which styles itself as feminist. Similarly, whilst my call for participants asked for feminist women, this may have precluded women of colour who define themselves differently, from responding.

[9] Dandelion argues that British Friends have a 'prescription of seeking' (in this volume), and the questions raised by Dandelion about the extent to which Quakers of the liberal British tradition can be called Christian (1996) and Mellor (in this volume) about the way British Quakers define 'Christian' indicate that there may be many Quakers who value a 'personal spiritual quest' and are disconnected from 'traditional sources of meaning' regardless of whether or not they are Quaker Pagans.

[10] When Quagans argue that Goddess Feminism is not all 'sweetness and light', there is a subtext which they are keen to point out. As Peter Collins writes, 'the dominant symbol of Quakerism is 'the Inner Light' (1996, 285). This is a symbol

which Quagans question because 'light has dark in it, surely; dark has light—they need each other. ...For me, the dark is fruitful and juicy and alive. We need the cycle of both. ...We need to untie the notion that dark is evil and wrong' (Gwen). However, the theology behind the concept of the inner light is part and parcel of Quagan beliefs. Similarly, Goddess Feminists are careful to differentiate themselves (and pagans in general) from the New Age emphasis on light (Heelas 1996; Harvey 1997) for the same reasons.

[11] It would be interesting to know what the gender split is in Pilgrim's work, but her analysis is not 'gendered'.

[12] The 'second shift' refers to women's unpaid work in the home which is on top of their paid occupation. Such work includes both material and emotional work, the majority of which still falls to women in most households (Hochschild 1989, Brannen and Moss 1991).

[13] Though the term 'spiritual supermarket' was coined by Lyon, Luckmann used a similar phrase as far back as 1967 when he called it a 'market of ultimate significance'. Aupers and Houtman have recently done a good job tracing and challenging this discourse (2006).

[14] This is a closed email group to which one must apply to join, but a website is planned and more information may be obtained by emailing postfriend@quakergoddessnetwork.org.uk.

[15] The Venus of Laussel is a carving of a woman of generous proportions from the entrance to a cave in France. She holds a curved horn inscribed with thirteen lines. Paleolithic 'Venus figurines' such as this one have been used by Goddess Feminists to point to a)evidence for ancient Goddess worship, b)as images of 'the Goddess' or goddesses, c)as positive images of the female body and its cycles.

[16] See Dandelion, Chapter One, this volume, for a comprehensive list and analysis of the reasons Quakers object to 'belief creeds'.

[17] Note that the author of this entry does not capitalise 'truth', and uses 'one' not 'we', implying that truth is neither static, nor universal. Again, to me this is consistent with Liberal Quaker belief.

[18] Other-than-human beings would include animals, but also trees, rivers, rocks, etc.

[19] Pilgrim (2004) argues that 'the utopian vision quest of Quakerism with regard to peace, justice and social equality has become mainstream within the wider society' (2004, 212). I find this difficult to believe. To take but one example, regardless of thirty years of equality legislation in the UK(the Equal Pay Act came into force in 1975), the gender wage gap remains significant, the average difference being 17.1% (or median 12.6%) according to the government Women and Equality Unit report (2007: 12). .

[20] Not all Quakers are as active as this may imply, but these testimonies were certainly stressed by my Quagan participants.

[21] Thealogy is discourse on the female divine, as used by Goddess Feminists.

[22] Shieffelin builds here on Bourdieu's 'practices' (1977) which also influence Collins' thought (in this volume), and the differering approaches to 'performance' of theorists such as Schechner (1982) and Goffman (1959).

---

[23] Dandelion shows how the interpretation of this phrase, especially what is meant by 'God' is diverse within contemporary British Quakerism and is a move away from the traditional Christian notion of God of previous generations of Friends (1996, 162, 268).

[24] One of the main influences of Goddess Feminism is Wicca, especially feminist forms of Wicca.

[25] For two interesting takes on how this can work in paganism see Salomonsen 2002, 138-42 on re-membering Tiamat in feminist Wicca, and Griffin 2000, 73-88 on embodied narrative in Goddess spirituality.

[26] This may be one reason why Catholic defectors do not seem drawn to Quakerism, unlike former members of protestant denominations (Rutherford 2003, unpublished research).

[27] The other women I interviewed (Elise and Gwen) have a much more personal relationship with goddesses and spirits.

[28] This an ancient Celtic myth about the goddess Cerridwen who brews the potion of knowledge and inspiration in her cauldron. She is a shape-shifter, a transformer.

[29] Elise works with health professionals, so healing and transformation are very much lived experiences in her professional life.

[30] I remember a great deal of (feminist) negativity to the word expressed on one Goddess Feminist e-list to which I belong. I suspect the word 'channel' (used by two Quaker Pagan participants) is language inherited from Quakerism. Certainly, it is a concept that early Quakers used for whom 'their bodies and lives were merely sites and channels to communicate the word of God, the living Christ, to others' (Dandelion 2005, 4).

[31] I use the singular here, but pagan polytheists are common (eg., See the Association of Polytheist Traditions website at www.manygods.org.uk accessed 12.10.2007 or http://www.paganfed.org/paganism.php accessed 12.10.2007).

[32] This phrase is one amongst many that were first used by early friends and preserved in successive editions of *Quaker Faith and Practice*, so that they are 'stock' Quaker phrases. This particular phrase occurs in the current edition of *Quaker Faith and Practice* in seven entries, three of which date from the seventeenth century (1995, 2.41, 21.03, 28.02).

[33] This chant, originally written by Starhawk, is possibly the most widely known and sung pagan chant, and is endlessly improvised upon.

[34] Of Dandelion's sample, 53.8 per cent claimed that 'listening' was the best way to describe what they do in Meeting for Worship (1996, 111).

[35] I am aware that both Dandelion and Pilgrim's research indicates that not all Quakers use Meeting for Worship in this way, but what is key here is that my participants *do*.

[36] And in the Goddess Feminist/Quagan context 'power' must also be read as 'empowerment'.

[37] Though there has recently been much web-based 'chatter' about Quaker Pagans by scholars studying contemporary paganism, I am not aware of any other academic publications resulting from the study of this form of spirituality.

CHAPTER ELEVEN

ADOLESCENT QUAKERS: A COMMUNITY OF INTIMACY

SIMON BEST

Introduction

Research into the spiritual beliefs and religious practices of adolescent Quakers (Best forthcoming) shows that this group finds the content of religious/spiritual belief[1] unimportant and non-definitional; values are broad, generalised and open to individual interpretation and, in some cases, indistinguishable from secular values. Corporate worship[2] is central, internal discipline is strong, involvement is extensive, commitment is high and the sense of belonging great. Adolescent Quakers form close bonds, both as a group and through individual friendships. The group has a strong perception of difference from other groups, both Quaker and non-Quaker. The group values inclusion and acceptance, and has a strong sense of allegiance to the community and its members.

In this chapter I argue that the adolescent Quaker group represents a 'Community of Intimacy'. The core features of a Community of Intimacy are that: 1) the members of the group feel a sense of belonging and affiliation to the group; 2) the group has a set of shared values which are expressed in internal and external behaviour; 3) this behaviour contributes to feelings of difference between the Community of Intimacy and other group which it is juxtaposed to; 4) this results in the group occupying separate physical and psychological spaces.

This research focuses on Quakers aged 11 to 18. Current estimates place the size of this group at approximately 1900 individuals in Britain (Best forthcoming). A total of 418 individuals took part in the project representing 22% of the constituency. Questionnaires were completed by participants at several residential Quaker events for young people. Focus group interviews were carried out at week-long or weekend residential gatherings.[3]

Affiliation, Friendship and the Networked Community

Adolescent Quakers place a high degree of importance on their involvement in Quakerism: 85% stated that their involvement in Quakerism is either quite important or very important to them. Through their participation in events individual adolescent Quakers gain a feeling of belonging to the group.

The majority of adolescent Quakers (58%) affiliate most closely with exclusively adolescent Quaker groups;[4] a further 10% said that the Quaker group they felt most part of was Britain Yearly Meeting, which many of them would have experienced through the separate programme for young people. Just over a quarter felt most part of their local congregation.[5] Figure 11-1 shows the groups that individuals feel most part of.

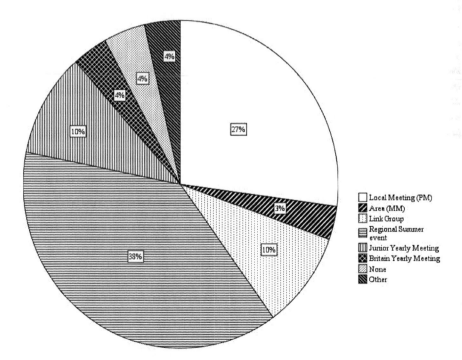

Figure 11-1: 'Which Quaker Group do you Most Feel Part of?' (n = 307)

Green emphasises the role of the 'gathering function' (2005, 12-13) in the understanding of adolescent Quaker identity and states that 'gathering together supports Quaker children and young people, giving them a chance to explore their identity with other Quakers in light of their likely geographical, religious and philosophical isolation' (Green 2005, 12). By enabling adolescents to gather together in community, Quaker events for young people are key in forming Quaker identity: 93% stated that going to Quaker events for young people made them think or feel that they were 'more Quaker' and had a stronger individual Quaker identity and a greater sense of belonging to the adolescent Quaker group.

> Although I have always gone to meeting ...before Summer School I didn't really think of myself as a Quaker, I just went coz my mum did (Female, 14).

> I found out who I was [at JYM], I am a Quaker and now I'm sure (Female, 18).

> [As a result of going to Quaker events] I feel more part of Quakerism at all levels – my local meeting up to Yearly Meeting (Female, 19).

Within the Quaker group, personal friendships act to secure unity and function as a dimension of religious identity (Dandelion 1996, 311). Friends and friendships are an important aspect of adolescent Quaker identity. Crucially for adolescents, these friendships are with other adolescent Quakers. Adolescent respondents identified the importance to them of the opportunity to meet and develop friendships with:

> like-minded people (Female, 18).

Through their participation in events, adolescent Quakers form ongoing friendships with other young people. Friends and friendships are an important aspect of adolescent Quaker identity: 66% stated that they had either a lot or some Quaker friends of their own age; 92% of those that had Quaker friends their age[6] stated that these were close friendships.

By enabling adolescents to gather together in community Quaker events for young people are a key feature of their Quaker identity: 93% stated that going to Quaker events for young people made them think or feel that they were 'more Quaker' and had a stronger individual Quaker identity and a greater sense of belonging to the adolescent Quaker group.

Events enable adolescents to gather and make connections with other adolescents, to develop friendships, and create networks: 85% stated that they had gained friendships from going to Quaker events:

> I've made a lot of very good friends (Female, 15).

Amongst adolescents, 'friends…are likely to go to the same class in the same school in the same neighbourhood' (Erwin 1998, 75). In contrast to this adolescent Quakers' friendships are spread over a wide geographical distance:

> I've gained lots more contacts all over England (Male, 15).

Despite not meeting frequently adolescents are often closer emotionally and functionally closer to their Quaker friends than others:

> closer than all school friends (Male, 14).

> we don't see each other often but every time we do meet, it's like we've never been parted (Female 18).

> most of my best friends are Quakers (Female,15).

These individual friendships exist within, and serve to sustain and are sustained by the larger networked community. The sense of community at events is often highlighted: 'We found confidence in each other's company, and were able to build a close community in this short time' (Junior Yearly Meeting Epistle 2003).

This is reflected in individual responses:

> [I like] being part of an understanding and supportive community (Female, 15).

> [It] feels like a big Quaker family (Female, 14).

This is a community where:

> individuals never feel left out (Male, 13).

The sense of community is not restricted to events but young Quakers form what can be described as a continuing community:

JYM doesn't end, it goes on in all of us (Field Notes, Female, 17).

Allan states that:

> because of the solidarity and trust that has been generated over time,
> [people] remain close friends, but, because of circumstances, actually
> spend little time socialising together (1989, 19).

Because of the small numbers of adolescent Quakers, and the
atmosphere of acceptance that is fostered at Quaker events for young
people, once adolescent Quakers establish contacts they develop these
friendships, because they provide social support especially relating to
issues of personal identity (Erwin 1998, 8). For the current generation of
adolescents, there has been a rise of 'communities of interest' increasingly
facilitated by new media (Salvation Army 2001, 60). Pahl states that
'modern technology in the form of telephone and email helps people to
nurture friendships' (Pahl 2000, 172). Internet chatrooms and discussion
boards[7] are a popular form of alternative community with adolescent
Quakers as with other teenagers (Salvation Army 2001, 60). Given the
geographical dispersal of adolescent Quakers these forms of
communication are used in order to maintain friendships and provide
support to each other:

> most of us have got MSN[8] now so most of us talk quite frequently anyway
> – or we get in touch by phone or letter or something (Male, 16).

Through their participation in Quaker events adolescent Quakers form
ongoing friendships, which in turn foster the feeling of belonging and
enable adolescent Quakers to continue to be part of an ongoing, networked
community between gatherings and outside Quaker-time.

Worship and Ritual

For adolescent Quakers ritual, in the form of communal worship, is
key in connecting individuals and forming and sustaining community:

> The silence has a unique ability to form bonds between people. A really
> deep meeting can form bonds that last a lifetime (Female, 16).

> The silence gives an overwhelming feeling of presence of those around.
> The appreciation of everyone as an individual is a thought I always begin
> silence with (Male, 17).

Adolescent Quaker worship[9] has two distinctive features. Firstly there is a lower level of differentiation than in the adult group. Collins emphasises the importance of the arrangement of participants and the lack of differentiation with all participants are seated at the same level and no one being marked off in any way (Collins 2005, 328). However a differentiation in the height of participants occurs when an individual stands to minister. Amongst adolescent Quakers, standing when ministering is very infrequent. In participant observation of semi-programmed worship with over 150 vocal contributions only one individual stood to minister (Field Notes). In unprogrammed worship amongst adolescent Quakers, approximately one third remained seated when ministering (Field Notes). Although it could be argued that ministering is in itself an act of differentiation, I argue that not standing when ministering signifies a lower-level of differentiation amongst adolescent Quakers than in the adult group. Adolescent Quakers frequently sit in one large circle, often on the floor, without lines or rows. Dandelion cites the extension of the ritual of shaking hands from just the elders to the whole Meeting as an example of the democratisation of the creedal form of worship (2005, 111). This democratisation is further extended by the adolescent group where worship is often closed by the whole group joining hands in a circle (Field Notes).[10] The lack of differentiation in ritual, especially the way of closing worship is a symbol of community togetherness. This does occur in the adult group but not as often.

Secondly, adolescent Quaker ritual includes programmed and semi-programmed, as well as unprogrammed worship. Silence remains the basis of worship, periods of worship begin and end with silence and programmed contributions are made out of the silence. Silence therefore still 'marks the boundaries of the collective worship' (Dandelion 1996, 15) however it gives religious and spiritual value to contributions through speech, music, song and dance by making them an integral aspect of worship:

I have spoken in meetings but only when it has been a reading, or in structured meetings or ones when it is encouraged (Female, 16).

I have never spoken in meeting, because I do find it intimidating, but I have spoken (and sung!) in epilogue (Female, 18).

There are greater opportunities for individuals to share their beliefs and this is often explicitly encouraged:

Our worship together... will hopefully be a time for reflection and we hope
that people will feel comfortable and safe enough to share their thoughts
(Field Notes).

I think a lot of people my age [13] find it very hard to get up and say
something in front of all those people, and Summer School was a good
place for it to happen (Female, 13).[11]

Although adolescent Quaker religious experience does occur in silence,
because speech and sound is an integral element of worship for adolescent
Quakers their attitude towards silence is non-creedal and significantly
there is the possibility of religious experience occurring at other times.
Other speaking that occurs in Quaker time is part of the religious
experience of adolescent Quakers and can influence the formation of
individual beliefs which are created to make sense of this experience. In
the adult group where, because of a caution about making overt
theological statements individual beliefs are rarely vocalised in ministry
(Dandelion 1996, 259), the theological diversity of the group remains
unknown (Dandelion 2005, 110). In contrast, in the adolescent group,
increased opportunity to share individual belief stories in Quaker-time
means that the theological diversity within the adolescent Quaker group is
both known, and accepted. Because there is increased vocalisation of
individual's beliefs the consequence of silence is avoided and, instead, the
reaction is more likely to be to encourage others to vocalise their beliefs.
The marginal position of theology and the acceptance of theological
diversity means that there is only a very minimal threat of a
confrontational reaction to the expression of beliefs which appear to be
outside the popular theology of the group. Changes in popular Quaker
theology do not need to be covert.

The consequence of programmed and semi-programmed worship is
that the group ritual operates a 'Culture of Contribution' which militates
against the consequences of Dandelion's 'Culture of Silence' (1996, 258):
this is shown in Figure 11-2.

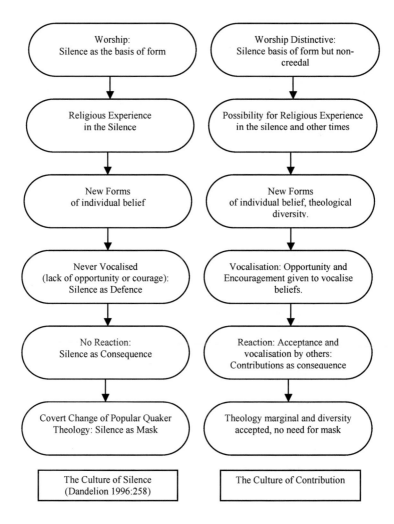

Figure 11-2: The Culture of Silence and the Culture of Contribution

Belief

For the adolescent group, belief operates at the periphery to the extent that a multiplicity of belief stories does not undermine the unity of the group. Although belief is marginal, the culture of contribution which is a consequence of the form of adolescent Quaker ritual leads to increased

opportunities and encouragement to share individual beliefs both during
worship and outside worship (but during Quaker-time) which results in a
greater vocalisation of individual belief stories.

There is no unified theology within the group and belief in God is not a
necessary part of being an adolescent Quaker. Although more adolescent
Quakers believe in God (41%) than do not (18%) almost as many as do
believe are not sure of their belief (40%)[12] Respondents gave 27 different
descriptions of God the most popular of which were 'inward light' with
50% 'love' with 48%, spirit 40% and 'a life force' 37% only 13%
described God as a being and 9% as a father figure.

The popular religion of the adolescent Quaker group portrays God as
an abstract non-personal spiritual presence or feeling that is shared by all,

[God is] sort of like sharing with everyone else something special (Male,
14).

It is more of a feeling of connectedness with other life and the landscape
(Male, 18).

Adolescents often use the word 'Light' rather than 'God' or use the
two terms interchangeably. For some adolescent Quakers 'light' has come
to indicate an abstract non-personal, non-Christian, concept of God:

You don't have to believe that God is a big angry man in the sky to believe
that the light within is God (Male, 16).

For adolescents the description of God as 'a spirit' or 'the Inward
Light' is closely related to the idea of 'that of God in everyone' indicated
by the use of the term 'light in us all' (Field Notes). The majority (80%) of
mentions of God in group interviews focused on the idea of 'that of God in
everyone'. However the focus is often not on God but rather on that of
'good' in everyone both self and others:

I put much less [importance] on God and more on good in everyone.
(Female, 18).

He [God] like does good in everything but that's just human nature and
nothing greater than that. (Male, 16).

Dandelion identifies a belief of that of God in everyone as 'the
parameter of acceptability of popular Quaker theology' (Dandelion 1996,
300). Adolescents have less connection with this key Quaker belief and

have re-interpreted and re-defined it, changing the language to reflect the absence of belief in a personal God.

Only 14% of adolescent Quakers state that Jesus is important in their spiritual lives, many of those do not ascribe divinity to him. Jesus is described as a non-divine teacher or prophetic figure with significant and important beliefs. If the uniqueness and importance of Jesus is definitional of Christianity (Hampson 1993, 25) then the popular religion of adolescent Quaker group is distinctively not Christian and not Quaker-Christian (Dandelion 1996, 176). Mellor (this volume, Chapter 4) argues that a broader definition of Christianity should be used for Quakers using self-definition, attitudes towards Jesus and use of the Bible as measures. Within the adolescent group only 12.6% said that they thought of themselves as Christian. 28.7% of respondents included divine characteristics (Son of God, Saviour) in their description of Jesus 42.5% stated that they had read the Bible, or parts of it, and found it helpful However they do not necessarily view it as having divine authority. One respondent stated that they had read the Bible and found it helpful added

> but I don't agree or believe most of it (Male, 17).

Another stated that it had been helpful:

> in relation to understanding other's beliefs (Female, 17).

Other respondents suggest that many have an ambivalent attitude towards the Bible:

> some parts are helpful ... the Old Testament [is] depressing and terrible (Female, 18).

Others view it as irrelevant:

> not really either [helpful or unhelpful] it just seems irrelevant (Female, 18).

Even using a broader definition of Christianity I argue that the popular religion of the adolescent Quaker group has moved beyond the post-Christian neo-orthodoxy of liberal-Liberal Quakerism (Dandelion 1996, 319) and can most appropriately be described as non-Christian.

Values

Because belief is marginal, many adolescent Quakers exhibit their Quaker identity in part through the identification with and assimilation of Quaker values. Adolescent Quakers' values are manifested in two interrelated ways: internal rules that operate within the group and Quaker-time, and external behaviour outside the group and Quaker-time.

At Quaker events for young people there are group rules, usually called 'boundaries' (Field Notes). This terminology distinguishes them from school rules and presents them as more liberal and less demanding. Official boundaries vary according to the age of participants but generally include the prohibition of drinking alcohol, taking illegal drugs and sexual activity. Boundaries do not necessarily correspond to the legality of the act. Indeed adolescent Quakers may actually be supported in acts which are not legal. At some events participants are permitted to smoke even if they are under the age of 16 (Field Notes).[13] Conversely other rules prohibit behaviour which is legal for some members of the group, for example alcohol consumption by over 18s. Justification for these rules is not usually given in terms of the law but in terms of the necessity of these rules to build an inclusive community:

> They [adolescent Quakers] know that… if they are legally able to drink or smoke when others in their group are not, to do so would exclude some members of the group (Quaker Action on Alcohol and Drugs 2006, 100).

Rather than reflecting the law, boundaries are often framed in terms of prohibiting 'exclusive behaviour' (Field Notes) and justified with reference to Quaker values, to ensuring that all participants feel included and to the need to maintain the community

> As we believe in equality, it is important to the success of JYM that everyone … attempts to get on well with others in order to build a sense of community and boundaries are necessary for this to happen (Field Notes).

Boundaries attempt to control the behaviour of adolescents during Quaker-time while expressing the centrality of principles of inclusion and of the primacy of group needs over those of individuals. The maintenance of the Community of Intimacy underpins a range of boundaries some of which are exceptionally liberal and others which are more conservative and demanding. In addition to formal boundaries a series of less formal norms also operate to moderate behaviour within the group. These informal rules are also justified in terms of maintaining the community. Dandelion states that the rules on Quaker form are accepted by the group *en masse* as legitimate (1996, 104). Similarly, I suggest that for the adolescent group, behavioural rules which are clearly aimed at protecting the Community of Intimacy are accepted. Behaviour that contravenes these informal rules is sometimes explicitly mentioned, as being unacceptable or 'unQuakerly' (Field Notes). One adult volunteer said, in response to a young person who had been teasing other participants:

> I told him that it wasn't the kind of thing that it was ok to do at Summer School (Field Notes).

In the adolescent Quaker group the final authority for acceptability of behaviour rests with the group, which locates itself in a physical (during Quaker-time) and a psychological (beyond Quaker-time) space that is separate from and different to the world that surrounds it. Within the adolescent Quaker group, loyalty to the community is used as the primary justification for having both formal boundaries and less formal rules of group behaviour. Within the adolescent Quaker group there is a high level of internal discipline which is secured by the individuals' loyalty to the group. This is similar to the virtue ethics approach identified by Scully (this volume, Chapter 6) however for the adolescent Quaker group the foundation is not 'that of God in everyone' but rather the 'good adolescent Quaker' is one who acts in a way that enables the community to be maintained and flourish and recognises the potential for good in themselves and others:

> [it's] as though it's inside of you its not as though its God but just goodness...it just makes you want to be good and try and be a better person (Female, 16).

Similar to the pluralisation of belief, there is a pluralisation of values and an individualisation of the behaviour that is an expression of these values. Adolescents identified 23 ways in which they consider being a Quaker makes a difference to how they live their lives, ways in which Quaker values are manifest in their behaviour. Only one (pacifism and the Quaker peace testimony) was shared by more than one quarter of respondents and only four were held in common by more than 10% of the sample. The group has little authority over the behaviour of members when outside the group and few demands are placed on members in terms of outward witness to Quaker values. However there is an optional influence on individuals' external behaviour, especially relating to non-violence, tolerance and acceptance and equality.

Respondents identified behaviour that reflects the influence of Quaker testimonies such as buying Fair Trade products and participating in anti-war demonstrations:

> My belief in non-violence makes me confident to search [for] non-violent solutions to problems (Female, 18).

> [Being a Quaker] helps me make a conscious choice to live a bit simply (Female, 18).

The Quaker testimonies provide 'a template for action' (Coleman and Collins 2000, 322) and responses indicate that adolescents recognise this:

> I try and live with the testimonies. I think I am less violent and more honest that most of my friends because of this (Male, 15).

Adolescents referred to the Quaker testimonies as being:

> not set in stone ... people take notice of them because they're considerate human beings (Male, 16).

Behavioural norms especially in terms of inclusion, anti-discrimination and treating others with respect that operate within the group influence individuals behaviour outside the group. The individualization and non-definitional status of belief places greater weight on ritual and behaviour which are critical to the operation of the Community of Intimacy.

Within liberal-Liberal Quakerism the interpretation of testimony has become individualised and 'what any part of Quaker testimony means, whether on peace or integrity or gambling or moderation is now up to the individual' (QAAD 2006, vi). Dandelion argues that the double-life between individual and corporate ethics represents 'an attempt to live out the duality of a personal and public ethic. But still both are interpreted individually' (QAAD 2006, vii). For the adolescent group, the influence of the Community of Intimacy as a networked community lessens the duality between the two aspects. The personal ethic becomes more public amongst Quakers and, in turn, the public Quaker ethic is reflected to a greater extent in the personal.

Authority and Influence

Although the group has a low formal authority over individuals' private lives, considerable influence exists through behavioural boundaries within the group and ethical choices made by group members. The values that are the basis for group boundaries and unspoken norms of behaviour provide individuals with a model for external behaviour.

Adolescent Quakers associate certain patterns of behaviour with Quaker-time experiences and the positive experience of being part of the Community of Intimacy and through this with the explicit and implicit rules that operate within the group. Adolescents draw a conscious link between Quaker-time activities and behaviour which is different to that of groups they are part of in their non-Quaker lives. Adolescent Quakers' behaviour in their private lives outside Quaker-time is influenced by the rules that govern Quaker-time activities because of a desire to recreate that positive experience and continue the sense of belonging and connection with the Community of Intimacy:

> We leave having identified our values and beliefs… eager to apply them to our daily lives (Junior Yearly Meeting Epistle 2003).

Through a process of modelling behavioural conformity to a particular set of values, which are expressed through the formal and informal rules that operate in the adolescent group, individuals are provided with an example of how to live in the world: 'You just go back, you try to apply summer school and senior conference as your actual life and it's really good' (Pearmain 2005, 238).

Difference and Separateness

Adolescent Quakers identify and perceive differences between themselves and other Quakers and between themselves and other young people. These differences are both inward and outward:

> You've got your alternative clothes and different ways in which you stand out rather than blend in but you've also got different views … to do with sort of world issues things like that and your views which aren't sort of thought of as the right view but can often be quite educated views (Male, 17).

> At Quaker events I can find other young people with similar views to mine rather than always being the odd one out (Male, 16).

This is a group that is seen from the outside as religious but which exists in an adolescent society where:

it's now looked at as a bad thing if you're religious and have morals (Field Notes).

Adolescent Quakers may face having their beliefs derided because:

people at school think religion and God are stupid (Field Notes).

In one focus group interview half of the group of adolescents had been bullied because of their beliefs:

Because we don't feel we have to justify our beliefs, we become easy bullying targets to people who don't understand us (Field Notes).

They know that there are differences. They want to pick on us because not only are we different but they know we're kind of like accepting and they don't understand (Male, 15).

Adolescent Quakers' perceptions of difference are often located in the reaction of others to their attempts to express Quaker values through their behaviour outside Quaker-time:

Some people at school may not be violent there but will tell me about incidents when their brother or sister was nasty so they hit/kicked/threw something at them - they then always are surprised when they hear I would never do that (Stanger 2004).

There is also a perception of difference between adolescents and adult Quakers in terms of Quaker belief and practice:

Older Quakers have their defined Quaker values that they believe in ... whereas I think lots of young Quakers are unsure whereabouts they are (Female 17).

[Young Quakers] put less value on going to meeting and God worshiping but [more on] just holding their own beliefs. (Field Notes).

Coleman and Collins argue that outwardly expressed non-conformist behaviour represents 'explicit signalling of religious identity in relation to others' (Coleman and Collins 2000, 326). Quaker beliefs and values may still prevent adolescents from doing things that most other children are able to do and 'state schools are, on the whole, secular institutions attended by young children whose behaviour is not governed by world-renouncing tenets' (Holden 2002, 137). Collins and Coleman mention the case of a child whose Quaker beliefs became apparent when she refused to buy a raffle ticket in front of her class (Collins and Coleman 2000, 322). The behaviour of adolescent Quakers both within and outside the group represents the manifestation of a particular set of values. Perceptions of difference are consequential to this and are, in part, a result of this behaviour having its basis in religious values.

Adolescents' involvement in Quaker activities also represents an outward expression of belonging to the adolescent Quaker group where individuals place themselves in a space which is separate from their other lives and the world. For adolescent Quakers the Community of Intimacy represents a 'safe haven' (Pearmain 2005, 277), a separate space that is seen as qualitatively different from the rest of their lives:

> I found it awkward trying to explain to [my friend] where I was going this weekend because he might think that I was weird or something... It's like if I tell someone I'm going to a Quaker weekend they think its some kind of religious, freaky activity and that I'm weird. It's as though Quakers are an alien breed that isn't accepted in human society! (Clark 1995).

> I feel like I'm two different people when I'm with my friends and among Quakers (Female, 15).

> I cannot add my Quaker life to my school life as they are incomparable (Male, 15).

These activities are often separated from those of the adult Quaker group, both through choice, of adolescents as well as adults, and circumstance. Collins argues that the Quaker group is 'striated' according to the differentiating social categories to which different members belong, and that Quaker identity, rests on the suppression of these 'contradictory positions' (Collins 2002b, 83). Because of their age, adolescent Quakers share membership of a social category which is contradictory to that of the rest of the Quaker group and is not suppressed but rather, at least partially, separated from the Quaker group as a whole. Adolescent Quakers meet at different times and in different places to the adult Quaker group, including at 'all-age events'; this leads to the creation of a separate psychological as well as physical space.

In the Community of Intimacy, particularly at Quaker events for young people, adolescent Quakers experience a temporary existence in alternative social structure, which operates according to rules which emphasise the primacy of the community. Adolescent ritual is a significant aspect of the creation of this separate space. . It represents a visible differentiation from the everyday and from adult Quaker ritual:

> [Quaker worship] is so different from modern life (Male, 18).

> I enjoy Meeting for Worship at Holiday School because there is a real sense of community and belonging and unity in the silence. (Female, 17).

> There is more group togetherness in epilogue. In epilogue its kind of more like a peer group than your own meeting for worship [where] you're like the youngest there and its made a point of that you're the youngest there and in epilogue you're more relaxed (Female, 18).

It also demonstrates an alternative theological ordering. Durkheim emphasises the significance of 'effervescent collective assemblies' which 'heighten people's passions and energies' (Allen *et al* 1998, 10). The intensity of these gatherings 'serves as a social glue' and binds individuals to the group (Ramp 1998, 137). 'The charged emotional environments call individuals out of themselves, imbuing them with a heightened sense of their participation in the collective' (Ramp 1998, 141). Communal worship at Quaker events for young people has this effect on adolescent Quakers:

> The silence is different in meeting for worship in Quaker events where you have been doing it for a least a day because everybody is in 'Quaker mode' whereas with meeting everybody is coming in from outside (Female, 15).

Adopting this 'Quaker mode' represents a transformation that occurs at Quaker events for young people in which worship is instrumental. Individuals cross a temporal or spatial threshold of the event and are transformed in that act (Ramp 1998, 141-42). For adolescent Quakers worship may not represent transformation by means of 'a conscious and internal giving way' (Collins 2005, 336) but is transformative because of the context. Quaker worship is a visible differentiation from the everyday and a means of binding individuals to the group. Individuals experience both a separation from the world and a sense of themselves as a distinctive worshiping community separate from adult Quakers:

> At holiday school I felt like much more connected to people when I was sat in meeting … cos like I went to meeting the other day to my normal meeting and although I know everybody there I didn't feel as connected to them (Female, 16).

It is through distinctive Quaker worship, and self-identification by adolescent Quakers as a distinctive worshiping community, that individuals experience both a separation from the world and from adult Quakers. Through ritual the adolescent group maintains cohesion and integration (Dandelion 2005, 121) but this ritual is separate from that of adults and set apart from the world. For adolescents, ritual, including programmed and semi-programmed worship, provides a space in which their experiences can be realised, claimed and articulated (Stringer 1999, 204).

The adolescent Quaker group has both a high level of internal integration and a high degree of differentiation from other groups (Fenn 1997, 41). Adolescent ritual involves the creation of a separate space that reflects an ideal social order and the transformation of individuals to being members of the adolescent Quaker group, the Community of Intimacy.

The Adolescent Quaker Community of Intimacy

The adolescent Quaker group represents a 'Community of Intimacy'. The features and their interrelationship of the adolescent Quaker Community of Intimacy are illustrated in Figure 11-3.

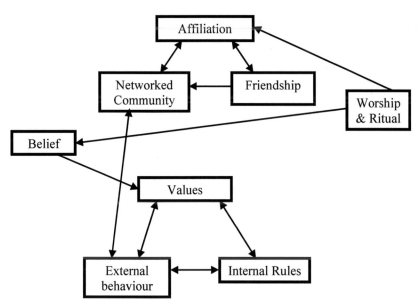

Figure 11-3: The Adolescent Quaker Community of Intimacy

The Community of Intimacy is a collective grouping, affiliation to which comes from individuals' involvement in Quakerism. This sense of belonging, together with friendships formed and fostered during Quaker-time leads to the creation and sustaining of a networked community which continues beyond this.[14]

For the adolescent group, belief operates at the periphery to the extent that a multiplicity of belief stories does not undermine the unity of the group. Although belief is marginal, there is a high level of vocalisation of individual belief stories. The individualisation and non-definitional status of belief places greater weight on ritual and behaviour which are critical to the operation of the adolescent Quaker Community of Intimacy. Adolescent Quaker ritual is an embodiment of the community and transforms individuals into members of the community; this transformation is crucial to creating a sense of belonging.

The individual interpretation of Quaker values through external behaviour is contrasted with a high level of authority over behaviour within the group, and the modelling of formal and informal rules within the group influences individuals' behaviour outside the group. The operation of the Community of Intimacy as a networked community which exists outside formal Quaker-time ensures that the influence and example set through behavioural rules in the group extends to behaviour outside Quaker-time.

Heterotopia

Pilgrim (this volume, Chapter 3) argues that liberal-Liberal Quakers obtain a sense of identity and unity through the creation of a heterotopic space by offering an alternate ordering to the rest of society. The Adolescent Quaker group is juxtaposed to both adult Quakers and the world: this is in contrast to the Experimenters described by Meads (this volume, Chapter 12) whose heterotopic impulse operates only within the Quaker group. However I suggest that adolescent Quakers are not heterotopic in the same way as adults whose energies, Pilgrim argues, are directed towards negotiating the playing out of their heterotopic stance within their own organisation. Adolescent Quakers' sense of otherness is a consequence of the features of the Community of Intimacy and their interrelationship and the utopian vision quest that it represents.

Double-Culture and Triple-Culture

Dandelion's Quaker double-culture is comprised of the liberal belief culture, and the behavioural creed, which demands conformity to form and practice (Dandelion 1996, 118). Dandelion argues that the double-culture functions as twin components of the culture of the Quaker group, operating within the organisational life of the group. For the adolescent group there is a triple-culture formed by ritual (the 'Culture of Contribution'), the networked community, and narrative and behaviour. This triple culture is a function (i.e. a consequence) of the Community of Intimacy and is the means by which adolescent Quaker identity is formed and sustained. The components of the triple-culture are also features of the Community of Intimacy. Table 11-1 shows the features of the adolescent Quaker triple-culture.

Ritual
• Setting: communal space separate from other Quakers and the world
• Radical in terms of form (silence as basis but non-creedal)
• Radical content (semi-programmed)
• Opportunity and encouragement given to vocalise beliefs
• Marginal – not primary within Quakerism as a whole
• Transformational
• Initiation of the individual into the community
• Separate space – not primary within Quakerism as a whole
Networked Community
• 'Gathering function'
• Feeling of belonging through participating in events despite small numbers and geographical distance
• Ongoing personal friendships sustain and are sustained by the larger community
• Acts to secure unity
• Continuing community- not restricted to Quaker-time
• Facilitated by new media
• Friendships provide support especially relating to issues of personal or social identity
• Quality and closeness of friendships despite not seeing each other frequently

Narrative & Behaviour
• Community is justification for formal and informal rules of group behaviour • Low formal authority over individuals' private lives • Aspirational and inspirational stories providing a model for behaviour within and outside Quaker time • Narrative: stories that individuals tell about and with their lives reflects the groups' values, rules and internal norms of behaviour • Desire to recreate positive Quaker-time experience and continue connection with community • Rules that govern Quaker-time activities exert influence over behaviour outside Quaker-time • Creation of a physical and a psychological space that is seen and felt to be separate from and different to the world

Table 11–1: The Features of the Adolescent Quaker Triple-Culture

In the adult Quaker group 'culture is the system of transmission of meaning constructed in the relationship between popular and institutional forms of religion' (Dandelion 1996, 120)[15]. The institutional religion and access to it is controlled by the adult Quaker group and adolescents are excluded from this in structural and implicit operational ways. For the adolescent group, the Community of Intimacy represents the popular religion.

Within the adolescent Quaker group the triple-culture represents the creation and preservation of a separate physical and psychological space, which occurs as a result of both the gathering function and the similarity of adolescent Quakers and their exclusion from the adult group. The three aspects of the triple culture are in dynamic interrelationship – all are focused on maintaining and sustaining the Community of Intimacy. This is illustrated in Figure 11-4.

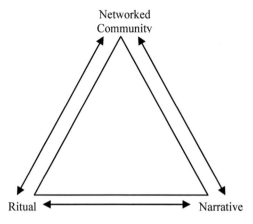

Figure 11-4: The Adolescent Quaker Triple-Culture

Conclusion

Adolescent Quakers are Quakers not by virtue of believing the same thing or by doing the same thing but by being the same thing – where this 'being' is universal and essential. They are part of a network of personal friendships with other adolescent Quakers; they behave as Quakers in both Quaker-time and non-Quaker time and most significantly the groups they belong to is a distinctive group of Quakers, which practices in different ways and gathers in separate spaces to other Quakers.

For the adult group, according to Dandelion, 'it is the way in which Quakers practise their religion which is definitional' rather than the content of Quaker belief and the behavioural creed which acts to 'generate unity and maintain cohesion' (2004b, 222-23). For the adolescent group unity is achieved not by orthopraxis but rather through the initiation of the individual into the community and the creation of an ideal social order, by establishing a separate physical and psychological space through ritual in the adolescent group. Unity and adolescent Quaker identity are strengthened by connection to the group through a networked community of personal friendships and by narrative, the stories adolescent Quakers tell in and by their lives. In liberal-Liberal Quakerism the behavioural creed serves as 'social glue' (Dandelion this volume, Chapter 1); for adolescents this social glue is provided by the Community of Intimacy.

Notes

---

[1] Religious belief is contrasted with a broader worldview, which may include spiritual, moral and political values. This term is used to make explicit that despite being members of a religious group, explicitly religious beliefs are unimportant for adolescents and are not a basis for individual identity or group unity.

[2] In this chapter I use the term worship because, although it may imply a shared belief which does not exist for this group, it is a term commonly understood by the group and used to describe corporate ritual. The focus of corporate worship is not on having shared beliefs but on sharing individual beliefs with others. For adolescent Quakers having shared beliefs is not important (although they may in fact share some beliefs); the sharing of beliefs with each other is important.

[3] Quotations from questionnaires, group interviews and participant observation undertaken as part of this research are indented throughout.

[4] Regional summer events 38%, Junior Yearly Meeting 10%, and Link Groups 10%.

[5] 3% felt most part of their area (Monthly) Meeting, which is the primary Meeting for church affairs amongst Quakers in Britain. 4% identified other Quaker groups and 4% stated that they did not feel part of any grouping of Quakers.

[6] 75.6% of total respondents.

[7] There is an internet discussion boards dedicated to adolescent Quakers (www.friendlink.org.uk) and as of August 2007 there were approximately 15 groups for British adolescent Quakers on Facebook, a social networking site (www.facebook.com).

[8] MSN, sometimes referred to by the name 'Messenger' is an online instant messaging programme. This allows individuals connected to the internet to have conversations in real-time. People can have simultaneous conversations with several people at the same time, or have three-way (or more) conversations and use webcams.

[9] 'Worship' refers both to Meeting for Worship which usually occurs at the beginning of the day and can either be programmed or unprogrammed and to Epilogue a period of worship at the end of the day which more usually includes a programmed element as well as silent worship.

[10] This practice is occasionally observed in the adult group but usually only in programmed or semi-programmed worship.

[11] http://www.friendlink.org.uk/boards/viewtopic.php?t=1868, accessed on 11.09.2006.

[12] Of those who self-identified as Quakers 46.7% stated that they believed in God, a slightly lower percentage than for the group as a whole, 12.7% did not believe in God and 40.1% were unsure of their belief.

[13] 16 is currently the legal age for buying cigarettes or tobacco in the United Kingdom.

[14] Frith (this volume, Chapter 9) indicates that these friendships continue from one life stage to another.

[15] Institutional religion is religion as described by the organisation, its content is located within parameters established by the organisational process, popular religion is 'where the personal interpretation of organisational religion is collectively shared or shared within the collective frame' (Dandelion 1996, 21).

CHAPTER TWELVE

'EXPERIMENT WITH LIGHT': RADICAL SPIRITUAL WING OF BRITISH QUAKERISM

HELEN MEADS

In this chapter I argue that 'Experiment with Light' represents a radical spiritual wing of British Quakerism and that, as a practice, it is not more widespread nor better understood because of tensions between the nature of the practice and accepted Quaker ways of behaving. I am here using 'radical' in both its more common sense of 'advanced' and 'extreme' and in its original sense of 'pertaining to roots', 'inherent in the nature or essence of a thing', 'fundamental' or 'forming the root, basis or foundation' (Onions 1970, 1648). I describe it as a 'wing' because it reflects an undefined element of British Quakers who seek religious/spiritual experience as a basis for their being in the world. Wing connotes 'outlying or portion of a space or region', that is, its position on the fringes of Britain Yearly Meeting (BYM), and its being a 'section of a party, holding views deviating in one direction or the other from those generally held' (Onions 1970, 2433). It is radical in that what Experimenters experience is often uncomfortable, but can also lead them to 'Truth', 'right relationship with God' and fundamental changes in their lives; their Experimenting together magnifies this experience. Also, Experimenters share intimate details of their lives and spiritual experience and this binds them together closely into local 'communities of intimacy' (Best this volume, Chapter 11) within, but not consisting entirely of, recognised Meeting structure, and into a 'community of love'. Such explicit sharing, common among early Friends, is uncommon in twenty first century British Quaker Meetings.

I first discuss the origins, process, practice and organisation of the Experiment, then why it is radical and not more widespread nor better understood. There are in-built tensions within the Experiment which both bind Experimenters closer to each other in a community of love, like early Friends, and also differentiate them within their own Meetings, especially where conflict arises and Experimenters receive little help and support within their Meetings. I argue that Experimenters operate an heterotopic impulse.

The Experiment

Origins

The 'Experiment with Light' was devised by Rex Ambler after reading early Friends' writings and thinking about the nature of Quaker experience in worship (Ambler 1994; 1997a; 1997b; 2001; 2002). Ambler led the first Experiment with Light in 1996 at a General Meeting of British Quakers (2002, 37).

Ambler says he found that George Fox[1] in particular told people not what to believe, but what to do, directing them to the truth they have in them (Ambler 1997a, 12) by conducting 'an experiment with light' (1997a, 14), that is, by undergoing a process.

Ambler says 'seeing in the light' is different from 'thinking and imagining, and all human activity, so that in a mode of inner as well as outer silence we can become aware … of the reality of the world, beneath its images and illusions.' He refers to early Quakers' finding 'self-will' as a fundamental obstacle to realising God and the truth, but distinguishing Quaker light by its moral content: 'what we come to see in the light is not just illusion, falsehood, deceit, but also evil', so that:

> following the light comes to be a matter of living with the truth as we have
> come to see it … giving up our customary, all-too-human, characteristically
> modern habit of deciding everything for ourselves; for a condition of
> seeing in the light is that we surrender to it, recognising that a true vision
> of the world comes from beyond ourselves, and that it becomes clear to us
> only as and when we can be free of the ego that obscures our vision
> (Ambler 1997a, 20).

The 'truth' that emerges is maintained in the practice of sharing discernments with each other, testing discernments over time and trusting the process (1997b, 163-64), as Quakers have long done. Experiment with Light is thus based on the steps which Ambler believes led seventeenth century Quakers to their 'convincement' or encounter with God and the resulting dramatic changes in their lives. Its aim is to follow the same process as early Quakers did and to see what happens, literally to experiment, and to see if the light can be experienced as it had been by early Quakers, to resolve issues and find peace (2002, 37-38).

Process and Practice

The Experiment is usually undertaken in 'Light groups' based in Quaker Meetings,[2] although some Experimenters do practise individually. There are no statistics either for the numbers of Light groups, nor for Experimenters. How widespread the practice is varies from year to year as groups fold and new ones begin. I would estimate that there were between twenty and thirty groups active in Britain during the period of my fieldwork.[3]

Some Light groups are 'closed', that is participants may join only at the beginning of the group's life or by specific invitation, whilst others are 'freeflowing' and may be joined at any time by anyone from the Meeting in which it operates.[4] Groups are small, generally varying between four and twelve members. Some Meetings have more than one group.

The Experiment itself comprises a forty minute meditation, consisting of six steps interspersed with periods of silence. The meditation is usually guided by a tape or compact disc, but in some groups one member reads it. Usually the meditation is followed by silence for individual personal reflection, making notes or drawing representations of the Experimenter's experience. Finally, and very importantly, participants share what has come up for them.[5] There is no typical experience of an Experiment with Light; some Experimenters see images, others hear, feel what they experience bodily, are in the experience as in a dream or suddenly become aware of something.

Experimenters do not specifically seek 'convincement' or encounter with God, because they do not want to assume that God will come when called. In this, Experimenters are perhaps not much different in their intention from Friends in Meeting for Worship (MfW), but the Experiment has more process structured into it and largely its focus is on the individual,[6] whereas MfW is more communal (*Quaker Faith and Practice* 1995, 2.35-2.40). Experimenters say they find the Experiment both deeper and more personal than MfW, some expressing frustration at MfW getting stuck with the 'dreadfulness of the world', containing too much ministry from the head, or at too many Friends limiting their spiritual practice only to MfW on Sundays, making it clear that for them MfW lacks something which the Experiment provides.

Experience: transformation, immanence and transcendence

Experimenters said that in their Experimenting they came to find truths about themselves and their relationships, how their own attitudes and behaviour had prevented them living their lives as honestly as they would like or being fully at ease with themselves and others; their Experimenting led to different ways of being, conducting their relationships and experiencing the world.[7] Different interviewees variously described becoming vegetarian, being unable to tell white lies for social convenience, being able to retire and giving up long-held Quaker jobs, coming to understand the true nature of feelings for family and beginning to discern what underlay an obsession with sex.   I observed one Experimenter weeping silently at a pain she could not share except to say that she knew she had to accept the way things were, another ceasing to struggle with one daughter's twenty year refusal to speak to another daughter and others letting go of 'toxic anger' and facing past violent acts. Making these discoveries was uncomfortable for all of them.

Some of these realisations came from the most unlikely Friends: one of the incidents of violence was told by a Friend well known for adherence to the peace testimony; another revealed potential mistakes he had made in life-or-death decisions, saying: 'I need to forgive myself.' To share these things was risky and exposed their vulnerabilities to others at the same time as they became aware of them themselves and expressed great trust in fellow Experimenters. I observed that when they shared with each other in depth their relationships changed.   The combination of Experimenting together and then sharing amplified the experience, not least because they would then carry around others' images as well as their own. They also carried their fellow-Experimenters' sharing including these images under the protocol of confidentiality. The protocol served to bind them still closer and increased their sense of intimacy.

What Experimenters had in common went beyond uncomfortably facing themselves, to sharing more transcendent experiences. On one occasion two Experimenters shared the same image, of a pool of water and its significance, of peace. Another said: 'I had an image of Experiment with Light as a mountain spring, and in the biblical sense of the water of life, which when you drink it, you don't get thirsty any more.' One described her Experimenting as 'an experience of relating to something beyond me that was illuminating me, so that there was a separate entity which was very real, very alive,' then later as 'a dynamic going on between something beyond me but also in me' and as bringing her into 'right relationship with God.' Another wrote a poem exploring her transportation in the meditation through all five senses. One described strange shifting scenarios he did not himself understand. More than one talked of feeling a very deep sense of peace, tapping into and being guided by a force or energy, an inner spiritual resource, infinite potential, 'external intentionality'; some named it as 'the Light', outside or other than themselves, yet part of themselves, both immanent and transcendent.

Experimenting led to their listening more, paying more attention to spiritual matters and deepening both daily spiritual practice and experience in MfW.

Intimacy, Vulnerability and Love

Best (this volume, Chapter 11) discusses how adolescent Quakers form a 'community of intimacy'. He argues that the members of the group feel a sense of belonging and affiliation to the group, that they share a set of shared values which are expressed in internal and external behaviour. This behaviour contributes to feelings of difference between the Community of Intimacy and those to which it is juxtaposed so that the group occupies separate physical and psychological spaces.

Light groups form local communities of intimacy, in that what they do is separate from other Quaker activity and different. For example, they may meet in the Meeting House, but their Experimenting takes place separately and is different from MfW, the primary (and, increasingly for more Friends, only) regular Quaker activity. The knowledge which Experimenters share of each others' inward and outward lives and the protocol of confidentiality under which they share it binds them into a local community of intimacy not shared by the others in their Meetings; they indicated that they consider themselves different in the extension of their 'Quaker-time' (Dandelion 1996, xii) from Friends who found once-a-week MfW sufficient.[8]

The Experiment differs from MfW not only in its focus, but also in how Experimenters understand each others' experience. For Experimenters the ritual around MfW provides little or no opportunity to share individual experience of worship in depth,[9] whereas it is built into Light groups' meetings. To share requires an ability to be both vulnerable and trusting. I observed Experimenters softening towards each other both as they exposed their vulnerability, thus demonstrating trust of the others in the group, and as the other group members held their Friend's vulnerability. For example, a Friend may have been aloof and distant, even unco-operative, but when the underlying cause was revealed in an Experiment as a painful personal experience or low self-esteem, understanding and compassion was engendered. Similarly when an Experimenter described a transcendent experience, the other participants said or demonstrated that they were honoured at and awed by being allowed to know of it, and to know they were present when it happened.

Whilst most Experimenters' practice is in their local Light groups, there is also a wider network from the weeks held at Glenthorne in 1998 and 2004, from courses[10] and from the recognition of each other in other settings. The recognition and acknowledgement of Experimenters' common experience often goes unnoticed, so is not understood by other Friends in those different settings. This private knowledge of what Experimenting entails binds them with each other at a subtle level and differentiates them in their own understanding from the other Friends present who have not had similar experience.

Like early Quakers, Experimenters are a 'community of love', a community of intimacy based on experience of the spiritual foundation (Dawson 2004, 160-62) which underlies everyday existence; a community of love is derived from the inward investigation of that spiritual foundation (Meads forthcoming). As Howgill wrote in the seventeenth century, early Quakers were gathered and caught 'as in a net' separate from the world: 'our hearts were knit unto the Lord *and one unto another* [my emphasis] in true and fervent love' (*Quaker Faith and Practice* 1995, 19.08).

Organisation

Some Light groups are established under formal business method, by a minute in a Preparative Meeting (PM), but most are established informally, although the Elders of the Meeting in which they operate should keep a watching brief, since Elders have a responsibility for the spiritual health of the Meeting including all its peripheral activities (*Quaker Faith and Practice* 1995, 12.11, 12.12h and 12.20). If a member of a Light group is an Elder, that is co-incidental.

Groups may form as a result of a critical mass of Friends in local Meetings wanting to Experiment or by one enthusiast leading an initiative. Some Meetings invite Ambler, or someone else with experience, to speak or lead a workshop locally, some Experimenters may have been introduced to the practice on an organised course, or have read Ambler's exposition of the Experiment (Ambler 2002) and then try to set up a group in their Meeting without any further input.

In 1998 a group of invited Friends spent a week at Glenthorne with the intention that they should train to run workshops to introduce the

Experiment.[11] Some of them then met periodically afterwards, but there has never been a formal central organisation for the Experiment; indeed, both the group which met periodically and those at the second retreat held at Glenthorne in 2004 actively decided there should be no formal separate organisation. The earlier group felt it would stifle the Experiment's impulse (Collier 1999). Glenthorne's 2004 Experimenters felt that the Experiment should permeate the whole of BYM ('Epistle from Experiment with Light Gathering at Glenthorne', 2004) and they took no action beyond distributing the epistle to all Monthly Meetings in the hope that it would make the Experiment more widely understood (Field Notes).

Since the Experiment was never tested through BYM's formal hierarchy of business Meetings, neither BYM's 'Quaker Life' department nor any one Meeting or group of Meetings provides resources for dissemination of the practice, nor is it legitimated with the authority of any level of Meeting within BYM, except in the rare occurrence of a Light group's establishment under a minute from its local Meeting. The nearest the Experiment comes to recognised corporate structure is that a Light group is a small group within a local Meeting (*Quaker Faith & Practice* 1995, 12.20-12.21). All events are self-financing, or, in the case of administration for the Glenthorne retreat in 2004 and the distribution of the epistle, funded by surpluses from selling the tapes and CDs (Field Notes). The website is hosted by an individual Experimenter. Thus, none of the Experiment's activity beyond local Meetings has any structured accountability.

There was one contact person for queries (Ambler 2002, 60), but since 2004 there have been regional contacts although three regions have no contact person ('Experiment with Light Contacts'), so that in much of Britain the Experiment is not able to respond in any organised way to Quakers' 'spiritual hunger' (Heeks 1998), nor even to requests for assistance in establishing new Light groups.

At a local level, as a result of their intimacy, Light groups can be perceived as exclusive and unavailable, even to Friends who might wish to join a group. Controversy regarding their closed nature surrounded one group I observed which was closed, but an Experimenter in another group I observed thought (before she joined it) that she would not be able to do so, even though it was in fact freeflowing and its meetings were announced after MfW and in the Meeting's newsletter (Field Notes).

Challenge

Interviewees expressed frustration that many Friends in their Meetings appeared to them to experience the Religious Society of Friends at only a superficial level. The criticism was explicit in that confidential setting, but is implicit publicly in Meetings. Experimenters who enthuse about their Experimenting may do so in conversation or even in ministry in MfW, 'coming out' about their Experimenting if it is not already known. So, by their additional practice of Experimenting, they imply MfW is not enough for them and that it is lacking in some respect, and thus they potentially implicitly criticise those who do find it sufficient.

I observed conflict surrounding three light groups (and informants described other instances). In one Meeting, a Light group could not be established because one Elder was very opposed and the other Elders dared not disagree. Some years later a group was established in the same Meeting, but it was severely undermined by one of its members directly upsetting all the other members of the group. Even though some Friends were clearly becoming very deeply hurt, and in some cases damaged, the Elders did not intervene until they were directly asked by so many of the group that they could no longer ignore it. Even then one Elder felt she had to stay away from MfW during her handling of the situation. In the two other Meetings, Elders declined to intervene and any resolution of the issue was left entirely to the Light group's initiative.

These Light groups could not understand why they were perceived as presenting any difficulty, nor why they had to make so much effort to maintain their position as informal small groups within their Meetings (*Quaker Faith and Practice* 1995, 12.20-12.21), because they felt their Experimenting was core Quaker practice. Their Meetings, however, did not understand what was happening in the Light groups and, perceiving Experimenting to be only an optional extra and not core, did not feel any responsibility to deal with any difficulty. Light groups asked for Elders' help and were not immediately met with dialogue.

The instances of conflict added more tension than that caused by the conflict itself, since it offended the 'behavioural creed' (Dandelion 1996, 100-10) presumption that conflict does not exist within British Quaker Meetings (Robson 2005, 10). The continued practice of the Light groups in the face of conflict was seen as what Plüss terms 'idiosyncratic conduct' and failure to 'adapt' to the common source of Friends' insights (1995, 114).

Since Experimenters do not usually tell Friends outside their Light groups of their experiences in the Experiment, it may be that the positive effect on Experimenters' lives of their realisations about themselves and the way they had hitherto lived their lives are so gradual that they are not visible to other Friends in their Meetings and so those others do not feel any personal imperative to enquire about nor to embrace it, nor to assist when difficulties surround it. Of its nature, the Experiment is radical without communicating its benefits effectively, except in the rarer cases where Light groups sought full Meeting endorsement by way of formal minute.

The Nature of the Experiment

Mysticism is implicit in Quaker experience, which is predicated upon an unmediated relationship with God. Although mystical experience does feature in the main British canonical work (*Quaker Faith and Practice* 1995),[12] in the normal run of Quaker life Friends do not speak to each other of their unbidden mystical experiences.[13] One Experimenter said: 'I am concerned about what I feel is the intellectual treading on the rose petals of my experience, my felt experience.' Another Experimenter encouraged me to talk openly about peak experiences precisely because Friends are reluctant to talk about them and a third Experimenter told me that when enthusiastic Experimenters have spoken of them, their experience was diminished by discussion amongst those who did not Experiment, so that that pressure from those not in Light groups led to their breaking up.

In other contexts, Leonardo Boff has described how the meeting of divine centre and personal centre in mystical encounter can reintegrate the 'opaque' and 'brutal facticity' of human experience with the spiritual foundation which underlies everything (Dawson 2004, 160-62). The result of this encounter is that the individual becomes true, existentially, to the way things really are, ontologically, overcoming humankind's spiritual estrangement. In other words, human experience becomes more transparent to spiritual foundation: 'transcendence within immanence and immanence within transcendence'. This captures exactly what Experimenters have told me in interview and what I have observed of their Experimenting. For example one interviewee said:

> When we began, our expectation was that Light would simply flood into personal relationships, work situations, which it did, tangled areas where there'd been loss of communication and so on, all of that happened, [then] we found that there was nothing to share, that no one was dialoguing internally about problems or personal issues but we were coming into a sort of floating, resting in the Presence of God. I believe that the group has

been touched in a very, very deep way, experientially, spiritually. You are able to communicate in silence and uphold and treasure and help and heal.

Only those people with a predilection for exploration and spiritual encounter persist with the Experiment. Not all Friends who seek spiritual encounter Experiment, nor is the type of experience engendered by the Experiment unique to Experimenters. What distinguishes Experimenters' experiences from those of Friends who may have similar experiences in other contexts is the visibility of the Experiment's process and the fact that what is experienced can easily be and is often explicitly shared with other Experimenters. Experimenters' reluctance to explain their experience more widely is partly a result of BYM's Culture of Silence (Dandelion 1996, 238-50) and partly, as informants described, because of fear or experience of unsettling reaction from other Friends, including incredulity and accusations of conceit.

Robson finds that by and large Quakers prefer the theoretical and imaginative approach over the practical and factual (Robson 2005, 6) and this was evident in particular in relation to an early attempt to organise dissemination of the practice. When faced with a long agenda, the group conducted an Experiment in which they decided to abandon a formal approach to the work:

> In the meditation a strong leading was felt by a number of friends that the work was to be carried lightly; a feather on the breath of God, a lighting of candles one by another and a butterfly in flight were images offered. As this was the sense of the meeting we agreed to depart from the agenda in the afternoon session (Collier 1999).

Practical business organisation is considered of subsidiary importance. The underlying assumption is that the Light will work where it chooses, independently of any need for organisation.[14] At Glenthorne in 2004 it was also said that the Experiment should not become a Listed Informal Group ('Epistle from Experiment with Light Gathering at Glenthorne') as that would demean its fundamental importance.[15] Without an infrastructure, however, there is no mechanism for the practice to be sustained where it does exist, nor to become more widespread.

Heterotopic Impulses

Pilgrim has developed a theory of Quakers operating an heterotopic impulse, that Quakers are and always have been '*simultaneously* marginal and embedded in the prevailing social order' and express their 'alternate ordering' directly through the society from which they seek to be different: they must be juxtaposed to be heterotopic (2004, 209 and this volume) and to do this effectively, they need to inhabit spaces which are sufficiently central to render their alternate ordering visible (2004, 211). She also points out that by the mid-twentieth century, the experience of being 'convicted' by the Light had diminished in power, if it had not disappeared altogether, so that early Friends' experience of being convicted by Christ and visibly transformed was no longer seen as essential among British Quakers (2004, 216).

Experimenters go through a process of transformation in stages similar to those early Friends went through (Dandelion 2003; Meads forthcoming).[16] Thus, those who persist with the Experiment and are transformed, albeit that it is a gradual dawning rather than a single visible conviction and albeit that they talk about 'Light', not the 'Light of Christ', feel themselves to be different from the rest of the Meetings to which they belong. Particularly in smaller Meetings, they are also visible as Experimenters,[17] although, since they do not talk about what they experience outside their Light groups, that experience is inherently invisible to other Friends in their Meetings. Experimenters are a radical wing in that, by their seeking spiritual experience and sharing it with each other explicitly, they operate an heterotopic impulse in juxtaposition to the other Friends in their Meetings. Unlike early Friends and Adolescent Quakers, however, Experimenters' heterotopic impulse operates only within BYM. As Pilgrim observes, in a pluralist society British Quakers end up defining their difference against each other (2004, 222-23). The Experiment is one example of this.

Pilgrim also defines those in BYM as 'Inclusivist' or 'Syncretic' (2004, 220-21).[18] Inclusivists hold to Friends' mainstream traditions and the behavioural creed (Dandelion 1996, 100-10), believe in God and the possibility of discernment and value the discipline and authority of the corporate body over the Syncretists' individualised privatised spirituality. Pilgrim says that Inclusivists tend to regard themselves as a 'moral elect'. Syncretists, on the other hand, have a sense of disconnection from traditional sources of meaning, place great emphasis on freedom, authenticity, the recovery of rejected knowledge and a synthesis of spiritualities.

Experimenters have a Syncretic attitude to business method where the establishment of a Light group is concerned. Although Quaker origins are not formally 'rejected knowledge', Experimenters fit Pilgrim's Syncretic model in their attraction to the Experiment's claimed link with early Friends, whose separation from the world has been outgrown by developments in BYM since the mid-nineteenth century, as Pilgrim shows (2004, 213-16). The essence of the first Friends' ways of being and early Friends' significance may no longer be seen as mainstream tradition by Inclusivists. Indeed some Experimenters told me that in their Meetings reference to Fox was felt to be controversial, if not irrelevant. If Inclusivists are the majority of British Quakers, Experimenters' Syncretism (in Pilgrim's terms) again places them in an heterotopic space, different from and defined in contradiction to BYM generally and this, combined with Experimenters' reluctance to proselytise, also contributes to the Experiment's limited spread and limited understanding of it. Indeed, those who gathered at Glenthorne in 2004 acknowledged they were struggling to make the Experiment more widely known and better understood ('Epistle from Experiment with Light Gathering at Glenthorne'); Experimenters are trying to bring others in BYM to a similar experience and have no desire to be exclusive.

Behaviour

Plüss concluded from her study of belief differences between two Quaker groups that the glue which holds Quakers together is their socialisation process (1995, 91). She found that how Friends define quality of truth, that is, how they define the will of God, together in MfW, underlies Quaker institutional conduct, so that adherence to the group's discernment is a necessary characteristic of that institutional conduct (1995, 62). Implicitly the requirements of Quaker membership 'stipulate' that Quakers should not consider their individually held beliefs as being of foremost importance, rather their epistemology is collective (1995, 129).

What matters to Quakers collectively, as Dandelion also observed in his discussion of a 'behavioural creed' (1996, 100-31), is how they behave, not what they believe: their behaviour in 'Quaker-time' is policed by Quakers holding the time-limited offices of Elders and Clerks and Quaker business matters are conducted in formally constituted business meetings. Whilst liberal in belief, British Quakers are conservative and conformist in attitudes to behavioural deviation in the Meeting House (Dandelion 2004b, 221).

Dandelion and Plüss' conclusions on behaviour emerged out of their focus on *belief*, so they did not consider the importance of behaviour in relation to spiritual *experience*. Robson (2005) looked at behaviour, but in a specific context and so did not examine this either. My work focuses on experience in a way these scholars did not and also identifies that the Experiment can provide a new way of engendering spiritual experience, in the context of the requirement for conformist institutional conduct which Dandelion, Plüss and Robson identify.

Some Light groups meet in Experimenters' homes, thus extending their 'Quaker-time' into a different space and potentially creating ambiguity about Elders' and Clerks' jurisdiction, especially in the case of one group which did not operate in any one particular Monthly Meeting. In the course of my fieldwork I came across only two groups which had been established under accepted Quaker business method, by formal minute of a Quaker Meeting for Worship for business; all of the others, including those which I observed, those other informants described and the group in my own Meeting, were either set up informally or under an adapted form of approval, advising Elders of their intentions and thus implicitly seeking their approval.[19] Without the endorsement of Quaker business process there is no accountability, evidenced by Elders reluctance to become involved where conflict arose. In some respects, however, Experimenters do follow the behavioural creed. Ambler exhorts Friends to try the Experiment for themselves, just as early Friends declined to be spiritual directors (Grundy 2007, 157-58). Similarly Experimenters' not shouting their transforming and transcendent experiences from the Meeting House rooftops conforms to institutional conduct (the Culture of Silence (Dandelion 1996, 238-50)).

Quakers claim they are Quakers because of what they experience, not because of what they believe. Thus, although the Experiment conforms to the behavioural creed in its central search through experience and by directing Friends to have their own experience, by side-stepping formal business method, and breaking the Culture of Silence *within* Light groups, it simultaneously does not. Thus not only does it occupy an heterotopic space both within local Meetings and nationally in BYM, but also it makes it difficult to disseminate the practice in any organised way or even to respond to requests for support in satisfying local demand when it arises.

BYM takes more note of worldly concerns,[20] but individual spiritual experience is rarely explicitly shared, exactly the reverse of the case when the Society was founded. Since the Experiment has not been tested as a concern through the recognised method, its *raison d'etre* is neither recognised nor understood and it has not been embraced, except in small pockets.

Conclusion: the Experiment illuminates its context

Experimenters' experience can be so fundamental to how they live their lives and see the world, that it is precious to them. Some of their experiences in the Experiment rivet them and feel extraordinary. Such experience is embodied, literally felt and understood and they can be transformed by it. Deep trust and love is engendered in the intimacy of Light groups' sharing and that is precious to Experimenters, too. This shared experience, intimacy and love defines them as different from other Friends in their Meetings at the same time as it is for them fundamentally Quaker experience, reinforcing their Quaker identity. Early Quakers were a community of love and so too are Experimenters with Light.

Experimenters' privilege the spiritual nature of the Quaker experience over organisation and disseminating their practice: they largely bypass the accepted Quaker business method, the most formal expression of the Quaker behavioural creed which Plüss and Dandelion showed carries more weight in BYM than belief.

The Experiment is radical in the sense not just of its advanced or extreme attention to spiritual experience, but also in that it refers to the foundations of Quakerism, to early Friends' experience which is no longer felt to be so important in BYM. It seeks to permeate BYM, deliberately not being a Listed Informal Group, but in its heterotopic stance instead it occupies an outlying space, practised within only a few Meetings. It is a wing, an element operating simultaneously within BYM's Meetings, but against the flow of how non-Experimenters behave. Its lack of organisation, failure to communicate its benefits and bewilderment at the indifference (and sometimes hostility) it meets, leave it making only marginal localised impact.

Plüss and Dandelion forefronted behaviour in relation to belief, but my research shows that *explicitly shared* spiritual experience in twenty first century BYM, whatever belief underlies it, is also in juxtaposition. Where Experimenters instigate dialogue with their local Meetings, it is not about their spiritual experience, which they share only with each other.

Early Friends were highly organised and committed, they were 'convinced' and communicated their experience to each other freely so that they had a common understanding and then proselytised avidly, creating the network of Meetings in which the Experiment with Light, itself reflecting their founding impulse, is now heterotopic.

Notes

---

[1] George Fox (1624-90) was one of the first Quakers. He travelled, wrote extensively and led the early movement. He is seen by most Quakers as the founder, as he was the most prominent and longest surviving of the earliest group of Friends.

[2] Light groups are usually based in and draw their members from a PM or several PMs within a Monthly Meeting.

[3] My fieldwork consisted of nineteen semi-structured interviews and three periods of participant observation, as well as other meetings with informants, over a three year period (2003 to 2006). The participant observation was of an eight-member Light group in thirty three Experiments over a seventeen month period, of a nine-member group on one occasion, which included an inter-active discussion, and of the weeklong Experiment with Light retreat in 2004 at Glenthorne Country Guest House and Quaker Conference Centre in Grasmere, Cumbria. The one-off participant observation also had an attendant series of interviews with some of the group members and Elders from the Meeting to which the group was attached. I also subsequently had conversations and e-mail exchanges with some of the interviewees, some of the members of the group I observed longer term and other informants. Throughout most of this period I was Experimenting in a Light group in my own Meeting and this informed my understanding, although Friends' experience in that group was not the object of the research. I have struggled with the difficulties thrown up by how much I am an insider to the practice of Experiment with Light but have also shown how crucial my insiderness is in this type of research (Meads 2007).

[4] Closed groups tend to require more commitment from members; some closed groups re-open at given times to allow new members and then close again. Freeflowing groups allow any person from the Meeting to join without commitment and to leave at any time.

[5] Preferably in a 'worship sharing' manner (*Quaker Faith and Practice* 1995, 12.21: 4th and 5th paragraphs).

[6] Most of the fieldwork referred to Experiments on the individual, but there was some reference to Experiments on the group. I think it likely this reflects practice generally. There are also Experiments on other people and on the world.

[7] Some of this experience was described to me in the interviews and therefore is claimed by Experimenters, but I also observed some of this experience in the participant observation: it was clear from Experimenters' realisations in the course of the Experiments undertaken, their reports in the sharing and subsequent descriptions of situations in later conversations, including the sharing following later Experiments. It is also hinted at in the Glenthorne epistle.

[8] I am indebted to Simon Best for pointing out two of the links between Light groups and communities of intimacy: the extension of Quaker-time and the separate space occupied in Quaker-time.

[9] In his detailed anthropological study of one Quaker meeting, Collins refers only to discussion over tea after MfW of others' spoken ministry, not of individual

spiritual experience: 'It is spoken ministry which is discussed following Meeting for Worship, not the quality of the silence.' (1994, 188)

[10] Periodically such courses are held at Quaker centres, such as Charney Manor Quaker Conference Centre and Retreat House in Oxfordshire, Swarthmoor Hall in Cumbria or Woodbrooke Quaker Study Centre in Birmingham.

[11] 31 August to 4 September 1998, originally with the intention of training key invited Friends to lead workshops, but it became more of a retreat where those present explored their own issues (field notes).

[12] In December 2007 I interviewed a member of the Book of Discipline Revision Committee, responsible for the draft compilation of *Quaker Faith and Practice* (1995). Her recollection was that the index (which does not include 'mysticism') did not reflect new trends, but was largely based on preceding editions. She went on to say that the content of Chapter 26 'Reflections' was representative of BYM's then (1986-1994) contemporary understanding of mystical experience, since it was selected by a Committee sub-group from collated submissions and preceding editions. Mysticism is not indexed in *Christian Faith and Practice* (1960) either.

[13] Collins cites an example of a discussion group where most Friends chose to represent MfW pictorially by leaving the sheet of paper blank and comments that these Quakers understand that their beliefs are not explicable in words (1994, 240). I wonder how those who did draw pictures felt when faced with the others' blank sheets. It is also interesting that Collins, who elsewhere acknowledges that Quakers privilege practice over belief (1994, 245), understands the blank sheets in terms of belief, rather than in terms of experience. Although in a conversation in October 2006 Collins rejected this, I suggest that if Friends present at the discussion had any religious experience, they might well have not felt secure enough in the context of the Meeting generally to share that.

[14] Although one informant said she thought this was sometimes used as an excuse for not meeting commitments.

[15] A group may be listed in BYM's annual *Book of Meetings* if it meets certain criteria: the group's aims, purpose and manner of proceeding should be consistent with Friends' testimonies and methods; the group should be specifically for Friends and Attenders within Britain Yearly Meeting or the wider Religious Society of Friends - it should not be part of a wider grouping outside the Society, although might affiliate with other groups; the group should be open to all Friends and Attenders who qualify, on a Yearly Meeting basis; the group should be properly constituted, with officers as appropriate; membership levels should indicate a continued interest within Britain Yearly Meeting and should not normally be merely a very few individuals; the group should be ongoing, i.e. not set up merely for a short period of time; a copy of the aims of the group should be sent to the Assistant Recording Clerk, Friends House (*Listed Informal Groups: Status and Criteria for Recognition* 2003). Most Light groups would not meet these criteria: some are not open to all; they do not have formal officers; some may be established for only a limited time and they do not have formal aims. Similarly there are no formal officers of any central organisation (as there is no formal central organisation).

[16] I am using the word 'convincement' with its original connotation of conviction. Conviction is the second stage of the steps of convincement (Dandelion 2003; Meads forthcoming). This use is different from late twentieth century BYM usage, particularly in connection with membership, as something lesser than encounter with God (Dandelion 1996, 273-74).

[17] During the course of my fieldwork I was aware of only one Light group which did not operate within the Preparative or Monthly Meeting to which its members belonged. The Experimenters in this group were, however, largely so closely identified with the Experiment that they would be visible as Experimenters in their own Meetings. Subsequently new Light groups have formed where members are drawn from more than one Monthly Meeting, so this may be changing.

[18] Pilgrim's example of Exclusivist Quakers is a group who broke away from BYM in 1993 and formed their own Yearly Meeting.

[19] When, as I was first drafting this chapter in 2006, I became aware of the significance of this, I suggested that the group in my own Meeting be recognised with the whole of the Meeting's involvement, by a formal PM minute, and this was done.

[20] As happened for example in the work of two of its Central Committees, Quaker Stewardship Committee and Quaker Finance and Property Central Committee, in April 2006 when they produced draft governing documents to Meeting for Sufferings to conform with proposed charity legislation, seeking to alter over 350 years of Quaker organisation and method.

GLOSSARY

Attenders

Regular participants at local Quaker Meetings who have not applied for formal membership.

Book of Discipline

An anthology of extracts from previous minutes or Quaker writings compiled to guide and nurture Quakers and their Meetings in their discipleship. Each Yearly Meeting has its own book of discipline and they are regularly revised. The latest British book is entitled *Quaker Faith and Practice* (1995, 1999).

Business Meeting

A Meeting for Worship concerned with decisions to do with the life of the Meeting, eg finance, property etc. No votes are taken but the Clerk prepares a minute reflecting 'the sense of the Meeting' which is agreed in the Meeting. Unity is seen as a sign of discerning God's will accurately, disunity as a sign that further work needs to be done, perhaps at a later date.

Centring Down

The process by which Quakers deepen their experience of worship in the silence.

Clerks

Those who guide the process of Quaker business Meetings. They also typically handle the correspondence of the Meeting.

Concern

A 'leading' from God to action. Quakers talk of having a 'concern laid on them'.

Convincement

Whilst technically meaning conviction, one of the elements of the transformation experienced by early Friends, the term is used more popularly to refer to the whole of the transformation experience. Today it can also be used les specifically to refer to those who have come into membership as adults, 'by convincement'.

Discernment

The process by which Quakers decide what is truly from God.

Disownment

The process by which Quakers lose their formal membership. This is a Meeting decision and is typically based on major misdemeanour or misrepresentation of Quakerism. The practice was very prevalent in the eighteenth century, particularly for 'marrying out' (ie marrying a non-Quaker) but is rare today.

Elders

Those appointed to nurture the ministry of the Members and the Meeting for Worship. Elders can be associated with the disciplining of the Meeting and Friends talk of having been 'eldered' when reminded of Quaker practice.

General Meeting (GM)

A regional grouping, midway in size between a Monthly (or Area) and Yearly Meeting. In Britain, General Meetings used to be called Quarterly Meetings.

Leading

A sense of being directed by God in a particular direction. Quakers talk of 'having leadings.'

Liberal Quakers

Based on a rationalist expression of Christianity, one of the three main Quaker traditions in the world today. Beginning in the late nineteenth century, it is characterised today by a permissive attitude to belief and a caution over explicit theology.

Meeting for Sufferings

Originally set up to petition government on behalf of Friends suffering in prison, these committees became powerful interim committees of their Yearly Meetings. In Britain, Meeting for Sufferings is concerned with major policy decisions. It is comprised of representatives from each Monthly or Area Meeting.

Meeting for Worship

The term used to refer to Quaker worship, rather than 'service'. Quakers talk of 'going to Meeting' rather than going to church.

Meeting House

The name given to the places built intentionally to house Quaker worship.

Members

Those who have formally applied for membership.

Minister

Those believed to have a 'gift' of ministry. In some Yearly Meetings, this term is used for those who are specifically 'recorded' by the Monthly Meetings as having the gift of ministry.

Ministry

In its broadest sense, the term used to describe the particular calling given to everyone by God. For example, somebody may be described as having a ministry of hospitality. Also and more commonly used to refer to vocal ministry given in Meeting for Worship.

Minutes

Quakers have proved to be assiduous record keepers over time, one principal source being the minutes of all their Meetings. These are always agreed by the whole Meeting (be it monthly or yearly) within the Meeting.

Monthly Meeting (MM)

The body of Friends which holds responsibility for membership and property and also the name of the monthly business meeting to discuss these and other matters. A Monthly Meeting, retitled Area Meeting in 2008, is part of the Yearly Meeting. It has its own constituent Preparative or Local Meetings. In Britain, there are 72 Monthly Meetings.

Nominations Committee

The Committee who 'discern' whose name should be suggested to a business meeting for appointment to a particular role, such as Clerk or Elder.

Non-Realism

Within theology, the philosophical idea that God does not exist and as such that theological statements cannot be true.

Overseer

The name traditionally given to those who are concerned with the pastoral needs of the Meeting.

Peculiarities

The collective term for the numerous ways Friends traditionally separated themselves from 'the world', such as plain speech and dress, the numbering of days and months instead of naming them.

Plain Dress

The term used to describe the way in which Friends dressed in uniform and simple manner, distinctive in its grey or black colour and plain style from worldly fashions. This practice began with the first Friends and lasted until the twentieth century. A very few Friends still adopt plain dress.

Plain Speech

The refusal to use the polite form 'you' to social superiors but to use 'thee' and 'thou' to everyone. The term also refers to the way in which Quakers attempted to cut any superfluity from their conversation such as small talk.

Preparative Meeting (PM)

A constituent meeting of a Monthly Meeting, usually holding its own monthly business meeting in preparation for the Monthly Meeting. In Britain, Preparative Meetings were renamed Local Meetings in 2008. There are about 500 in Britain.

Progressivism

The doctrine maintaining humanity necessarily learns more about the nature of God over time. Future generations will know more than the present one as God reveals more in each age.

Quietist Quakers

The name given to eighteenth century Friends influenced by the mysticism of the continental quietists such as Guyon, Fenelon, and Molinos. They emphasised the inward nature of true spirituality and a desire for humility and obedience.

Realism

Within theology, the philosophical idea that God exists and that theological statements can be true and accurate.

Semi-Realism

Within theology, the philosophical idea that whilst God exists, statements about God necessarily fall short in their attempt to match words to experience and cannot be considered to be objectively accurate or true.

Travelling in the ministry

The term used to describe the way in which Friends travel 'under concern' to other parts of the Quaker and wider world to share their ministry. This is typically supported with a minute from the Friends' home Meetings.

Universalism

The idea that there are many different equally valid spiritual paths.

Yearly Meeting

The term used to describe an independent body of Friends comprised of various Monthly Meetings, as well as the annual gathering of those Friends. Thus, someone can both be a part of a Yearly Meeting and attend Yearly Meeting sessions. Britain Yearly Meeting has about 15,000 Members and 8000 Attenders..

REFERENCES

Acheson, Robert J. 1993. *Radical Puritans in England 1550-1660*. London: Longman.

Advices and Queries. 1995. London: Britain Yearly Meeting.

Allaire, Y. and Firsirotu, M. 1984. 'Theories of Organizational Culture.' *Organization Studies* 5: 193-226.

Allan, Graham. 1989. *Friendship: Developing a sociological perspective*. London: Harvester Wheatsheaf.

Allen, N.J., W.S.F. Pickering and W. Watts Miller, eds. 1998. *On Durkheim's Elementary Forms of Religious Life*. London and New York: Routledge.

Ambler, Rex. 1989. *Creeds and the Search for Unity*. London: Quaker Home Service.

—. 1994. *The End of Words: issues in contemporary Quaker theology*. London: Quaker Home Service.

—. 1997a. 'The Discipline of Light.' *Proceedings of the Quaker Theology Seminar 1995/6*, Birmingham: Woodbrooke, 10-24.

—. 1997b. 'Quaker Truth or, the Way of a Ship in the Sea.' *Proceedings of the Quaker Theology Seminar 1996/7*, Birmingham: Woodbrooke, 151-67.

—. 2001. *Truth of the Heart: an anthology of George Fox 1624-1691*. London: Quaker Books.

—. 2002. *Light to Live By: an exploration in Quaker spirituality*. London: Quaker Books.

Amit, Vered and Nigel Rapport, 2002. *The Trouble With Community: anthropological reflections on movement, identity and collectivity*. Sterling USA, Pluto Press.

Ammerman, Nancy. T. 1997. *Congregation and Community*. New Brunswick NJ: Rutgers University Press.

Argyris, C., and D. Schön, 1996. *Organizational Learning II* Reading, MA: Addison-Wesley.

Auksi, Peter. 1995. *Christian Plain Style: the evolution of a spiritual ideal*. Montreal and Kingston: McGill-Queens University Press.

Aune, Kristin, Sonya Sharma and Giselle Vincett, eds. 2008. *Women and Religion in the West: challenging secularization*. Aldershot: Ashgate.

Aupers, Stef and Dick Houtman. 2006. 'Beyond the Spiritual Supermarket: the social and public significance of New Age spirituality.' *Journal of Contemporary Religion.* 21: 201-22.

Baier, Annette. 1985. 'What do women want in a moral theory?' *Nous.* 19: 53-64.

Bailey, R., 1992. *New Light on George Fox and Early Quakerism: the making and unmaking of a God,* San Francisco: Mellen Research University Press.

Baines, Anne. 1998. 'A Critique of the Originality of George Fox.' *The Friends Quarterly,* January: 26-35.

Banks, Sarah, Jackie Leach Scully and Tom Shakespeare. 2006. 'Ordinary ethics: lay people's deliberations on social sex selection.' *New Genetics and Society.* 25: 289-303.

Bannister, Donald, 1966. 'Psychology as an Exercise in Paradox.' *Bulletin of the British Psychological Society* 19: 21-26.

—. 1985. 'The Experience of Self' in *Anticipating Personal Construct Psychology*, F. Epting, F. and A. W. Landfeld, eds. Lincoln, NE: University of Nebraska Press, 39-45.

Barbour, Hugh. 1964. *The Quakers in Puritan England.* New York: Yale University Press.

Bauman, Richard. 1983. *Let Your Words Be Few: symbolism of speaking and silence among 17th century Quakers.*

Becker, Howard S. 1963. *Outsiders: studies in the sociology of deviance.* New York: The Free Press of Glencoe.

Becker, Penny. E. 1999. *Congregations in Conflict: cultural models of local religious life.* Cambridge: Cambridge University Press.

Bell, Sandra and Peter Collins. 1998. 'Religion and the Performance of Silence', *Journal of Quaker Studies* 3: 1-26.

Berger, Helen A., Evan A. Leach, and Leigh S. Shaffer, eds. 2003. *Voices from the Pagan Census: a national survey of Witches and Neo-Pagans in the United States.* Columbia, SC: University of South Carolina Press.

Berger, Peter. 1967. *The Sacred Canopy: elements of a sociological theory of religion.* Garden City, NY: Doubleday.

Berger, Peter, Brigitte Berger, and Hansfried Kellner. 1974. *Homeless Mind: modernization and consciousness.* New York: Vintage.

Best, Simon. Forthcoming. *The Spiritual Beliefs and Religious Practices of Adolescent Quakers.* Unpublished PhD thesis, University of Birmingham.

Bibby, R.W., and Brinkerhoff, M.B. 1973. 'The Circulation of the Saints: a study of people who join conservative churches'. *Journal for the Scientific Study of Religion* 12: 273-83.

Bibby, R.W., and Brinkerhoff, M.B. 1983. 'Circulation of the Saints Revisited: a longitudinal look at conservative church growth.' *Journal for the Scientific Study of Religion* 22: 153-62.

Bock, Elmer, John Cochran, and Leonard Beeghley. 1987. 'Moral Messages: The Relative Influence of Denomination on the Religiosity–Alcohol Relationship.' *The Sociological Quarterly* 28: 89-103.

Book of Meetings 2005. 2005. London: Britain Yearly Meeting.

Boulton, David, ed. 2006. *Godless for God's Sake: nontheism in contemporary Quakerism.* Dent, Cumbria: Dales Historical Monographs.

Boulton, David. 2007. 'Are Quakers Christian?' *The Friend*, 165 (44): 8.

Bourdieu, Pierre. 1977. *Outline of a Theory of Practice.* Cambridge: Cambridge University Press.

—. 1997 [1987]. 'The Forms of Capital' in *Education: culture, economy, society,* A.H. Halsey, H Lauder, P. Brown, and A.S. Wells, eds. Oxford: Oxford University Press, 49-55.

Brand, Stewart. 1999. *The Clock of the Long Now: time and responsibility.* London: Weidenfeld and Nicolson.

Brannen, J. and P. Moss. 1991. *Managing Mothers.* London: Unwin Hyman.

Brierley, Peter, ed. 2007. *UK Christian Handbook: religious trends 6 (2006-2007).* London: Christian Research.

Brown, Callum. 2001. *The Death of Christian Britain: understanding secularisation 1800 – 2000.* London: Routledge.

Bruce, Steve. 2002. *God is Dead: secularization in the west.* Oxford: Blackwell.

—. 2003, 'The Demise of Christianity in Britain,' in *Predicting Religion: Christian, secular, and alternative futures* Grace Davie, Paul Heelas, and Linda Woodhead, eds., Aldershot: Ashgate, 53-63.

Bruce, Steve and A. Glendinning, 2003. 'Religious Beliefs and Differences' in *Devolution: Scottish Answers to Scottish Questions?,* Bromley, C., Curtis, J., Hinds, K., Park, A., eds, Edinburgh: Edinburgh University Press, 86-115.

Burkett, Steven R. 1980. 'Religiosity, Beliefs, Normative Standards and Adolescent Drinking.' *Journal of Studies on Alcohol* 41: 662-71.

Burkett, Steven, and Mervin White. 1974. 'Hellfire and Delinquency: Another Look.' *Journal for the Scientific Study of Religion* 13: 455-62.

Burton, P., 2005. 'Keeping the Light Shining? The end of British Quakerism revisited', *Quaker Studies* 9: 249-56.

Calhoun, Cheshire. 1989. 'Responsibility and Reproach.' *Ethics.* 99: 389-406.

Cary, Mark S. and Pink Dandelion, 'Three Kinds of British Friends: a latent class analysis.' *Quaker Studies* 12: 145-56.

Cary, Mark S. and Anita L. Weber, 'Two Kinds of Quakers: a latent class analysis.' *Quaker Studies* 12: 134-44..

Carter, Max. 1999. 'Early Friends and the Alchemy of Perfection'. *Journal of Friends Historical Society* 58: 235-50

Cave, Elizabeth., and Ros Morley, eds, 2000. *Faith in action: Quaker social testimony.* London: Quaker Home Service.

Ceadel, Martin. 2002. 'The Quaker Peace Testimony and its Contribution to the British Peace Movement: an overview.' *Quaker Studies* 7: 9-29.

Chadkirk, Bill. 2004. 'Will the Last (Woman) Friend to Leave Please Ensure the Light Remains Shining?' *Quaker Studies* 9: 114-19.

Chapin-Bishop, Cat. http://quakerpagan.blogspot.com., accessed 20.07.2006.

Child, J. 1984. *Organization: a guide to problems and practice.* London: Harper and Row.

Christian Faith and Practice in the Experience of the Society of Friends. 1960. London: London Yearly Meeting of the Religious Society of Friends.

Clarke, Thom. 1995. 'How do you do it? Explaining link weekends.' *Interlinx* 29: 3.

Clegg, S. 1990. *Modern Organizations: organization studies in the postmodern world.* London: Sage.

Cochran, John, and Ronald Akers. 1989. 'Beyond Hellfire: an Exploration of the Variable effects of Religiosity on Adolescent Marijuana and Alcohol Use.' *Journal of Research in Crime and Delinquency* 26: 198-225.

Cohen, Anthony P. 1986. *The Symbolic Construction of Community.* London: Routledge.

—. 1994. *Self Consciousness: an alternative anthropology of identity.* London: Routledge.

Cohen, Stanley, N Ben-Yehuda, J Aviad. 1987. 'Recentering the World: the quest for "elective" centers in a secularized universe.' *The Sociological Review* 35: 320-436.

Cohen, Stanley, and Laurie Taylor. 1992 *Escape Attempts: the theory and practice of resistance to everyday life.* London: Routledge.

Coleman, Simon and Collins Peter. 2000. 'The Plain and the Positive: ritual, experience and aesthetics in Quakerism and charismatic

Christianity.' *Journal of Contemporary Religion* 15: 317-29.

Coleman, Simon and Collins, Peter. 1996. 'Constructing the Sacred: the anthropology of architecture in the world religions.' *Architectural Design* 124: 14-18.

Coleman, Simon and Collins, Peter. 2006. 'The Shape of Faith or The Architectural Forms of the Religious Life' in *Materialising Religion,* Elisabeth Arweck and William Keenan , eds . Aldershot: Ashgate, 32-44.

Collier, Brian. 1999. 'Experiment with Light: report on the meeting at Cheltenham', 26 June 1999.

Collins, Peter. 1994. 'The Sense of the Meeting: an anthropology of vernacular Quakerism.' Unpublished PhD Thesis, University of Manchester.

Collins, Peter. 1996a. 'Auto/biography, Narrative and the Quaker Meeting', *Auto/biography* 4(2/3): 27-38.

—. 1996b. ' "Plaining": the social and cognitive practice of symbolisation in the Religious Society of Friends (Quakers).' *Journal of Contemporary Religion* 11: 277-88.

—. 1998. 'Quaker Worship: an anthropological perspective.' *Worship* 72(6): 501-15.

—. 2001. 'Quaker Plaining as Critical Aesthetic.' *Quaker Studies* 5: 121-39.

—. 2002a. 'Habitus and the Storied Self: religious faith and practice as a dynamic means of consolidating identities.' *Culture and Religion* 3(2): 147-61.

Collins, Peter J. 2002b. 'Connecting Anthropology and Quakerism: transcending the insider/outsider dichotomy' in *Theorizing Faith: the insider/outsider problem in the study of ritual,* Elisabeth Arweck and Martin Stringer, eds, Birmingham: University of Birmingham Press, 77-95.

Collins, Peter. 2002c. 'Both Independent and Interconnected Voices: Bakhtin among the Quakers' in *Best of British: The Anthropology of Britain,* Nigel Rapport, ed., Oxford: Berg, 281-98.

—. 2002d. 'Discipline: the codification of Quakerism as orthopraxy, 1650-1738.' *History and Anthropology* 13(2): 17-32.

—. 2003. 'Storying Self and Others: the construction of narrative identity.' *Journal of Politics and Language* 2: 243-65.

—. 2004. 'Congregations, Narratives and Identities: a Quaker case study' in *Congregational Studies in the UK: Christianity in a post-Christian context,* Mathew Guest, Karen Tusting and Linda Woodhead, eds, Aldershot: Ashgate, 99-112.

—. 2005. 'Thirteen Ways of Looking at a "Ritual".' *Journal of Contemporary Religion* 20: 323–42.

—. 2006. 'Reading Religious Architecture' in *Reading Religion in Text and Context: reflections of faith and practice in religious materials* Elisabeth Arweck and Peter Collins, eds. Aldershot: Ashgate, 137-56.

—. 2008. 'The Practice of Discipline and the Discipline of Practice' in ✓ *Exploring Regimes of Discipline: the dynamics of restraint,* Noel Dyck, ed.,. Berg: Oxford, 135-55.

Collins, Peter and Dandelion, Pink. 2006. 'Wrapped Attention: revelation and concealment in nonconformism' in *Materialising Religion,* Elisabeth Arweck and William Keenan, eds, Aldershot: Ashgate, 45-61.

Conflict in Meetings. 2000. London: Quaker Home Service.

Cooper, Wilmer. A. 1990. *A Living Faith: a historical study of Quaker beliefs.* Richmond, IN: Friends United Press.

Cortese, Anthony J. 1990. *Ethnic Ethics: the restructuring of moral theory.* Albany, NY: State University of New York.

Cresswell, Tim. 1996. *In Place/Out Of Place.* Minneapolis, MN: University of Minnesota Press.

Crisp, Roger and Michael Slote, eds. 1997. *Virtue Ethics.* Oxford: Oxford University Press.

Cronk, Sandra. 1991. *Gospel Order: a Quaker understanding of faithful church community.* Wallingford, PA: Pendle Hill Publications.

Cross. F.L. 1957. *The Oxford Dictionary of the Christian Church.* London: Oxford University Press.

Crossley, Nick. 2004. 'Ritual, Body Technique, and (Inter)Subjectivity' in *Thinking Through Rituals: philosophical perspectives,* Kevin Schilbrack ed., London and New York: Routledge, 31-51.

Csikszentmihalyi Mihaly. 2001. *Finding Flow: the psychology of engagement with everyday life.* New York: Basic Books.

Csordas, Thomas J. 1994. 'Introduction: the body as representation and being-in-the-world' in *Embodiment and Experience: the existential ground of culture and self,* Thomas J. Csordas, ed., Cambridge: Cambridge University Press, 1- 26.

—. ed. 1994. *Embodiment and Experience: the existential ground of culture and self.* Cambridge: Cambridge University Press.

Culpepper, Emily Irwin. 1987. 'Contemporary Goddess Thealogy: a Sympathetic Critique' in *Shaping New Vision: gender and values in American culture,* Clarissa W. Atkinson, C. Buchanan and M. Miles, eds, Ann Arbor, MI: UMI Research Press, 55-71.

—. 1991. 'The Spiritual, Political Journey of a Feminist Freethinker' in *After Patriarchy: feminist transformations of the world religions,* Paula Cooey, William R. Eakin and Jay B. McDaniel, eds. New York: Orbis Books, 426-46.

Dale, Jonathan. 1996. *Beyond the Spirit of the Age.* London: Quaker Home Service

Dandelion, Ben Pink. 2003. *Convinced Quakerism.* Melbourne Beach, FL: Southeastern Yearly Meeting of the Religious Society of Friends.

Dandelion, Ben Pink, Douglas Gwyn and Timothy Peat. 1998. *Heaven on Earth: Quakers and the second coming.* Birmingham: Woodbrooke College.

Dandelion, Pink. 1996. *A Sociological Analysis of the Theology of Quakers: the silent revolution.* Lampeter: Edwin Mellen Press.

—. 2002. 'Those Who Leave and Those Who Feel Left: the complexity of Quaker disaffiliation.' *Journal of Contemporary Religion* 17: 213-28.

—. 2004a. *The Creation of Quaker Theory: insider perspectives.* Aldershot: Ashgate.

—. 2004b, 'Implicit Conservatism in Liberal Religion: British Quakers as an 'uncertain sect.' *Journal of Contemporary Religion* 19: 219 – 29.

—. 2005. *The Liturgies of Quakerism.* Aldershot, UK and Burlington, VT: Ashgate.

Dandelion, Pink, and Homan, Roger. 1995. 'Questioning Quakers.' *Social Compass* 42: 487-95.

Davie, G. 1994. *Religion in Britain Since 1945: believing without belonging.* Oxford: Blackwell.

Davie, Martin. 1997. *British Quaker Theology since 1895.* Lampeter: Edwin Mellen Press.

Davies, Alan. 1988. 'Talking in Silence: ministry in Quaker Meetings' in *Styles of Discourse,* N. Coupland, ed., London: Croom Helm, 105-37.

Davies, Douglas. 2002. *Anthropology and Theology.* Oxford: Berg.

Davison, A. 1982. *The Fires of Levana.* London: Leaveners Press.

Dawson, Andrew. 2004. 'Mystical Experience as Universal Connectedness: Leonardo Boff's "Trans-Cultural Phenomenology".' *Journal of Contemporary Religion* 19: 155-69.

Eller, Cynthia. 1993. *Living in the Lap of the Goddess: the feminist spirituality movement in America.* Boston: Beacon Press.

'Epistle from Experiment with Light Gathering at Glenthorne, Grasmere, 1 to 5 November 2004' http://www.charlieblackfield.com/light/04glenep.pdf., accessed 20.04.2005

Epistle of Ireland Yearly Meeting 2006, http://www.quakers-in-ireland.ie/archive/YM06.htm, accessed 08.08.2006

'Experiment with Light Contacts'
http://www.charlieblackfield.com/light/contacts.htm,   accessed
23.03.2006.

Fenn, Richard K. 1997. *The End of Time: religion, ritual and the forging of the soul*. London: SPCK

Flanagan, Kieran, and Peter Jupp, eds. 2000. *Virtue Ethics and Sociology: issues of modernity and religion.* London: Palgrave.

Foucault, Michel. 1977. *The Order of Things: an archeology of the human sciences.* London: Tavistock Publications.

—. 1986. 'Of Other Spaces.' *Diacritics.* Spring 16 (1): 22-27.

Francis, Diana. 2006. 'Faith and Practice: Believing, Acting and Witnessing' in *Endeavours to Mend Perspectives on British Quaker Work in the World Today*, Brian Phillips and John Lampen, London: Quaker Books, 104-117.

Franzosi, Roberto. 1998. 'Narrative Analysis – or why (and how) sociologists should be interested in narrative.' *Annual Review of Sociology* 24: 517-54.

Furseth, Inger, and Repstad, Pal. 2006. *An Introduction to the Sociology of Religion: Classical and Contemporary Perspectives.* Aldershot: Ashgate.

Gabriel, Y. 2000. *Storytelling in Organizations.* Oxford: Oxford University Press

Garnett, Jane, Matthew Grimley, and Alana Harris, eds. 2007. *Redefining Christian Britain: post 1945 perspectives.* London: SCM.

Giddens, Anthony. 1998. *The Third Way, the renewal of social democracy.* Cambridge: Polity Press.

—. BBC 1999 Reith Lecture.
www.news.bbc.co.uk/hi/english/static/events/reith_99, accessed 2. 10. 2005.

Gill, Catie, 2005. *Women in the Seventeenth-Century Quaker Community: a literary study of political identities, 1650–1700.* Aldershot: Ashgate.

Gilligan, Carol. 1982. *In a different voice: psychological theory and women's development.* Cambridge, MA: Harvard University Press.

Gledhill, Ruth. 'Church admits shortage of cash threatens one third of clergy.' www.thetimesonline.co.uk, accessed 8.6.2005.

Gorman, George. 1973. *The Amazing Fact of Quaker Worship.* London: Friends Home Service Committee.

Green, Maxine. 2005. *Report to Quaker Life on the work of the Children and Young People's Section.* London: Quaker Life.

Griffin, Wendy, ed. 2000. *Daughters of the Goddess: studies of healing, identity and empowerment.* Walnut Creek, CA: Altamira.

Grundy, Martha Paxson. 2007. 'Learning to Be Quaker: spiritual formation and religious education among early Friends.' *Quaker Studies* 11: 151-65.

Guest, Matthew J., Karen Tusting, and Linda Woodhead, eds. 2004. *Congregational Studies in the UK: Christianity in a post-Christian context.* Aldershot: Ashgate.

Gwyn, Douglas. 1995. *The Covenant Crucified: Quakerism and the rise of capitalism.* Wallingford, PA: Pendle Hill Publications.

—. 2000. *Seekers Found: atonement in early Quaker experience.* Wallingford, PA: Pendle Hill Publications.

Haidt, Jonathan. 2001. 'The Emotional Dog and its Rational Tail: a social intuitionist approach to moral judgment'. *Psychological Review* 108: 814-34.

Hanegraaf, Wouter J. 1998. *New Age Religion and Western Culture: esotericism in the mirror of secular thought.* Albany, NY: State University of New York Press.

Haralambos, Michael and Martin Holborn. 2000. *Sociology: themes and perspectives.* London: HarperCollins.

Harré, R., and L. Van Langenhove, eds. 1999. *Positioning Theory.* Oxford: Blackwell.

Hartshorne, Susan. 1993. 'Quaker Justice in Seventeenth Century Pennsylvania.' *Friends Quarterly*, October 1993: 348-64.

Harvey, Graham. 1997. *Listening People, Speaking Earth: contemporary paganism.* London: Hurst and Company.

—. ed. 2005. *Ritual and Religious Belief: a reader.* London: Equinox.

Harvey, Graham. 2007. *What Do Pagans Believe?* London: Granta.

Hay, David. 'Spirituality in a Secular Age.' Paper presented at the SPIDIR AGM 2003.

Hay, David and Rebecca Nye. 1998. *The Spirit of the Child.* London: HarperCollins.

Hearts and Minds Prepared. 2003. Birmingham: Woodbrooke Quaker Study Centre

Heathfield, Margaret. 1994. *Being Together: Our Corporate Life in the Religious Society of Friends.* London: Quaker Home Service.

Heeks, Peggy. 1994. *Reaching into Community.* York: Joseph Rowntree Charitable Trust.

—. 1998. *Growing in the Spirit: learning and nurture in Britain Yearly Meeting.* York: Joseph Rowntree Charitable Trust.

Heelas, Paul. 1996. *The New Age Movement: the celebration of self and the sacralization of modernity.* Oxford: Blackwell.

Heelas, Paul, Linda Woodhead, Benjamin Seel, Bronislaw Szerszynski, and Karen Tusting. 2005, *The Spiritual Revolution: why religion is giving way to spirituality.* Oxford: Blackwell.

Heilman, Samuel C. 1976. *Synagogue Life.* Chicago: University of Illinois Press.

Held, Virginia. 2005. *The Ethics of Care.* Oxford: Oxford University Press.

Hendry, Joy, 1995. *Wrapping Culture: politeness, presentation, and power in Japan.* Oxford: Oxford University Press.

Heron, Alastair. 1992. *Caring, Conviction and Commitment: dilemmas of Quaker membership today.* London: Quaker Home Service.

—. 1995. *Quakers in Britain: a century of change 1895 – 1995.* Kelso: Curlew Graphics.

Hervieu-Léger, Daniéle. 2000. *Religion as a Chain of Memory.* Translated by Simon Lee. Cambridge: Polity Press.

Hetherington, Kevin. 1996. *The Badlands of Modernity: heterotopia and social ordering.* London: Routledge.

—. 1998. *Expressions of Identity, Space, Performance, Politics.* London: Sage

Higginson, Francis. 1653. *A Brief Relation of the Irreligion of the Northern Quakers.* London.

Hill, Christopher. 1975. *The World Turned Upside Down: radical ideas during the English revolution.* London: Penguin.

—. 1998. *England's Turning Point: essays on 17th century English history.* London: Bookmarks.

Hinds, H. 1996. *God's Englishwomen: seventeenth-century radical sectarian writing and feminist criticism.* Manchester: Manchester University Press.

Hobbs, Dick. 1989. *Doing the Business: entrepreneurship, the working class and detectives in the East End of London.* Oxford: Oxford University Press.

Hobby, E. 1989. *The Virtue of Necessity: English women's writing 1649-88,* Ann Arbor, MI: University of Michigan Press.

Hochschild, Arlie R. 1989. *The Second Shift: working parents and the revolution at home.* New York: Viking.

Holden, Andrew. 2002. *Jehovah's Witnesses: portrait of a contemporary religious movement.* London and New York: Routledge.

Homan, Roger, and Pink Dandelion, 1997. 'The Religious Basis of Resistance and Non-response: a methodological note.' *Journal of Contemporary Religion* 12: 205-14.

Houtman, Dick and Stef Aupers. 2008. 'The Spiritual Revolution and the New Age Gender Puzzle: the sacralisation of the self in late modernity (1980-2000)' in *Women and Religion in the West: challenging secularization,* Kristin Aune, Sonya Sharma and Giselle Vincett, eds, Aldershot: Ashgate, in press.

Huber, Klaus. 2001. 'The Spirituality of Buddhist Quakers.' Unpublished M.Phil thesis, University of Sunderland.

Hursthouse, Rosalind. 1999. *On Virtue Ethics*. Oxford: Oxford University Press.

Inman, Kendra. 'Families Today', www.channel4.com/health, accessed 29.9.2005.

Isichei, Elizabeth. 1970. *Victorian Quakers.* London: Oxford University Press.

Jackson, Bernard, S. 1990. 'Narrative theories and legal discourse' in *Narrative in Culture: the uses of storytelling in the sciences, philosophy and literature,* Christopher Nash, ed., London: Routledge, 23-50.

Jessor, Richard, and Shirley Jessor. 1977. *Problem Behaviour and Psychosocial Development: a longtitudinal study of youth.* New York: Academic Press.

Jolly, Sarah, and Jim Orford. 1983. 'Religious Observance, Attitudes towards Drinking, and Knowledge about Drinking amongst University Students.' *Alcohol and Alcoholism* 18: 271-78.

Jones, T.Canby, ed. 1989. *The Power of the Lord is Over All: the pastoral letters of George Fox.* Richmond, IN: Friends United Press.

Jönsson, Bodil. 2003. *Ten Thoughts About Time: a philosophical enquiry.* Translated by Anna Paterson. London: Constable.

Junior Yearly Meeting Epistle 2003, Minute 5, in *Proceedings of the Yearly Meeting of the Religious Society of Friends (Quakers) in Britain 2003.* London: Britain Yearly Meeting.

Keane, Webb. 2007. *Christian Moderns: freedom and fetishism in the mission encounter.* Berkeley, CA: University of California Press.

Keith, Michael, and Steve Pile, eds. 1993. *Place and the Politics of Identity.* London: Routledge.

Kelley, D.M. 1972. *Why Conservative Churches are Growing.* New York: Harper and Row.

Kelly, G.A. 1963. *A Theory of Personality: the psychology of personal constructs.* New York: Norton.

Kelly, Thomas. 1944. *The Gathered Meeting*. London: Friends Home Service Committee.

Kennedy, Thomas C. 2001. *British Quakerism 1860-1920: the transformation of a religious community.* Oxford: Oxford University Press.

Kirkby, Joanna. 2001. *The Two Oceans: the dark and the light.* York: William Sessions.

Kline, D.A. 2002. 'Quakerly Conflict: the cultural logic of conflict in the Religious Society of Friends'. Unpublished PhD Thesis, University of Edinburgh.

Krieger, Susan. 1985. 'Beyond "Subjectivity": the use of self in social science.' *Qualitative Sociology* 8: 309-24.

Krohn, Marvin, Ronald Akers, Marcia Radosevich, Lonn Lanza-Kaduce. 1982. 'Norm Qualities and Adolescent Drinking and Drug Behaviour: the effects of norm quality and reference group on using alcohol and marijuana.' *Journal of Drug Issues* 12: 343-59.

Lamont, William. 1969. *Godly Rule: politics and religion 1603-1660.* London: Macmillan.

Latour, Bruno. 1993. *We Have Never Been Modern*. Cambridge, MA: Harvard University Press.

Lederach, J. P. 1999. *The Journey toward Reconciliation*. Scottdale, PA: Herald Press.

Leonard, Alison. 1995. *Telling Our Stories: wrestling with a fresh language for the spiritual journey.* London: Darton, Longman and Todd.

—. 2003. 'Journey Towards the Goddess.' *Feminist Theology* 12 (1): 11-35.

Lindemann Nelson, Hilde. 2001. *Damaged Identities, Narrative Repair.* Ithaca, NY: Cornell University Press.

Listed Informal Groups: status and criteria for recognition. 2003. London: Britain Yearly Meeting.

London Yearly Meeting, 1783. *Extracts from the Minutes and Advices of Friends held in London.* London: W. Phillips.

Long, Asphodel. 1997. 'The One or the Many?' *Feminist Theology* 15 (2): 13-29.

Loring, Patricia. 1999. *Listening Spirituality Volume 11: corporate spiritual practice among Friends.* Washington Grove, MD: Openings Press.

Lynch, Gordon. 2002. *After Religion: 'Generation X' and the search for meaning.* London: Darton, Longman and Todd.

Lyon, M.L. and J.M. Barbalet. 1994. 'Society's Body: emotion and the "somaticization" of social theory' in *Embodiment and Experience: the existential ground of culture and self,* Thomas J. Csordas, ed, Cambridge: Cambridge University Press, 48-68.

Mack, P. 1992. *Visionary Women: gender and prophecy in seventeenth-century England.* Berkeley, CA: University of California Press.

Marin, Louis. 1984. *Utopics: spatial play.* London: Macmillan.

—. 1992. 'Frontiers of Utopia: past and present'. *Critical Enquiry* 19: 397-420.

May, William F. 1994. 'The Virtues in a Professional Setting' in *Medicine and Moral Reasoning,* Kenneth William Musgrave Fulford, Grant Gillett and Janet Martin Soskice, eds, Cambridge: Cambridge University Press, 75-90.

McCloskey, Donald, N. 1990. 'Storytelling in Economics' in *Narrative in Culture: the uses of storytelling in the sciences, philosophy and literature,* Christopher Nash, ed., London: Routledge, 5-22.

McLaren, Margaret. 2001. 'Feminist ethics: care as a virtue' in *Feminists Doing Ethics,* Peggy DesAutels and Joanne Waugh, eds, Lanham, MD: Rowman and Littlefield, 101-17.

Meads, Helen. 2007. 'Insider Research into "Experiment with Light": uncomfortable reflexivity in a different field.' *Quaker Studies* 11: 282-98.

—. Forthcoming. 'Experiment with Light: Radical Spiritual Wing of British Quakerism 1996 To ?' Unpublished PhD thesis, University of Birmingham.

Meek, V.L. 1988. 'Organizational Culture: origins and weaknesses.' *Organization Studies* 9: 453-73.

Merton, Robert. K. 1968 [1948]. *Social Theory and Social Structure,* New York: Free Press.

Miller, William R. 1998. 'Researching the Spiritual Dimensions of Alcohol and other Drug Problems.' *Addiction* 93: 979-90.

Minutes of Hardshaw Monthly Meeting. 1691. Deposited in Manchester Central Library.

Mizruchi, Ephraim, and Robert Perrucci. 1962. 'Norm qualities and Differential Effects of Deviant Behavior: an exploratory analysis.' *American Sociological Review* 27: 391-99.

Moore, Rosemary. 2000. *The Light in Their Consciences: early Quakers in Britain 1646-1666.* State Park, PA: Pennsylvania State University Press.

Morton, Nelle. 1989. 'The Goddess as Metaphoric Image' in *Weaving the Visions*, Judith Plaskow and Carol P. Christ, eds, New York: Harper Collins, 111-18.

Mullen, Kenneth, Rory Williams and Kate Hunt. 1996. 'Irish Descent, Religion, and Alcohol and Tobacco Use.' *Addiction* 91: 243-54.

Nelsen, Hart, and James Rooney. 1982. 'Fire and Brimstone, Lager and Pot: religious involvement and substance use.' *Sociological Analysis* 43: 247-56.

Nesbitt, E. 2002. 'Quaker Ethnographers: a reflexive approach' in *Theorizing Faith: the insider/outsider problem in the study of ritual*, Elisabeth Arweck and Martin Stringer, eds. Birmingham: University of Birmingham Press, 133-54.

Newcastle Meeting. 1998. *What Do You Do In Meeting For Worship?* Colchester: The Millrind Press.

Nickalls, John L. ed. 1952. *The Journal of George Fox*. Cambridge: Cambridge University Press.

Nussbaum, Martha. 2000. 'Non-relative virtues: an Aristotelian approach' in *Moral Disagreement: classic and contemporary readings*, Christopher W. Gowans, ed., London and New York: Routledge, 168-79.

Onions, C.T., ed. 1970. *The Shorter Oxford English Dictionary on Historical Principles*. Third edn. London: Oxford University Press.

Orford, Jim. 1985. *Excessive Appetites*. Chichester: Wiley.

Osborn, Lawrence and Osborn Diana. 1993. *The Time of Your Life*. London. Darton, Longman and Todd.

Ouchi, W.G., and Wilkins, A.L. 1985. 'Organizational Culture.' *Annual Review of Sociology* 11: 457-83.

Pahl, Ray. 2000. *On Friendship*. Oxford: Blackwell.

Parsons, Talcott. 1960. *Structure and Process in Modern Societies*. Glencoe, IL: Free Press.

Pearmain, Rosalind. 2005. 'Transformational Experiences in Young People: the meaning of a safe haven.' *International Journal of Children's Spirituality* 10: 277–90.

Perrin, R.D. and Mauss, A.L. 1991. 'Saints and Seekers: sources of recruitment to the Vineyard Christian Fellowship.' *Review of Religious Research* 33: 97-111.

Peters, Kate 2005, *Print Culture and the Early Quakers*. Cambridge: Cambridge University Press.

Pettigrew, A.M. 1979. 'On Studying Organisational Cultures.' *Administrative Science Quarterly* 24: 570-81.

—. 1986. *The Awakening Giant: continuity and change in Imperial Chemical Industries.* Oxford: Blackwell, 1986.

Phillips, Brian. 1989. 'Friendly Patriotism: British Quakerism and the imperial nation 1890-1910.' Unpublished Ph.D thesis, University of Cambridge.

Phillips, Brian and John Lampen, eds. 2006. *Endeavours to Mend.* London: Quaker Books.

Phipps, John-Francis. 2004. 'Time and Peace.' *The Friends Quarterly* 34: 145-52.

Pilgrim, Gay. 2003. 'The Quakers: towards an alternate ordering' in *Predicting Religion: Christian, secular and alternative futures,* Grace Davie, Paul Heelas and Linda Woodhead, eds., Aldershot: Ashgate, 147-58.

—. 2004. Taming Anarchy: Quaker alternate ordering and 'otherness' in *The Creation of Quaker Theory: insider perspectives,* Pink Dandelion, ed., Aldershot: Ashgate, 206-25.

Plummer, K. 1995. *Telling Sexual Stories.* London: Routledge.

Plüss, Caroline. 1995. 'A Sociological Analysis of the Modern Quaker Movement.' Unpublished D.Phil. thesis, University of Oxford.

Proceeding of Britain Yearly Meeting. 2001. London: Britain Yearly Meeting.

—. 2006. London: Britain Yearly Meeting.

Punshon, John. 1984. *Portrait in Grey: a short history of the Quakers.* London: Quaker Home Service.

—. 1989. *Letter to a Universalist.* Pendle Hill Pamphlet No. 285, Wallingford, PA: Pendle Hill.

Putnam, Robert D. 2000. *Bowling Alone: the collapse and revival of American community.* New York: Simon and Schuster.

Quaker Action on Alcohol and Drugs (QAAD). 2006. *To Use or Not to Use? Quaker views on alcohol, drugs and gambling.* Gloucester: Quaker Action on Alcohol and Drugs.

Quaker Faith and Practice: The Book of Christian Discipline of the Yearly Meeting of the Religious Society of Friends (Quakers) in Britain. 1995. London: Britain Yearly Meeting.

—. 1999. Second edn. London: Britain Yearly Meeting.

Quaker Peace and Social Witness. 2004. *Role Over: National Lottery funding and the Quaker testimony against gambling.* London: Quaker Books.

Quaker Work in 2006, 2007. London: Britain Yearly Meeting

Ramp, William. 1998. 'Effervescence, Differentiation and Representation' in *On Durkheim's Elementary Forms of Religious Life,* N.J. Allen,

W.S.F. Pickering and W. Watts Miller, eds. London and New York: Routledge. 136-48.

Reay, Barry. 1985. *The Quakers and the English Revolution.* London: Temple Smith.

Ritzer, George. 1983. 'The McDonaldization of Society'. *Journal of American Culture* 6: 100-07.

Roberts, Brian. 2004. 'Political Activism and Narrative Analysis: the biographical template and the meat pot' [30 paragraphs]. *Forum Qualitative Sozialforschung / Forum: Qualitative Social Research* [On-line Journal], *5*(3), Art. 10. http://www.qualitative-research.net/fqs-texte/3-04/04-3-10-e.htm , accessed May 1 2007.

Robson, Susan. 2005. 'An Exploration of Conflict Handling Among Quakers.' Unpublished PhD Thesis, University of Huddersfield.

—. 2006. 'Quakers and conflict: an oxymoron' *Friends Quarterly* 36: 156-64.

Roe, Emory. 1994. *Narrative Policy Analysis: theory and practice.* Durham, NC: Duke University Press.

Roof, Wade Clark. 1993. *Generation of Seekers: the spiritual journeys of the baby boom generation.* San Francisco, CA: Harper San Francisco.

—. 1999. *The Spiritual Marketplace: baby boomers and the remaking of American religion.* Princeton NJ: Princeton University Press.

Rooney, James F. 1977. 'Conflicting Standards for Use of Mood-altering Substances among American Youth.' Paper presented at the Annual Meetings of Society for the Study of Social Problems, Chicago.

Rose, Gillian. 1993. *Feminism and Geography.* Oxford: Polity.

Roseneil, Sasha. 'Towards a More Friendly Society?' *The Edge, Issue 15,* March 2004, www.leeds.ac.uk/cava/papers, accessed 23.1.2005

Rothman, J. 1997. *Resolving Identity Based Conflict.* San Francisco: Jossey Bass.

Rountree, Kathryn. 2004. *Embracing the Witch and the Goddess: feminist ritual-makers in New Zealand.* London and New York: Routledge.

Rush, David. 2003. 'They Too Are Quakers: a survey of 199 nontheist Friends'. *Woodbrooke Journal* 11.

Rutherford, Rosie. 2003. Survey data currently held by the Centre for Postgraduate Quaker Studies, University of Birmingham and Woodbrooke Quaker Study Centre.

Salomonsen, Jone. 2002. *Enchanted Feminism: the reclaiming witches of San Francisco.* London and New York: Routledge.

Salvation Army/The Henley Centre. 2001. *The Burden of Youth: Opportunities & aspirations - a report for The Salvation Army.* London: The Salvation Army.

Salzer, M. 1998. 'Narrative Approach to Assessing Interactions between Society, Community and Person.' *Journal of Community Psychology* 26: 569-80.

Sandy, S.V., Boardman, S.K., Deutsch, M. 2000. 'Personality and Conflict.' In *The Handbook of Conflict Resolution*, Deutsch, M. and Coleman P.T. , eds, San Francisco, CA: Jossey Bass, 289-315.

Sarbin, Theodore R., ed, 1986. *Narrative Psychology: the storied nature of human conduct*. New York: Praeger.

Schaefer, Roy. 1992. *Narrative Actions in Psychoanalysis*. Worcester, MA: Clark University Press.

Scheff, T.J. 2000. *Bloody Revenge: emotions, nationalism and war*. Lincoln, NE: iUniverse.com.Inc.

Schein, E. 1985. *Organizational Culture and Leadership: a dynamic view*. San Francisco: Jossey Bass.

Schiefflelin, Edward. 2005. 'Problematizing Performance' in *Ritual and Religious Belief: a reader*, Graham Harvey, ed. London: Equinox, 124-38.

Schilbrack, Kevin, ed. 2004. *Thinking Through Rituals: philosophical perspectives*. London and New York: Routledge.

Scott, Janet. 1980. *What Canst Thou Say? Towards a Quaker Theology*. London: Quaker Home Service.

—. 2002. 'Charitable Organisation of Meetings.' *Documents in Advance*. London: Britain Yearly Meeting.

—. 2003. 'The Peaceable Kingdom.' *Proceedings of the Quaker Theology Seminar 2002/03*, Birmingham: Woodbrooke, Pages.

Scully, Jackie L. 2002. *Quaker Approaches to Moral Issues in Genetics*. Lampeter: Edwin Mellen Press.

Scully, Jackie Leach, Sarah Banks and Tom Shakespeare. 2006a. 'Chance, Choice and Control: lay debate on prenatal social sex selection'. *Social Science and Medicine*. 63: 21-31.

Scully, Jackie Leach, Tom Shakespeare and Sarah Banks. 2006b. 'Gift Not Commodity? Lay people deliberating social sex selection'. *Sociology of Health and Illness*. 28: 749–767.

Scully, Jackie Leach. 2007. 'The Secular Ethics of Liberal Quakerism' in *Good and Evil: Quaker perspectives*, Jackie Leach Scully and Pink Dandelion, eds, Aldershot: Ashgate, 219-31.

Sered, Susan Starr. 1994. *Priestess, Mother, Sacred Sister: religions dominated by women*. New York: Oxford University Press.

Sheeran, Michael J. 1983. *Beyond Majority Rule*. Philadelphia, PA: Philadelphia Yearly Meeting.

Shellens, Hazel. 2004. *Was the Invisible Brought into the Light?*
    Birmingham: Woodbrooke Quaker Study Centre.
Shields, Rob. 1991. *Places on the Margin: alternative geographies of*
    modernity. London: Routledge.
Simpson, Diane. 2007. 'Where is Jesus?' *The Friend,* 165 (31): 8.
Spencer, Carole D. 2007. *Holiness: the soul of Quakerism,* Milton Keynes:
    Paternoster.
Stack, Carol B. 1979. *All Our Kin: strategies for survival in a Black*
    community. New York: Harper and Row.
Stanger, Jennifer. 2004. 'Being a Quaker Child.' *The Friend* 162(15): 14.
Starhawk. 1999 [1979]. *Spiral Dance.* San Francisco: Harper San
    Francisco.
Steer, M. 2001. 'The Quaker Shadow.' Paper presented at Worcester and
    Shropshire Monthly Meeting.
Stohr, Karen. 2006. 'Contemporary virtue ethics.' *Philosophy Compass* 1:
    22-27.
Stoller, Tony. 2006. 'Do Quakers Need God?' *The Friend,* 164 (23): 10-
    11.
Stringer, Martin. 1999. *On the Perception of Worship: the ethnography of*
    worship in four Christian congregations in Manchester. Birmingham:
    University of Birmingham Press.
Stroud Charles and Pink Dandelion. 2004. 'British Quakers and a new
    Kind of End-time Prophecy'. *Quaker Studies* 9: 120-25.
Taber, Fran. I. 1992. Paradoxical Understandings to Hold in Creative
    Tension. *Friends Journal,* 38 (7): 16-17.
Tarter, M. L. (2001), 'Quaking in the Light: the politics of Quaker
    women's corporeal prophecy in the seventeenth-century transatlantic
    world' in *A Centre of Wonders: the body in early America* , J. M.
    Lindman and M. L. Tarter, eds, Ithaca, NY: Cornell University Press,
    145-62.
Taylor, Charles. 1989. *Sources of the Self: the making of the modern*
    identity. Cambridge, MA: Harvard University Press.
Testimonies Committee of Quaker Peace and Social Witness. 2003. *The*
    Quaker Testimonies. London: Quaker Books.
The Meeting of Friends in Wales of the Religious Society of Friends
    (Quakers) in Britain - 'Opening the Door': The Spiritual Hospitality
    Project Report, www.beehive.thisissouthwales.co.uk/default, accessed
    22.11.2003.
Thomas, K.W. 1988. 'The Conflict-Handling Modes: toward more precise
    theory.' *Management Communication Quarterly* 1: 430-36.
Toffler, Alvin. 1980. *The Third Wave.* London, Pan Books.

Torbert, W. R. 1991. *The Power of Balance*. Newbury Park, CA: Sage.

Trevett, Christine. 2000. *Quaker Women Prophets in England and Wales 1650 – 1700*, Lampeter: Edwin Mellen Press.

Tronto, Joan. 1993. *Moral Boundaries: a political argument for an ethic of care*. London and New York: Routledge.

Turner, Victor. 1969. *The Ritual Process: structure and anti-structure*. London: Routledge and Kegan Paul.

Turner, Victor. 1982. *From Ritual to Theatre: the human seriousness of play*. New York: Performing Arts Publication.

UK Women and Work Commission. Women and Equality Unit Report. *Towards a Fairer Future*.
http://www.womenandequalityunit.gov.uk/women_work_commission/.

Vincett, Giselle. 2008. 'The Fusers: new forms of spiritualized christianity' in *Women and Religion in the West: challenging secularization,* Kristin Aune, Sonya Sharma and Giselle Vincett, eds, Aldershot: Ashgate, in press.

Voas D., and A. Crockett. 2005. 'Religion in Britain: neither believing nor belonging', *Sociology* 39: 11-28.

Wallis, Jack, 1999. *Jung and the Quaker Way*. London: Quaker Home Service.

Wallis, Roy, 1976. *The Road to Total Freedom: a sociological analysis of Scientology*. London: Heinemann.

Walliss, J., (2002), *The Brahma Kumaris as a Reflexive Tradition: responding to late modernity*, Aldershot: Ashgate.

Walvin, J. 1997. *The Quakers: money and morals*. London: John Murray.

Welch, Sharon D. 1985. *Communities of Resistance and Solidarity: a feminist theology of liberation*. New York: Orbis.

Welsch, Wolfgang. 1997. *Undoing Aesthetics*. London: Sage,

White, Hayden V. 1987. *The Content of Form: narrative discourse and historical representation*. Baltimore, MD: John Hopkins University Press.

Whitehouse, Derrick. 2005. 'Congregational Culture and Spiritual Nurture in Quaker Meetings in Britain.' Unpublished Ph.D. thesis, University of Sunderland.

Wildwood, Alex. 1999. *A Faith to Call Our Own: Quaker tradition in the light of contemporary movements of the spirit*. London: Quaker Home Service.

Williams, Fiona. 2004. *Rethinking Families.* London: Calouste Gulbenkian Foundation.

Wilson, Lloyd. L. 1996. *Essays on the Quaker Gospel Vision*. Wallingford, PA: Pendle Hill Publications.

Winslade, John. 2001. *Narrative Mediation: a new approach to conflict resolution.* San Francisco, CA: Jossey Bass.

—. 2003. 'Narrative Mediation: assisting in the renegotiation of discursive positions.' *The International Journal of Narrative Therapy and Community Work* 4: 64-75.

Woodhead, Linda. 2001. 'Feminism and the Sociology of Religion: from gender-blindness to gendered difference' in *The Blackwell Companion to Sociology of Religion,* Richard K. Fenn, ed., Oxford and Maldon, MA: Blackwell, 67-84.

—. 2005a. 'Gendering Secularisation Theory.' *Køn og Forskning* (Women, Gender and Research) 1(1): 24-35.

—. 2005b. 'Why So Many Women in Holistic Spirituality?' Presentation at Lancaster University.

—. 2007. 'Gender Differences in Religious Practice and Significance' in *Handbook of the Sociology of Religion,* James Beckford and N.J. Demerath III, eds, London: Sage, 550-70.

—. 2008. ' "Because I'm Worth It": religion and women's changing lives in the west'. In *Women and Religion in the West: challenging secularization,* eds. Kristin Aune, Sonya Sharma and Giselle Vincett. Aldershot, UK and Burlington, VT: Ashgate, in press.

Wrench, Jamie. 2006. 'Conflict in Meetings' *The Friend,* 164 (6): 14.

Wright, Andrew. 1999. *Discerning the Spirit: teaching spirituality in the religious education classroom.* Abingdon: Culham College Institute.

www.manygods.org.uk., accessed 12.10.2006.

www.paganfed.org., accessed 12.10.2006.

www.quakerpagan.org.,accessed 12.10.2006.

YFGM, Documents in Advance, 12/10/03.

Zielinski, Stan. 1975. *Psychology and Silence.* Pendle Hill Pamphlet No. 210. Wallingford, PA: Pendle Hill.

CONTRIBUTORS

Simon Best is completing a PhD at the Centre for Postgraduate Quaker Studies, Woodbrooke and the University of Birmingham. His thesis is on the spiritual beliefs and religious practices of adolescent Quakers. He has presented at a number of conferences and his article 'Quaker Events for Young People: Informal Education and Faith Transmission.' appeared in *Quaker Studies* in March 2007. He has worked with adolescent Quakers in a number of roles.

Helena Chambers completed her Ph.D. at the University of Birmingham in the Centre for Postgraduate Quaker Studies. Her thesis was the first investigation of its kind into the attitudes and behaviours of Quakers towards substance use and gambling, and integrates theoretical perspectives from sociological, psychological and theological disciplines. She is employed as the Director of Quaker Action on Alcohol and Drugs, where her role includes representing the charity's perspectives on matters of public policy.

Peter Collins teaches Anthropology at Durham University. His interests include religion, aesthetics, space and place, and qualitative methodology. He has recently co-edited *Locating the Field: space place and context in anthropology* (Berg, 2006), with Simon Coleman; *Reading Religion in Text and Context: reflections of faith and practice in religious materials* (Ashgate 2006), with Elisabeth Arweck; and *Religion, Identity and Change: perspectives on global transformations* (ed.). Ashgate (2004), with Simon Coleman. He is preparing *Continuity and Change: Bolton Quakers 1650-1990* (Edwin Mellen) for publication and *Keeping an Open 'I': memory and experience as resources in ethnography* (co-edited with Anselma Gallinat) is in press.

Pink Dandelion directs the work of the Centre for Postgraduate Quaker Studies, Woodbrooke and the University of Birmingham. He edits *Quaker Studies* and acts as Series Editor for the Edwin Mellen series in Quaker Studies. His books include *The Quakers: a very short introduction* (2008), *Good and Evil: Quaker perspectives (*2007, with Jackie Leach Scully),

Introduction to Quakerism (2007), *The Liturgies of Quakerism* (2005*)*, *The Creation of Quaker Theory* (2004), the co-authored *Towards Tragedy/Reclaiming Hope* (2004) and *The Sociological Analysis of the Theology of Quakers: the silent revolution* (1996).

Judy Frith is a PhD student in the Centre for Postgraduate Quaker Studies, Woodbrooke and Birmingham University. Her thesis on how British Quakers make choices about time at the beginning of the twenty first century focuses on how changes in work and family impact on the time available for service with and involvement in the Religious Society of Friends.

Jackie Leach Scully is senior lecturer in the School of Geography, Politics and Sociology at Newcastle University. Her publications include *Quaker Approaches to Moral Issues in Genetics* (2002),) *Good and Evil: Quaker perspectives* (2007, with Pink Dandelion), and *Disability Bioethics* (2008).

Helen Meads is a PhD candidate in the Centre for Postgraduate Quaker Studies, Woodbrooke and the University of Birmingham (and has a continuing career as a tax specialist in the finance sector, managing projects, writing technical advice papers and delivering continuous professional training). The working title of her thesis is 'Experiment with Light: The Radical Spiritual Wing of British Quakerism 1996 to ?'. She has presented papers at Quaker Research Studies Association and BSA Sociology of Religion Study Group conferences. Publications include, 'Insider Research into "Experiment with Light": uncomfortable reflexivity in a different field.' *Quaker Studies* 11 (2007), 282-98.

Kate Mellor has recently completed an MPhil in the Centre for Postgraduate Quaker Studies, Woodbrooke and the University of Birmingham, research that formed the basis of her chapter. An expatriate American, Mellor studied for her undergraduate degree in History at Columbia University in New York with the 'deconstructionist' historian R.O. Paxton. She also has an MBA from the Judge Business School at the University of Cambridge (Pembroke College).

Gay Pilgrim has previously been a part-time lecturer in Sociology and Social Policy at Wolverhampton University, and is presently an Associate Tutor at Woodbrooke Quaker Study Centre, Birmingham. Her research interests include religion and identity, religious/faith community, alternative spiritualities, and pilgrimage. She has published two book chapters on the sociology of Quakerism.

Susan Robson's first degree was in sociology. A practical career in social work using systemic and family therapy approaches led her towards social constructivist understandings. It was natural therefore that her return to academe in later life involved collaborative action research and observing participation in a Quaker context. Her doctoral thesis (University of Huddersfield, 2005) was titled 'An Exploration of Conflict Handling among Quakers.' Working independently, her current pre-occupation is making her conclusions accessible to both the wider academic community and to Quakers themselves.

Giselle Vincett's PhD. thesis 'Feminism and Religion: a Study of Christian Feminists and Goddess Feminists in the UK' was based upon an empirical study of Christian and Goddess Feminist women and those who fuse the two. A chapter in her doctoral thesis is based upon her research with Quaker Pagans, and the research introduced her to the Friends. Giselle is currently a research associate at the University of Edinburgh working on a project with Scottish Christian youth in Glasgow. She co-edited *Women and Religion: challenges to secularization theory* (Ashgate 2008).

Derrick Whitehouse completed his PhD at the Centre for Quaker Studies, University of Sunderland, entitled 'Congregational Culture and Spiritual Nurture in Quaker Meetings in Britain'. The thesis breaks new ground in charting the cultural factors which influence the life of local Quaker Meetings and how they inter-relate, work that is applicable to other congregations. He is currently working on a book of the thesis.

INDEX